Brands with
a Conscience

Brands with a Conscience

How to build a successful and responsible brand

Sandra Horlings and
Nicholas Ind

KoganPage

LONDON PHILADELPHIA NEW DELHI

Publisher's note
Every possible effort has been made to ensure that the information contained in this book is accurate at the time of going to press, and the publishers and authors cannot accept responsibility for any errors or omissions, however caused. No responsibility for loss or damage occasioned to any person acting, or refraining from action, as a result of the material in this publication can be accepted by the authors or the publisher.

First published in Great Britain and the United States in 2016 by Kogan Page Limited

2nd Floor, 45 Gee Street	1518 Walnut Street, Suite 1100	4737/23 Ansari Road
London	Philadelphia PA 19102	Daryaganj
EC1V 3RS	USA	New Delhi 110002
United Kingdom		India

© Sandra Horlings and Nicholas Ind 2016

The right of Sandra Horlings and Nicholas Ind to be identified as the authors of this work has been asserted by them in accordance with the Copyright, Designs and Patents Act 1988.

ISBN   978 0 7494 7544 4
E-ISBN   978 0 7494 7545 1

British Library Cataloguing-in-Publication Data

A CIP record for this book is available from the British Library.

Library of Congress Control Number

2016932619

Typeset by Graphicraft Limited, Hong Kong
Print production managed by Jellyfish
Printed and bound by CPI Group (UK) Ltd, Croydon CR0 4YY

To help offset the environmental impact of printing this book, the Medinge Group has made a contribution to the Grow Trees for Tigers project in India. You can contribute too at **www.grow-trees.com**

CONTENTS

Vegetalia: nourishing life 124

Guiseppe Cavallo

07 DNV GL: Back to the future: sustainability at DNV GL 127

Nicholas Ind

Unilever and the green bond 138

Nicholas Ind

08 Cosentino: Conversations carved in stone 140

Cristián Saracco

ABOUT THE COVER

The artwork on the cover is based on a painting by Phil Dobson, a London-based artist and member of the Medinge Group. The original painting can be viewed through the website **www.medinge.org**

ABOUT MEDINGE

Medinge: we stand for brands with conscience

The Medinge Group is a think tank of brand experts and visionaries from around the world whose purpose is to influence business to become more human and conscious in order to help humanity progress and prosper.

We believe that organizations have a broad responsibility to all their stakeholders. Yet many organizations still treat their customers and other audiences as objects and try to control their brands. Our argument is that a brand is created together with others to the benefit of the organization, its stakeholders and society. A brand with a conscience thinks differently. It builds sustainable thinking into the core of what it does and always tries to act responsibly. Our members share ideas, concepts and real-world experiences to continually learn and refresh their thinking and to generate meaningful initiatives to transform the way organizations think and act.

How did 'Brands with a Conscience' come about?

Sandra

It started with me heading a workshop on a doable initiative for the Medinge group to broaden its influence. And it ended by delivering this global collection of brand stories gathered and written down by a bunch of creative, charming, smart, eloquent, passionate and stubborn brand managers, professionals and professors. They were united by the contagious idea that brands can be a force for good. **But why is it titled Brands with a Conscience? Where did this come from?**

Nicholas

A bigger question – **can a brand have a conscience?** The key individual might be a founder or a manager who has the conscience, but it only becomes a 'brand' with a conscience when their principles become embedded in the culture. Then you feel that the idea can endure. That doesn't really answer your question does it? Typical for an academic to answer a question that wasn't asked.

Sandra

Don't get me started on the more philosophical debate – what is a conscience, how do you understand it (we do that in our half-year brain bending events don't we)? I am a professional, hands-on by nature and result-driven. **So please help me understand how building a brand with a conscience is worthwhile** – how is it of help in my daily profession as a brand consultant?

Nicholas

You'll feel better when you do the right thing – so it's just good to have a conscience. And I think that in the long run if you persuade brands to think responsibly they reduce risk and increase their relevance. It also makes them a more attractive employer. The book is designed to help companies think in this way and the cases should **provide inspiration** for how to do it.

Sandra

Plenty of inspiration. And accessible too. That's what I like. You can relate the stories to everyday dilemmas. There's a variety of personal stories and a geographical and cultural spread. It's magazine-style reading I guess. Browsing at first and cherry-picking. Leave it be for a while. And later examine a different chapter more closely. Or review the challenger brands and short stories of new and niche players. It wouldn't be fair to say that reading the first chapter is just an appetizer. Ava's opening chapter with tech innovation and growing consciousness as the pillars is thought provoking. But if you were to describe the true value of this book to our readers, **what would you say is our value proposition?**

Nicholas

What's special about the book is the combination of two things. First, the passion of the writers for their topics – that shows through in the way they express their ideas. Just look at Philippe's love for Merci or Jack's enthusiasm for Dilmah and you can see how personal their descriptions are. Second, is the way the brand stories build on one another. Sure the stories make different points, but as you read you begin to acquire a fuller idea of what 'brands with a conscience' means. So I think the book provides **both strong role models and usable ideas**. And it seems true to Medinge and what it stands for in that it doesn't provide simplistic solutions but instead rather encourages the reader to find their own insights and ideas in the text.

Medinge Group

Changing the relevancy of business and the role of brand leaders forever

AVA HAKIM

This is not a book on how to build a brand. This is a book on how to change the world through business. The business world is in the midst of a transformative change brought on by two evolutions – the evolution of technology and the evolution of the planet. Both of these are forcing mankind to rethink the way business works and the models on which business is built. The stories within this book represent how a growing quake of forward thinkers are changing the relevancy of business and the role of brand leaders forever.

A butterfly flaps its wings

Technology and the easy access it provides to information enables massive opportunity for growth in the form of knowledge, innovation and reach. Greater awareness and the ability to analyse situations from different viewpoints fuel an ever-increasing intelligence – 'meta-intelligence' – of each other and the world. Suddenly, we can see – and even model – the true impact and outcomes of seemingly small changes in initial conditions. The butterfly effect becomes suddenly more personal when we can use the molecular make-up of the fish we are about to purchase to determine just how clean the waters were where it was farmed.

Playing fields are levelled as technology wipes away the opacity of business workings. Physical and economic barriers to entry are removed, making it possible to start a business – a global business – in just a few clicks. Capital can be gained in ways not imagined just a few years or even months ago. Big is no longer the determinant of best. Niche players now have the ability to compete and challenge the bottom line of the large multinational. The flow of ideas has never been greater, or faster. Media companies are no longer the sole source of news, views and influence. Brands can be smashed just as fast as businesses can be built. Consider: 400 million tweets are sent per day by about 200 million monthly active users; 30 billion pieces of content are shared on Facebook each month;[1] and, in early 2015, mainland China registered 629 million active social media users – 46 per cent of its population – who are estimated to spend a daily average of 1 hour and 42 minutes on social media platforms.[2] Brand managers, PR agencies and marketing departments that want to control their brand experiences will need the mind of a super computer and, even then, their success will be questionable. Brand dictators are out. Democracy and 'crowd voice' are in.

It is no wonder that companies around the world are scrambling to find the next best way to use data to their business advantage, to keep up with their younger, more agile competitors and consumers, and to capitalize on the insights hidden within 2.5 quintillion bytes of data generated daily.[3] Technology is truly the catalyst of change. But it is not the panacea for business or for the challenges facing our world of consumerism. Adding to the drama is the second business-changing evolution – that of our planet.

The world changes

In *The Responsible Company: What we've learned from Patagonia's first 40 years*, the founder of one of the more responsible companies in the world, Yvon Chouinard, and Vincent Stanley (co-editor) write:

> Everything we make causes some kind of damage. No human economic activity is yet sustainable. We have borrowed from nature what we can't pay back.[4]

Record-breaking droughts now plague places like California. The water system and challenges facing the Central Valley illustrate the unintended and unplanned results of desire and commercial interests: 'We have altered the driest parts of California, Nevada, and Arizona to fulfil our ambitions, and for years we have been able to ignore their natural limits. Now a growing population and a changing climate are exposing those limits as never before.'[5] Water will one day be more valuable than oil. After all, humans cannot survive without water. Yachtswoman Ellen MacArthur, tells the story of limitations using her own experience of sailing around the world:

> When you set off around the world, you take with you everything that you need for your survival. So for three and a half months you're on a boat with everything that you have. You know that you only have so much food, you only have so much diesel, and you become incredibly connected to those resources that you use. And as you watch those resources go down, you realize just what 'finite' means, because in the Southern Ocean, you're 2,500 miles away from the nearest town. There is no more, you can't stop and collect more.[6]

We are on a boat with Ellen. The boat is called *Earth*. Every mobile phone, every appliance, everything we buy is on that boat devouring our sustenance. What will we do? Continue to use limited supplies to feed our ego with things designed to throw away? Or will we innovate what, and how, we produce to save and reuse our supply in order to feed the world? Sustainable design and development are critical to the long-term survival not only of business, but also of the supply chain of natural – and human – sources.

Although the number of undernourished people has decreased over the last decade by 167 million to approximately 795 million, obesity is on the rise.[7] In 2014, more than 1.9 billion adults globally, 18 years and older, were overweight. Of these, over 600 million were obese. In addition, more than 42 million children under the age of five were overweight or obese. Although obesity was once considered a high-income country problem (the richest country, the United States, still home to the biggest chunk of the obesity problem at 13 per cent), these numbers are now on the rise in low- and middle-income countries as well. In fact, many low- and middle-income countries are now facing the 'double burden' of undernourished obesity.[8] According to the World Health Organization:

> Children in low- and middle-income countries are more vulnerable to inadequate pre-natal, infant and young child nutrition. At the same time, they are exposed to high-fat, high-sugar, high-salt, energy-dense, micronutrient-poor foods, which tend to be lower in cost but also lower in nutrient quality. These dietary patterns, in conjunction with lower levels of physical activity, result in sharp increases in childhood obesity while undernutrition issues remain unsolved.[9]

But, this burden is really more like a 'quadruple burden', considering the individual, societal and planetary stresses it imposes. More than a gallon of water is required to manufacture a spoonful of sugar.[10] Add the expense of health care to the equation and the cost of sugary goodies goes even higher.

The production of empty calories that taste ever so sweet and sell so well not only undernourishes individuals, but also strains the health of society and the planet. These issues can be resolved through sustainable design and development. Instead of producing sugary goodies, why not produce vegetables? They too require water and resources, but far less per dollar of economic output. More importantly, they provide health benefits, and can help reduce obesity when consumed in place of sugar-full alternatives. Sustainable innovation can have serious individual, economic and social impact.

The growing gap between the rich and poor is yet another threat to global well-being. Inequality is often the source of negative emotions – jealousy, desperation and even hatred. It can lead to exploitation as wealthier, more educated factions look to capitalize on the misfortune of their weaker brethren. The main theory behind this inequality is the belief that poorer people invest less in education and self-improvement. But, without the ways and financial means, the cycle of poverty continues. The living standards of the bottom 40 per cent need to improve in order to grow as a society. Meaningful employment and education is the most effective path to sustainable growth and, ultimately, to improving the environment in which businesses operate. For business leaders, these challenges present intriguing opportunities to do something more profound than simply maximizing shareholder return. They provide the opportunity to impact the lives of the more than 7 billion shareholders inhabiting and invested in this planet.

The rise of business consciousness

The growing scale of the human enterprise is driving the extinction of an estimated 30,000 species per year (or three per hour). These changes are fundamentally different from those at any other time in history.[11] The *Bardo Thodol – The Tibetan Book of the Dead* – speaks of a clarity of light, a deep awakening of consciousness, as the passing of life occurs. This awakening is not so different from that in business enterprises, and the world, today:

> Perhaps the greatest change that we humans are experiencing is our rising consciousness. To be conscious means to be fully awake and mindful, to see reality more clearly, and to more fully understand all the consequences – short term and long term – of our actions.[12]

This transformational phase is the dawning of a business renaissance. Gathering force is a collective intelligence and revival of the human spirit that questions the importance of financial growth in the light of environmental and social degradation. Abundance, having failed to fulfil the promise of happiness, has lost favour to a rising desire for meaning, purpose and a return to the simple pleasures of living. One need only look at the Slow Food Movement, to see that our fast paths to cash through low-quality substitutes are no longer acceptable to a discerning consumer. The movement that started with one person in defence of traditional home-grown values and living has grown to global proportions, involving millions of people in thousands of projects related to lifestyle, nutrition, politics and preservation of those things that make life so pleasurable.

A 2014 survey by Havas Worldwide of over 10,000 people worldwide supports this view by showing a global population in search of a better way of living and consuming. Of the people surveyed, 70 per cent believe that overconsumption is actually putting the planet and society at risk and a vast majority believes that 'our current economic models are not working'.[13] Medinge Group, a global think tank on branding, had taken notice of these challenges nearly a decade earlier when, in 2004, they began awarding companies that are leading the change to more sustainable practices.

Perpetual growth and increasing consumption is not possible in a world of limited resources. For a growing number of consumers, business leaders and corporation stakeholders, business as usual is no longer sustainable or acceptable. These 'business activists' (business stakeholders not affiliated with an official cause or group) are seeking change and doing so by changing their own behaviour – first. The impact of their actions causes change to occur across the broader business environment. According to the Havas Social Business Study, three-quarters of consumers surveyed think that business bears as much responsibility for driving positive social change as governments. And 80 per cent of consumers believe they have the responsibility to censure unethical companies by avoiding their products.[14] And, more and more, that is exactly what they do.

The rise of awareness and the ability to connect have empowered business stakeholders (the planet included) to elevate their role in the company from 'customer' or 'resource' to 'chief conscience officer'. The power to cut spending at the sign of unfavourable behaviour, misuse of resources or untruthful claims simply by taking their purchasing power elsewhere or, more effectively, by tweeting a comment to their circle of friends, is slowly forcing businesses to shift their goals from pure financial profit to one of social, environmental *and then* financial profit. Economic gain can no longer be the goal. The result of connecting to the larger purpose and goal of the macrocosm will be the way to gain sustainability and maintain economic wellness.

The gathering force of the collective conscious is starting to quake. Traditional brand strategists who try to manipulate the brand message from the inside out will soon find that they need to focus on a far larger set of brand 'managers'. Employees, customers, suppliers and the world of natural resources are the ones responsible for bringing brand stories to life and are the true testimonial to the validity of companies' claims. Where the paid voice will report one thing, earned chatter will certainly bring forth the truth. Businesses and marketing departments worldwide are making greater use of social media and sentiment analytics to gauge the general temperature of this larger constituency – to help identify and manage the key influencers. But in reality, the simplest truth is the most effective guiding practice. As more companies invite their stakeholders to participate in all types of business operations and product development activities, the more honest and transparent a company has to be. As more business leaders implement ideas founded on humane and ecological values, and demonstrate how business can change the world, the more conscientious the world will become. In such an environment, brand becomes pervasive – embedded in the core of the business – and standard brand practices and approaches become obsolete.

Conscientious business: a force for good

'Enlightened leaders are making sustainability a core part of business strategy. Now we need business leaders everywhere to make business a force for good. Together, we can respond to the urgency of our global challenges and build a better tomorrow.'[15]

H E BAN KI-MOON, UNITED NATIONS SECRETARY GENERAL

The realization that things are changing is also occurring within organizations and across developed, emerging and digital economies. Business leaders, whether influenced by their stakeholders or through their own observations of the environments in which they operate, are moving into a new level of consciousness. As they do, they are forcing resounding change. Concerned with the current and future state of affairs, they are rethinking their business strategies, redefining profit, and innovating new production and business models. Many of these models are founded on similar principles of regeneration and the circular flow of goods in a 'cradle to cradle', no waste, manner of usage.

Others are tapping into governmental and non-governmental organizations to collaborate, learn from and broaden their efforts. All are connecting to goals beyond financial. These businesses are proactivating change and, in the process, forcing their stakeholders to think differently about their own behaviour and consumption habits. The stories that follow below are demonstrations of how leading companies are working to change the world. What will be your role?

Meaningful innovation

Royal Philips is a diversified technology company, focused on improving people's lives through meaningful innovation. Since the introduction of the first Philips light bulb more than 120 years ago, innovation and a people-centric approach have been their foundation. Philips is addressing impending resource constraints by embedding 'circular' thinking into the way they design products. Rather than designing products that are 'thrown over the wall to customers', Philips is designing products that are upgradable and maintainable, and that can be mined for materials and components when the product reaches its end of life. By starting with the end, they are designing for the future – 15 years out. By pushing for great innovative thinking, Philips is generating savings, superior margins and creating breakthrough ideas for a healthier and more sustainable world.[16]

Visionary leadership

Unilever is on a similar path with what some say is the 'most comprehensive strategy of enlightened capitalism of any global firm'.[17] Unilever's goal is to help 1 billion people to take steps to improve their health and well-being; halve the environmental impact of its products/'Brands with a Purpose'; source 100 per cent of agricultural raw materials sustainably; and enhance the livelihoods of people across the value chain. They are doing this through visionary leadership, company-wide innovation and broad stakeholder influence. Through recycling and efficiency drives, three-quarters of Unilever's manufacturing sites now do not send any non-hazardous waste to landfills. That's right, NO non-hazardous waste to landfills. With more than 400 brands being developed in over 250 sites globally, this is a wildly significant achievement with consequential environmental impact. The entire company is being motivated to adopt best practices and to look for ways to make a difference. But it doesn't stop with its 170,000+ employees.

'Project Everyone' looks to engage the masses at scale – Unilever suppliers (over 200,000), consumers (2bn users of Unilever products), peers and even competitors – to 'change attitudes and behaviours, transform systems and create movements for sustainable living'. Unilever is going beyond selling products, to becoming a source of inspiration. Brand and marketing managers in this kind of an organization take on a complex role that straddles business activism, social marketer and caring educator. They are speaking out through channels such as Ted, but also in community forums. The important thing to note is that many are not marketers or brand professionals at all. They are employees. They are real people.

Reimagining commerce

Etsy is home to 1.5 million sellers who use the platform to sell unique handmade goods, crafts and vintage items. Etsy's mission is to 'reimagine commerce' – to help the 'little guy' with a more organized, active marketplace. It is a values-based company with the goal to 'create a better world'. Etsy values are stated as: 'We are a mindful, transparent and humane business; we plan and build for the long term; we value craftsmanship in all we make; we believe fun should be part of everything we do; we keep it real, always.' As a certified B Corporation, Etsy has pledged to adhere to strict social and environmental accountability guidelines. In their initial public offering (IPO), Etsy demonstrated this commitment by setting aside 5 per cent of shares to sell to its vendors and an additional 10 per cent of shares for other small investors, many of whom are Etsy customers. Though there is a hint of irony in the IPO, given that the original founder thought that maximizing shareholder value was 'ridiculous' and could not imagine running a business founded on that goal,[18] the model is especially clever. Its alignment of financial goals is now directly connected to their original social and environment goals – helping them, perhaps, to 'do well and do good' at the same time. In any case, they have reimagined commerce for even the most traditional players.

Catalysts of change

Walmart's sustainability and more ethical practices started out defensively as a response to increasing public criticism from employees and consumers. Founded on small-town values and a strong sense of community, in the 1960s, Walmart has grown to be one of the largest companies in the world in terms of sales.[19] If Walmart were a country it would be the twenty-sixth largest economy in the world. It has over 2 million employees and, in one week, serves more than 200 million customers. But it was the voice of their stakeholders that catalysed Walmart's drive for sustainability and focus on three simple goals: 1) to be supplied 100 per cent by renewable energy; 2) to create zero waste; and 3) to sell products that sustain people and the environment. These are admirable goals, considering that Walmart is starting from a position of enormous environmental impact – over 900 million square feet of physical space.[20] Even the smallest improvements in sustainability can mean significant benefit for the environment.

The results of Walmart's efforts can be read in their Global Sustainability Report, where they report on their achievements, as well as their misses:

> By the end of 2014, we had improved US fleet efficiency by 87.4 per cent over the 2005 baseline – an improvement of 3.2 per cent compared with the year before. At this rate, we project that we will come close but will not quite achieve our goal of doubling fleet efficiency by October 2015. The evolving service requirements of our multichannel, multiformat business have slowed our progress. We continue to strive for greater efficiency through equipment innovation, using data to help our drivers drive more efficiently, and adopting the latest fleet technologies as they become commercially viable.[21]

In 2014, Walmart held its 'first-ever sustainability conference', where top chief executive officers (CEOs) from companies and organizations such as Procter & Gamble, PepsiCo and Campbell's Soup, attended and agreed to work towards more sustainable practices. Eight of the largest food companies announced pledges to help ensure that tomorrow's food supply is affordable and sustainable.[22] This is a big deal. It highlights the powerful potential of the private sector to encourage more efficient use of our resources and to force conscientious branding principles.

Emerging economies can leap beyond

State Grid of China ranks in the top 10 of the 2014 Global Fortune 500. It is the world's largest power company, serving more than 1.1 billion Chinese. As the sales and financial assets of Chinese companies have continued to grow, so has their need to refocus their operations on social and environmentally responsible goals. Leading Chinese companies now seek to become some of the world's most reputable and pre-eminent brands. It is no longer sufficient just to be big. They must also evolve their strategies to include social and environmental issues to maintain their competitiveness, but more importantly to sustain the physical environments in which they operate. They must curb overdevelopment and reduce the use of fossil-based energy. State Grid has a goal to connect the world's energy grids and create a global energy grid that 'ties together solar, hydro and wind energy installation with energy-hungry cities'. Working with governments, the UN Global Compact and social institutions, they are hoping to make this innovation a reality. By making sustainability an imperative, China and other emerging economies can leap beyond existing barriers and set new standards for the future of business.[23]

Conscientious brands: change the world

Brands are powerful ideas that embody our values. Those who are aware realize that a growing population seeks brands that do more than just deliver the goods – they must do so in an ethical, humane way. The Medinge Group had its first meeting in 2000, around the same time that the UN Global Impact was established to align corporate practices with ten universal principles; to mobilize the global business community to advance UN goals; and to build a sustainable, inclusive global economy in which both business and society can thrive, within the environmental limits of the planet. Medinge has recognized and celebrated the power of conscientious business and the potential for business to create positive social and environmental impact in line with these goals. At the core of what Medinge defines as conscientious brands are some basic, but necessary principles.

Conscientious brands:

- have a visible conscience;
- apologize when things go wrong;
- invest time and energy in relationship building;
- promote the value of caring for one another;
- acknowledge that we are all fundamentally equal;
- are visibly accountable for all their actions;
- take risks in line with their values.

Where politics and religions can separate people around the world, conscientious brands can unite them. Businesses have the financial resources, human capital, technological savvy, innovative capability and cross-border reach to create results beyond that of any governmental institution or political party. They can be as powerful as Gandhi and more powerful than an army. Brand leaders have to step up to the C-suite and fuel this force with honest, value-driven actions. Take the money invested in expensive advertising/marketing campaigns and reinvest it in doing good. Just stop and reflect on the lives you impact.

The enlightenment. A movement. Your imperative

No matter what industry or size, whether you are an entrepreneur or a global corporation, the principles of conscientious branding apply. No effort is too small. Let the stories in this book be your inspiration and motivation. The time has come – business must change. The world demands it. Technology can enable it. But only your actions can make it happen. What will you do?

> The longest journey that people must take is the 18 inches between their heads and their hearts – then the most important step any organization or individual for that matter can take is the first step of that journey.[24]

Notes

1 Quintero, D, William M Genovese, KiWaon Kim, Ming Jun MJ Li, Fabio Martins, Ashish Nainwal, Dusan Smolej, Marcin Tabinowski and Ashu Tiwary (2015) *IBM Redbooks: IBM Software Defined Environment*, IBM Corporation, p 192

2 Jacquot, E (2015) [accessed 2 December 2015] A Primer on the Evolving Social Media Landscape of China [Online] https://www.techinasia.com/talk/primer-evolving-social-media-landscape-china/

3 IBM [accessed 2 December 2015] Bringing Big Data to the Enterprise, *IBM Corporation* [Online] http://www-01.ibm.com/software/data/bigdata/what-is-big-data.html

4 Chouinard, Y and Stanley, V (2012) *The Responsible Company: What we've learned from Patagonia's first 40 years*, Patagonia Books, California

5 Nijhuis, M (2014) [accessed 2 December 2015] When the Snow Fails, *National Geographic Magazine* [Online] http://www.nationalgeographic.com/west-snow-fail/

6 MacArthur, E (2014) [accessed 2 December 2015] Navigating the Circular Economy: A Conversation with Dame Ellen MacArthur, *McKinsey* [Online] http://www.mckinsey.com/insights/manufacturing/navigating_the_circular_economy_a_conversation_with_dame_ellen_macarthur

7 Food and Agricultural Organization of the United Nations (2015) [accessed 2 December 2015] The State of Food Insecurity in the World 2015 [Online] http://www.fao.org/hunger/key-messages/en/

8 World Health Organization (2015) [accessed 2 December 2015] Fact Sheet No 311 [Online] http://www.who.int/mediacentre/factsheets/fs311/en/

9 Ibid

10 Perkins, S (2010) [accessed 2 December 2015] Water, Water Everywhere, *Science News* [Online] https://www.sciencenews.org/blog/deleted-scenes/water-water-everywhere

11 Center for Biological Diversity [accessed 2 December 2015] Human Population Growth and Extinction [Online] http://www.biologicaldiversity.org/programs/population_and_sustainability/extinction/

12 Mackey, J and Sisodia, R (2014) *Liberating the Heroic Spirit of Business: Conscious capitalism*, Harvard Business School Publishing Corporation, Boston

13 Havas Worldwide Prosumer Report (2014) The New Consumer and the Sharing Economy, pp 6–7

14 Jones, D (2012) *Who Cares Wins: Why good business is better business*, Pearson Education Limited, Harlow, pp 20–21

15 DNV GL, United Nations Global Compact (2015) [accessed 2 December 2015] Next Sustainable Business [Online] https://www.dnvgl.com/news/new-publication-looks-at-what-s-next-for-sustainable-business-28407

16 Fleming, T and Zils, M (2014) [accessed 2 December 2015] Toward a Circular Economy: Philips CEO Frans van Houten, *McKinsey Quarterly* [Online] http://www.mckinsey.com/insights/sustainability/toward_a_circular_economy_philips_ceo_frans_van_houten

17 Port Sunlight (2104) [accessed 2 December 2015] Unilever: In Search of the Good Business, *The Economist* [Online] http://www.economist.com/news/business/21611103-second-time-its-120-year-history-unilever-trying-redefine-what-it-means-be

18 Chafkin, M (2011) [accessed 2 December 2015] Can Rob Kalin Scale Etsy?, *Inc Magazine* [Online] http://www.inc.com/magazine/20110401/can-rob-kalin-scale-etsy.html

19 Forbes (2015) [accessed 2 December 2015] The World's Biggest Public Companies [Online] http://www.forbes.com/global2000/list/

20 Cold Fusion (2015) [accessed 2 December 2015] How BIG is Walmart? (2.2 million employees!) [Online] https://www.youtube.com/watch?v=Timt1H6eYw4

21 Walmart (2015) [accessed 2 December 2015] 2015 Global Sustainability Report Executive Summary; 13 [Online] http://cdn.corporate.walmart.com/34/c7/6762cc4f43bc929feddd8a4abdd8/2015-global-responsibility-report-executive-summary.13.15.pdf

22 Walmart Staff (2014) [accessed 2 December 2015] Walmart Sustainable Product Expo Gathers Top CEOs to Renew Sustainability Commitments [Online] http://blog.walmart.com/sustainability/20140429/walmart-sustainable-product-expo-gathers-top-ceos-to-renew-sustainability-commitments

23 Liu, M (2015) [accessed 2 December 2015] Is Corporate Social Responsibility China's Secret Weapon?, *World Economic Forum* [Online] https://agenda.weforum.org/2015/03/is-corporate-social-responsibility-chinas-secret-weapon/

24 Mackey, J and Sisodia, R (2014) *Liberating the Heroic Spirit of Business: Conscious capitalism*, Harvard Business School Publishing Corporation, Boston

Business is a matter of human service

01

JACK YAN ON DILMAH TEA

○ *The brand is defined by real experiences over a long period of time.*

○ *Its authenticity comes from value creation for all those involved in the whole value chain.*

○ *The success of the brand is measured by the people served.*

Dilmah Tea, the Sri Lankan tea brand, came into the Medinge Group's orbit in 2004. It was one of eight brands named in the second Brands with a Conscience awards in December that year. The Brands with a Conscience committee members agreed at the time that Dilmah qualified as a humanistic, ethical brand, having remained consistent throughout its history. Its eventual win prompted positive e-mails from those who had come to know the firm.

The announcement came on 20 December 2004; six days later, the Boxing Day tsunami obliterated the south and east coasts of Sri Lanka. Thousands lost their lives. Dilmah, which had set up the MJF Charitable Foundation in 2002, rapidly sprang into action. One of the MJF Charitable Foundation's first initiatives was to supply nets to affected fishermen on the coasts in order to ensure that they could at least continue their livelihoods. In time, other initiatives covered medical, educational, housing, environmental, conservation and water sanitation needs for affected families, with the MJF Charitable Foundation facilitating over 100 projects. If the world needed proof that Medinge had made the right choice in its Brands with a Conscience awards, nature provided the catalyst.

Tell the truth

I was introduced to Merrill J Fernando, the founder of Dilmah, at a lunch put on by its New Zealand distributor in mid-2004. New Zealand has figured hugely in the development of the Dilmah brand: it was while in New Zealand that a plan was hatched to have Fernando as the spokesperson in its marketing, something that has since been adopted in other markets.

Fernando originally resisted being the on-air spokesperson for his tea. 'I resisted for two years,' he told me on one of his many visits to New Zealand. 'At a dinner, there were people trying to persuade me. I said in a weak moment, "OK, but only if it could be done before I leave the following day." It was filmed at a mutual friend's house.'

The brand had launched in Australia in 1988 with a more generic advertisement featuring a Sri Lankan model. But no tea maker had been willing to put their face to the name. Daron Curtiss, of Dilmah's advertising agency Curtiss & Spence, decided that the personal approach could cut through the noise for the New Zealand market. Dilmah's share went from 3.9 per cent to 9 per cent within two months of the first television commercial's airing in July 1995; by the 2010s it was the market leader, with around a one-quarter share. Market research showed, according to Fernando: 'This man has an honest face. He does not say he has the best tea, only to try it. There was no hard selling – he was just talking about the product.'

Fernando began recording a personal statement on each of the Dilmah packages, 'reflecting my personality and my feelings. The brand is in the culture: I have told the truth.' Fernando became a local celebrity; at the time of writing, Curtiss & Spence still has the account.

Curtiss, as well as Nigel Scott, the head of Dilmah in New Zealand, and Fernando's son Dilhan (the *Dil-* in Dilmah; the *-mah* comes from Fernando's other son, Malik, with the extra *h* added to balance the look of the brand name) were present at the first luncheon, along with the founder, who eventually came forth with more of his story. That early conversation in the middle of 2004 revealed a few titbits about Merrill Fernando: he was serious about the MJF Charitable Foundation and the work it was doing in Sri Lanka to benefit its citizens, and that both of his sons, while working for the family firm, had to fight along with other applicants to secure their jobs, and neither should expect a legacy from their father. Fernando's rationale was that he had attended school with children who wound up squandering their forebears' fortune in adulthood, and what he had would, instead, go to the community.

None of this was marketing hype. Closer investigation showed that Dilmah's claims of 'ethically grown tea' were genuine, paying all its workers a fair wage – the company relied on the traditional method of hand-picking tea – and bucking the trend of forcing lower wages on workers while executives profited at their expense. But, most importantly for Medinge, every aspect of Dilmah was geared towards social responsibility. The plantation sector, which had suffered extreme poverty, was being looked after through on-site child development centres that saw to the nutrition and health of workers' children, for instance. Small local businesses were given grants to improve the quality of life for their owners and their families. The MJF Charitable Foundation was being funded by a minimum of 10 per cent of the pre-tax profits for Dilmah Tea and its associated companies. Fitting in with the ideas that Simon Anholt expressed in his book *Brand New Justice*, which was very influential in the early 2000s on how brands could lift countries out of poverty, Dilmah was created in Sri Lanka, with its value-added components such as design, packaging and marketing strategy done locally. Interestingly, Anholt found Sri Lanka to be a tough market in his analysis: companies were discouraged from setting up their own brands, which might be seen as competing with the businesses they supplied. As a consequence of the country's colonial heritage, with its emphasis on the production of raw materials, Sri Lankans were discouraged from creating Western-style entrepreneurs, and its educational system tended to emphasize 'faithful and scrupulous service to others'. Dilmah turned the model on its head, creating its own brand, and ensuring that the scrupulous service was devoted to its own nationals. Dilmah was founded on the principle that the tea is packed garden-fresh and is sourced from Sri Lanka, and that tea can be picked, packed and shipped directly from the origin by the growers themselves.

Fernando struck me as a very determined man who was fortunate in not needing to compromise one iota on his principles, ensuring that Dilmah stayed true to its brand. But over the last decade, I have learned, through keeping in touch with the Fernando family and seeing them during their many visits to New Zealand, that the story was not as clear-cut as it first seemed. Dilmah has indeed stayed very true to its brand but, considering that Fernando was in his fifties when he founded Dilmah, it has done so based on decades of learning from an ambitious tea professional who entered the industry aged 22.

The man behind the brand

Merrill Joseph Fernando was born on 7 May 1930 in Pallansena, Negombo, in the west of Sri Lanka, to P Harry and Lucy Fernando, described in Dilmah's own history as 'a middle-class couple of modest means'.

'I have spent most of my life in tea,' Fernando recalls. 'In my early school days, I spent my holidays on the plantations of my friends, watching the workers. I was very happy, and I had a nice life at that time.'

He attended Maris Stella College in Negombo, and St Joseph's College in Colombo, and his first job was with a US petroleum company, as an inspector. After gaining independence from Britain in 1948, when Ceylon became Sri Lanka, the mercantile professions that were once reserved for the British began to be opened up. Fernando applied to be a tea-taster in 1952 and was in the first batch of trainees to be sent to Mincing Lane, London.

'I trained as a tea-taster. At the time we [Sri Lankans] were not tea-testers. The British believed we could not do it. They took six people. They were usually from top-echelon schools. I don't know how I was chosen; this could not be credited to me,' he recalls humbly.

The British had pioneered the tea industry in Ceylon, and helped propel its reputation as the finest in the world, so it was no surprise that they were held in high esteem by the young Merrill Fernando. But what he observed in what was once the 'mecca' of the tea trade was dysfunction. In his interview for this book, he recalled that at 24 years of age, 'I was very disappointed, because I regarded British people of that era [as possessing] very high integrity, but I saw them mixing Ceylon teas with other teas and labelling them "Ceylon tea". These would include cruder teas from Africa. Ceylon tea was a major employer and a foreign-exchange earner, but there were African companies undercutting us... The thought of having my own brand haunted me.'

Fernando briefly worked for a tea business in London before returning to Sri Lanka, joining A F Jones & Co, a British-owned tea business. Within four years he had been appointed as a director, and when the British owners decided it was time to return to the UK, Fernando and a partner purchased their shares. He even helped supply the first consignment of Ceylon tea to the Soviet Union at the end of the 1950s. After selling up his shares in A F Jones, in 1962 he founded his own firm, Merrill J Fernando & Co, with the aid of a US$100 loan from his father.

He recalled how the tea was being supplied to reputable family firms in plywood tea chests initially, but soon multinationals moved into the field, acquiring each company. They were also buying the family-owned businesses in Sri Lanka, forcing the smaller ones to go out of business through discounting. 'There was an annihilation of small businesses,' Fernando says. 'Globalization only benefited the big boys in developing countries, and mass unemployment resulted.'

He has critical words for the multinational tea traders: 'Any trader is an opportunist and makes all their money outside the producing country. Soon they will change the quality and exploit consumers.

'When traders lower quality, their commitment is to eliminate competition by discounting the price. When the price drops 25 per cent, quality drops 30 per cent. The only promise is their brand name.'

The acquisitions resulted in poorer quality as the corporations continued their approach of mixing teas from different origins, 'making tea a commodity. They took away the right of consumers to buy Ceylon tea, and they were forced to pay extra for a brand name.'

The dysfunction also meant that the producers in Sri Lanka benefited little, with the value-adding components all being done in Europe. Middlemen and the multinationals were the winners in the transaction.

Nevertheless, Merrill J Fernando & Co continued to supply bulk tea, resisting the multinationals, and made useful contacts around the world. It became one of the top 10 bulk-tea exporters in Sri Lanka, and the only locally owned one. Fernando served on the Ceylon Tea Propaganda Board (CTPB), unique as a Sri Lankan who headed his own firm, rather than as a foreigner or as a local representative of a foreign firm. At the time, he highlighted the importance of developing one's own brand name, something that the CTPB ridiculed, including the then-chairman of Brooke Bond. CTPB also permitted the 'Ceylon tea' description to be used for blended teas that contained 50 per cent of the product. Fernando continued to believe that Ceylon tea was superior, saying that, 'Traders don't respect the quality.'

In 1971 he purchased Melton Estate, a tea plantation, to begin vertically integrating his operation. However, the socialist government that had just come into power decided to nationalize all plantations, a move that saw them become run down. Coupled with increasing regulation, Fernando sold the business with the intent to emigrate to Ireland, but was persuaded by friends and clients to remain in Sri Lanka. Having decided to stay, he established MJF Exports Ltd in 1977, and lobbied the government to give incentives to exporters of value-added teas. In the 1970s it became the fourth-largest exporter of bulk teas. He imported the first tea-bagging machine into Sri Lanka, and faced heavy criticism from other Sri Lankans and from his customers, who believed that the country should remain a commodity supplier. 'It was hard to innovate in the late 1970s,' he recalls.

'I do not know what made me do that… to start doing the process of value addition in Sri Lanka.'

The machine remained underutilized for years and Fernando had to weather those forces who wanted to keep Sri Lanka a supplier of raw materials. However, he persevered with his vision that if consumers wanted Ceylon tea then that was what they should have, not the diluted product that certain multinationals passed off as Ceylon tea. By supplying consumers from the point of origin, the tea could be fresher and of higher quality. A few were convinced, and decided to stick with Fernando and his vision.

The MJF Group, as it became, wound up being a key stakeholder in over 50 of Sri Lanka's best tea gardens. It controlled the second-oldest tea broker in the country, Forbes & Walker. But at this point it still had not changed the way in which tea was marketed or branded.

'You need total commitment to change the existing colonial culture in trade,' says Fernando, who says it was important that there had been integrity in his policy. 'People realized the need to, but believed they couldn't.'

Value creation for all

Fernando continued to push the idea through the 1980s, supplying Coles, Tetley, Woolworths and Franklins through own-brand deals in Australia, while learning about the marketplace. In 1988, Dilmah Tea was launched, the first producer-owned tea brand from Sri Lanka, at substantial risk and criticisms from some of his buyers, who said that he would never succeed because he was not close enough to the customer. 'I started with very little money,' says Fernando. 'I realized if it failed, I would have lost all the money I had made.' He credits his Christian faith: 'There was somebody encouraging me, guiding me. Divine guidance directed me to do everything right.

'I named the brand after my children: that showed total dedication. Conviction is the only way a country can benefit from agricultural crops, to stop foreign traders driving people deeper into poverty. For trade to be fair, the packaging must be done in the country, not by third parties. When traders do it [with other brands], they keep the people poor.'

But it wasn't just about selling the tea: it was everything about value creation. Initially, Dilmah was forced to import basic packaging materials from Japan and Singapore, in a very complex operation. After the 1988 launch Dilmah established its own printing and packaging company. Fernando notes: 'There were no graphic artists and no three-colour printing. No one could advise about designing labels or packaging. I invested $180,000 buying an American-manufactured printing press.'

The company is Printcare plc, co-founded with Krishnamurthy R Ravindran; Fernando still chairs it. In the 1980s it operated from an area no larger than a garage; today, it is the largest printing and packaging company in Sri Lanka, with the most modern equipment, housed on a 10-acre block. 'It is rated one of the top five printing–packaging facilities in the region,' says Fernando. 'I risked going bankrupt with packaging, and going with my own brand.

'I set an example of how a producer country could retain, in the country, all the profits taken away by traders in branding, marketing, printing and packaging that had been done in industrialized nations. There have not been any serious followers, because of the investment, and the people.'

He believes that the best people to market tea are those who produce the tea, namely the farmers: 'Apart from the money, their concern is to develop the industry. [Dilmah] is the only [brand] owned by tea farmers, a new culture that attacked the colonial culture.

'The quality is on the pack. Ceylon tea is twice the price. We survived price competition strictly on quality and loyalty. Dilmah tea is ethically produced: we don't want to be "fair trade" where you can buy an endorsement by paying a fee. There is no relation between fair trade and quality. "Fair trade" needs to mean as much to the consumers *and* the producers. We don't need fair trade labels: ours is the fairest trade.'

Dilmah now exports to 100 countries, but the elements of the brand came from decades in the tea business, witnessing first-hand the destructive tendencies of certain players. And with the value-adding components being done domestically, Dilmah has ensured that the profits stay within the country to benefit Sri Lankans themselves.

However, it goes further. Fernando recalls his earlier thinking: 'I'm going to promise to share some of my earnings with the poor, the disabled, and with the community at large. I proved to those friends who are big businessmen that business will grow if you spread it to the community. The more we give, the more we receive the following year. We get consumers who know that when you brew a cup of Dilmah tea, your contribution goes directly back to the producers, to the people.'

Spreading wealth

By the time that the MJF Charitable Foundation was formally set up by an Act of Parliament in 2002, Fernando was in his early seventies. It clearly had not been set up on a whim, and can trace its origins back to a philosophy of caring and sharing that began 40 years before. Its existence was designed to lock in the ongoing benefits to the people working in the Sri Lankan tea trade, guaranteeing them protection against political uncertainty. By tying its fortunes to Dilmah Tea itself, it ensures that the company can never be compromised by foreign traders without harming the charitable foundation. It is an expression of the Dilmah brand as it has been developed over decades in the tea trade: unsurprisingly for a first-generation venture (one that is still run by its founder), it mirrors Fernando's principles. The foundation even bears his initials.

Fernando is officially the foundation's settlor, and it initially had seven full-time staff. Both his sons Malik and Dilhan serve as trustees, along with Minette Perera, the former MJF Group finance director, and long-time allies such as Printcare's Ravindran, at the time of writing the president-elect of Rotary International, the first Sri Lankan to hold the office. Its aim is to help the most deprived in the community, through programmes that have been created in consultation with the people they are meant to help. Says Dilhan, 'My father established the foundation as a trust to ensure that the philosophy of making business a matter of human service was formalized and eventually integrated into the operation of the business from the articles of association, compelling future generations to honour the philosophy on which he founded the business.'

The programmes are also designed for economical and environmental sustainability. At our first meeting, still months before the Boxing Day tsunami, Fernando was excited about the foundation helping the children of the workers in the Dilmah Tea gardens. By the turn of the decade, the foundation would be helping the workers' 3,000 children in development centres, providing them with lunch each day (a programme that began in 2007). The idea was to remove the worry that workers had over the welfare of their children, and as a result their health, safety and nutrition have improved.

Special-education classes in maths, English and science reached 8,500 children. Beyond the plantations, Batticaloa, on the east coast of Sri Lanka, benefited from a sanitization project to 194 homes, while fishermen in the tsunami-affected areas got boats, outboard motors and ice plants in addition to the nets that the foundation provided in the immediate aftermath of the tsunami. Preschools were also built.

A sustainable approach

Since winning the Brands with a Conscience award, Dilmah has not veered from its path. It has followed it unswervingly; and as it expanded its interests, it ensured the continued growth of the charitable foundation. In 2007, the foundation announced a new programme, in cooperation with the Ministry of Justice, of rehabilitating prisoners – helping those released on parole to get back on their feet with a productive life.

Meeting up with Fernando and his son Dilhan in 2009, they told me about other work that the MJF Charitable Foundation was doing. They had expanded beyond their original aims, and now funded traditional Ayurvedic medicine in hospitals. The foundation would pay for practitioners to come into hospitals, giving more people the option to receive treatment from them. It ensured that the foundation's traditions would continue and tied in with Fernando's belief in Sri Lanka's abilities. But he is not one-eyed about the benefits of occidental medicine, either: the MJF Charitable Foundation funded equipment including a mammogram scanner and a kidney dialysis machine, and it financed an eye-screening project that provided thousands with new glasses. The Houpe Estate Hospital was refurbished by the foundation.

Fernando described this as the socialization of medicine, aiming to secure the future of the health system against less desirable, profit-driven trends. A Fernando family home had been converted into the Sadhasarana Home for Elders, run by an order of nuns called the Sisters of Perpetual Help, for elderly people who had no family to support them.

In addition, money was being put towards nature reserves through Dilmah Conservation, part of the MJF Charitable Foundation, assisting areas that could be preserved, especially for elephants and other wildlife (Sri Lanka's elephant habitat had been shrinking as the country developed). Orphaned elephants went through the Elephant Transit Home, supported by the foundation, to be rehabilitated and returned to the wild. Dilmah Conservation, with its principles in promoting biodiversity, also preserved species of plant life against the expansion of the human population in Sri Lanka.

With a similar aim of preserving traditions, the foundation's Animal Tracks Pottery project, in association with the International Union for Conservation of Nature (IUCN) and the Department of Wildlife Conservation, encouraged the Koulara community to preserve its pottery skills, making high-value ornaments and souvenirs that could sustain them in the modern world, giving unskilled people a chance to make a livelihood.

By this time, a subsidiary programme called MJF Kids had been launched (in 2006), helping underprivileged children, originally those in the Peliyagoda vicinity near Dilmah's head office. These were not plantation children, but they were in a desperately impoverished area. Its initial venture was a day of fun for children from remote parts of Sri Lanka: one has to remember that Sri Lanka had been affected by civil war for decades, so these fun days serve to be memorable for them. Training programmes were set up in English, arts and crafts, sewing, cooking, music, dancing and computer studies, and assistance with school curricula. The programme, free for those from marginalized communities, has since expanded to Maligawtta, Pallansena (Fernando's home town), Moratuwa and Point Pedro.

By the time of our 2014 meeting for this book, the MJF Charitable Foundation had 75 child development centres looking after workers' children and providing them with lunch. In Talawakelle, where the foundation had built a primary school, they had established a special-education programme for plantation children. There were now computer training programmes at the Kahawatte plantations for children aged 8 to 16. Educational scholarships were being provided at higher levels, including 100 students who had made their way through university. The first born-and-bred plantation child entered medical school.

Fernando was justifiably proud of the school at Peliyagoda, where MJF Kids began. He said that the programme brought the children, aged up to 16, to the school from 1.30 pm, supplementing whatever education they were being given elsewhere. 'The kids are taught English and two languages, arithmetic, and three other subjects. They learn drumming and dancing, with professional teachers.' Some children have stayed back to teach themselves: 'They appreciate what we do.'

Dilhan noted, 'Whether they are from slums or wherever, they can go beyond their circumstances. They can transform their dreams and [empower] the dreams within them.'

'The success of a business should flow to the poor and the community,' added Dilhan's father. Merrill Fernando spoke more slowly than at our first meeting but, if anything, he was more passionate and determined about what Dilmah and the MJF Charitable Foundation were doing: 'We practise the culture of sharing and giving.' He quietly acknowledges that through their activities they were even able to inspire the Sri Lankan government.

Staying the course

Dilmah is a 'Brand with a Conscience' that in some respects is easy to write about. Since it won the award in 2004 the company has not suffered any setbacks to its brand. The narrative has remained constant at every turn, with a total of five meetings between Medinge representatives and the company. But that was only over the last decade. Fernando's own history demonstrates that a brand with a conscience can come out of a long-term fight stretching over decades, including dealing with dysfunction, deception and doubt; and it was after fighting all of these that baby steps were taken in creating the brand.

It is a brand story that has been forged alongside that of the Sri Lankan nation itself. The abuses of globalization were witnessed first-hand by Merrill J Fernando himself, long before it became fashionable to criticize them – post-Reaganomics and Thatchernomics. Dilmah came out of a decades-long process where Fernando knew that branding was the only way to avoid Sri Lanka being positioned as a producer and exporter of raw materials. He did so despite pressures from Western countries who told him that only they were clever and close enough to occidental consumers to be able to do it properly; and despite resistance from his own country, which could not understand his vision. He saw that the abuses were not only ongoing, but worsening, enriching middlemen while keeping his own people in abject poverty. Knowing that he was going to do it, he spent most of the 1980s acquiring the means, including his own printing press. He made the right contacts over decades, with people who wound up being his importers or running his businesses internationally. Sri Lanka is waking up to the Dilmah formula and understanding just why it is important for the value-added components to be done onshore, rather than simply repeating the colonial model that stayed put after independence.

This was a long-term project, one that took decades to materialize. But Fernando knew from the 1960s on, when he set up the firm bearing his own name, that branding was key to profit. Without a brand name, and a sustainable brand strategy, the company would never have thrived. The next decades were spent acquiring the means to implement the strategy and creating a brand name, albeit hampered by the political environment. If Fernando had not stood his ground and decided to remain in Sri Lanka, Dilmah would never have materialized.

The brand has played out almost in textbook fashion. The brand name was not conceived as the first step; instead, the competences of the firm, in being able to sustain a brand, were put into place. The MJF Group integrated its supply chain vertically and acquired a printing press. It learned about the environments into which it exported, as an original equipment manufacturer (OEM) supplier, understanding each market and assembling networks. Only when Fernando knew he was ready did the Dilmah brand come into being. There was little compromise on how it was rolled out: his internal audiences and distributors knew what he had planned, and the external marketing followed.

Once launched, the Dilmah brand evolved, and Fernando was open enough to accept input from his distributors and advertising agencies. The company moved from an arguably ill-defined promotion featuring a Sri Lankan model to using Fernando himself as the figurehead, and even though the first advertisement featuring him was filmed in a short space of time, it has become fundamental to the brand's approach.

Fernando was also keen to ensure that the brand could not be easily duplicated. While the capabilities were well cemented at home, social responsibility became a major part of the Dilmah brand, spurred by what he had witnessed in his lifetime. This 'Brand with a Conscience' came from real experiences: the ingredients of a strong brand, one that lasts, emerged over a long period. There is an authenticity about the social responsibility. It has come through a founder who was determined enough not to sway from his vision: while crediting his faith, he also knew that it had to be done to counter the colonial model, even if it was a huge gamble.

Finally, Fernando's upbringing taught him to respect all people, regardless of where they were from, and through that he could not stand by and tolerate the poverty he saw around him. There was an intent, by the founder, by his family and by those who work with him, to make things better for the community. Dilmah's success is measured by the people served, and while 'Do try it' is the tagline most associated with the company, the quotation, 'Business is a matter of human service' recurs regularly in Fernando's speeches and its marketing. Dilmah has been consistent in all the years that Medinge has had contact with the firm.

This chapter has dwelled on a considerable amount of Dilmah's charitable work, to show that it has gone beyond lip service. Groups such as the Ethical Tea Partnership, of which Dilmah is not a member, do valuable work, but Dilmah has the advantage of being a Sri Lankan firm that directly benefits the Sri Lankan people, rather than a foreign organization working with certification programmes and other mediating groups. Dilmah sees its work as forming a large part of how it communicates, symbolizes and differentiates itself to all audiences.

Dilmah and the MJF Charitable Foundation are intertwined not only financially, but culturally. One is named for the sons and the other after the father. One is the outward brand that serves as the touchstone for consumers; the other brings credibility to Fernando's claims of 'ethically grown tea' and going beyond fair trade with 'ours is the fairest trade'. Visually the two are tied. Remove the foundation and the Dilmah brand is weakened: it is part of the same vision of Merrill J Fernando, now well known throughout the company, and no longer doubted in its export markets or its homeland. Its projects have helped over 100,000 people in Sri Lanka, empowering them to be ambassadors of Dilmah as well as their country.

By passing on the mantle to his sons, who are as deeply involved in the corporate social responsibility (CSR) activities as their father, Fernando is ensuring a level of continuity. Dilhan is the more public face of the two brothers and accompanies his father on business trips; he also runs the business on a day-to-day basis, and drives Dilmah's marketing. He is heavily involved in the foundation. On recent trips, his father has put him forward more. Malik, meanwhile, oversees the operations and develops the group's tourism business. Succession has not been far from his mind.

The continuation of Fernando's philosophy that business is a matter of human service is assured in perpetuity, with this enshrined in each business's articles of association. This entails that the pre-tax profits of each company must be used in humanitarian or positive environmental service, with the exception of Ceylon Tea Services Ltd, the one publicly listed entity in the group, where the humanitarian and environmental obligation is voted on and passed annually at the shareholders' meeting. Dilhan states that future generations will uphold this philosophy and all aspects of the brand.

As the world economic centre shifts East, and globalization continues, it would not be inconceivable to see the next generation of Fernandos establish CSR initiatives abroad. If Dilmah can export its teas, and if its initiatives have been so successful, then why not extend that knowledge to more markets, including the ones to which Dilmah products go – especially as some of those Western countries have become less fair and have seen a growing gap between rich and poor.

Reflective questions

- What brands do you know that create value for business and society?
- What brands will suffer most from globalization and a growing Eastern orientation?
- What should be on the agenda for the next generation at Dilmah Tea?

Star for Life

ANNETTE ROSENCREUTZ

In 2005, Swedish entrepreneur Dan Olofsson was building a private game reserve in KwaZulu-Natal, South Africa. After a few visits he noticed that half of his workers had been replaced. Out of 200 construction workers about 100 people were new. When this happened again three months later, he realized that something was wrong. Seriously wrong.

When he investigated he found out that the workers were dying of AIDS. And that more people were already seriously ill. He realized that he would not meet many of the people he saw at the construction site again. He also saw children being left without parents.

At the time, KwaZulu-Natal was one of the regions most struck by HIV/AIDS: 37 per cent of the population was already HIV-infected. Dan and his wife, Christin Olofsson, felt that they had to do something to create a breakthrough. Having built and succesfully grown several Swedish companies, they though they could address the problem from a humanistic and psychological approach. Even though they came across deeply rooted ways of thinking, prejudices, traditions and habits, the problem was too big to be ignored. Together they set out to prevent the next generation from getting infected, by reversing the HIV epidemic among young people in South Africa.

A brand for a better future

Thomas and Zaiga Magnusson, motivational coaches, were hired to develop a programme and methodology for students and teenagers. While they never intended to build a brand, that is exactly what they created – a brand platform with a strong mission and values, symbolized in the Star for Life logo. With an action plan, and Dan and Christin's entrepreneurial leadership skills, the foundation of a brand for a better future was shaped.

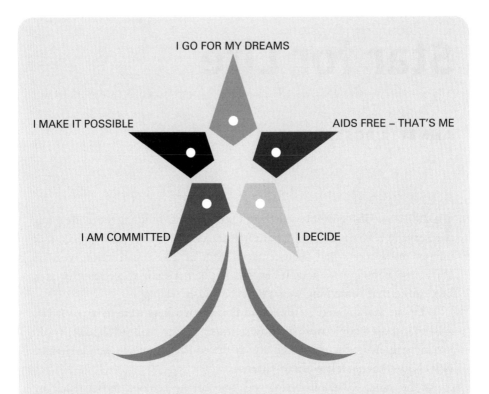

A programme filled with joy

The Star for Life (SFL) brand is built on a strong humanistic insight and a sense of what works. The basic idea is that young people with strong self-esteem and a belief in their ability to improve their lives will be more concerned about their sexual health and thus willing to protect themselves against HIV.

Star for Life works within the existing school structure. Twice a year over a period of three years, SFL conducts workshops on HIV and AIDS in high schools. In the workshops students formulate their own vision and goals for the future. SFL helps students to make the right decisions today so that they will have a better chance to achieve their dreams for the future.

The SFL programme focuses on strengthening teenagers' self-esteem, especially among girls, who often get pregnant in their teens and hence drop out of school. Higher self-esteem helps young people to adopt more positive attitudes towards life and education and improves HIV literacy, school performance, health behaviour and safer sex behaviour.

SFL celebrates life and thus the programme involves decisiveness, joy, determination, love for life, togetherness and dreams. And, above all, the power of music. Singing and playing together is at the very heart of South African culture and is also a way to give meaning. Each SFL programme has its own choir. Such has been the success of this that now students from different SFL schools perform around the world. Anyone who gets the chance to hear them sing will feel their passion and joy.

Breakthrough behaviour

Funding a school and creating a vibrant environment sounds like fun, but the proof of this concept is in the results:

- A 2009 survey showed that the pregnancy level of girls attending SFL dropped to 25 per cent compared to 40 per cent in the control group. Among girls with very high self-esteem it dropped to 18 per cent.

- The HIV literacy was also considerably higher among SFL girls: 59 per cent against 43 per cent of all SFL students and 23 per cent among those in the control group.

- The survey showed that SFL students, especially the girls, have considerably better grades in school than those in the control group from another school; 33 per cent of SFL girls with very high self-esteem received A in their best subject against 25 per cent among all SFL students and 18 per cent among the test group.

Not surprisingly, Dan Olofsson is a proud man: 'The outcome after 10 years' work is far better than we expected. The number of HIV positive individuals has been decreased by 50 per cent, the average life expectancy has increased by eight years and the life quality has increased.'

In 2015, the amount of HIV-infected citizens in South Africa has decreased by 50 per cent due to prevention and medicine; 16 per cent of the population aged 15–49 are HIV-infected. The figure for the KwaZulu-Natal region is 15.3 per cent in the age group 15–24.

Dan also notes that this success is the result of shared efforts on many levels. Medicine and prevention work is being done by a large number of different organizations. SFL only plays a small part, but it hits the right spot: improving self-esteem while focusing on a better future. 'We can say that we have been a driving force. Scientific studies show that we are one of the world's best preventive programmes.'

A borderless concept

Following this initial success, SFL has refined its structure. There are now programmes for primary-school children and for students after they have finished school, including help getting into university and an agreement with Volvo for trainees and mechanics, so that SFL students can get a job after they graduate.

Dan figured that the success of the methodology – including better school results – could be transplanted elsewhere. So he implemented the methodology in 11 schools with low results in Sweden as well. By focusing on increasing students' self-esteem and vision of the future, the results have been dramatic.

Now the idea is really spreading its wings. The SFL programme includes more than 100 schools, including 20 in Johannesburg, 8 in the Durban area and 20 in Windhoek, the capital of Namibia. It has now launched in Sri Lanka. Over 250,000 students around the globe have gone through the SFL programme, encouraging students and teachers to live a healthy life and to realize their dreams by increasing self-esteem and creating a better future for themselves.

Star for Life programme model

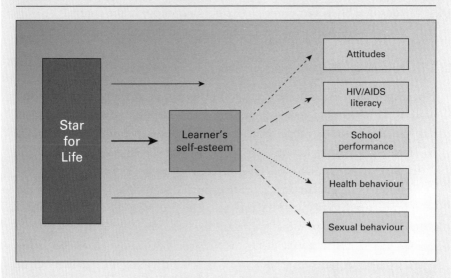

Partnership for all

02

ERIKA UFFINDELL AND SIMON PATERSON
ON THE JOHN LEWIS PARTNERSHIP

- ○ *Great people led by a humanistic vision and purpose, plus effective technology, create great customer experience.*
- ○ *Consensus and agile decision making are possible in partnerships.*
- ○ *Everyone wins when you connect all stakeholders together.*

> *The John Lewis Partnership was awarded a Brand with a Conscience award in 2005 for 'creating a sustainable, conscious and humanity-based brand and business model'.*

This is a story of one of the UK's most loved brands and successful businesses. John Lewis is a brand with a purpose and a business with the only large-scale 'employee ownership' model in the country. It's a brand and business that's in it for the long term.[1]

A conscious brand, a conscious business model

John Lewis has often been hailed as a beacon for 'a better way of doing business' and a benchmark for the way business should be run in the 21st century. And yet it is still, in a sense, one of its kind, the only large-scale 'employee ownership model in the UK' (the majority of the owner-run businesses in the UK have fewer than 10 people). But it is also one of the highest-performing brands in the sector and a flourishing business.

Where did it all start?

John Lewis was founded in 1864 by 28-year-old John Lewis, a draper who, with the help of a loan from his sisters, bought the stock for 132 Oxford Street, London where he began to build a business selling silks, laces, threads and ribbons. For the next 64 years until his death John Lewis actively ran what in effect became a department store and, in 1906, added to the business by acquiring a controlling interest in Peter Jones, a store based in Chelsea, handing this over to his son John Spedan Lewis to run in 1914.

In 1914, at the age of 21, Spedan Lewis was appointed chairman of Peter Jones, the Chelsea department store, while continuing to work in the John Lewis Oxford Street store. On the death of his father, John Lewis, in 1928, Spedan Lewis became the sole owner of John Lewis and Peter Jones and in 1929 created the John Lewis Partnership. The creation of the partnership had been an idea that had been taking shape for Spedan Lewis in his early twenties. He had begun to consider a new way of thinking about a business as 'not simply a machine for making money, but rather a living thing with rights of its own'. He began to plan 'a far-reaching experiment in industrial democracy' designed to 'limit the earnings of capital and divide the rest among the workers'. In his vision of this partnership model the management would be accountable to the employees 'sharing of gain, sharing of knowledge and sharing of power' – something that was radical at the time and still today would be unthinkable for many businesses. He proclaimed that: 'Partnership is justice. Better than justice it is kindness.'

In the 268-page partnership constitution published in 1929 Spedan Lewis set out that profits would be distributed to all partners. And in 1948 he published 'Partnership for all' – his manifesto for a new type of ownership model for business. The last paragraph of Spedan's 532-page manifesto sets out his vision for building a sustainable and humanity-based business:

> So far as general conditions in this country may allow, we should begin now to see how far producer cooperatives of this general type may be the answer to one of the great problems of our modern civilization, how to make our working lives as fruitful for ourselves and in all other ways as happy as they ought to be and so make ourselves work as well as for our own sakes we should...

What may be implied by working fruitfully for oneself is that this is a consequence of working in relationship with and in the service of others, rather than working for an entity.

In the early 1920s Spedan Lewis also introduced what would be John Lewis's enduring slogan 'Never knowingly undersold', which was initially conceived as a way to ensure that buyers got the best price from suppliers, but soon it became a message to customers that they were not paying more at John Lewis for the same goods that might be found elsewhere. This slogan in effect set in motion a value proposition that has stood the test of time and speaks to the integrity that sits at the heart of what makes John Lewis a brand with a conscience.

Today, the John Lewis Partnership is the seventh biggest retailer in the UK with annual gross sales of £10 billion. It has over 88,000 permanent staff who are partners and who, in turn, own 45 John Lewis shops, 341 Waitrose supermarkets, an online and catalogue business, a production unit and a farm. The John Lewis Partnership continues to demonstrate its relevance to today's consumer, with 35 per cent of its customers over the age of 55 and, perhaps unexpectedly, with 31 per cent under the age of 34.

Ahead of its time

When we think about the premise of a humanistic brand, Spedan's manifesto could not have been more pertinent. In some ways Spedan Lewis foresaw that capitalists would become their own worst enemy and he sought to reform society and provide a better way of running a business and exploiting the collective ingenuity of a group of people – this, after all, is what a business is – for their benefit and, of course, the benefit of their customers.

One of a kind

Not many brands have a written constitution. The John Lewis Partnership does for two reasons. One is historical, based on Spedan Lewis's vision and ideals, which he set out as a framework to define the partnership's principles and the way it should operate. The constitution has been updated a number of times but it gains its inspiration from Spedan Lewis's original document. The second reason is to ensure that a business, which is not driven by the demands of outside shareholders and that sets high standards of behaviour, can flourish in the competitive conditions facing a modern retailing business. The constitution provides the principles and rules within which the business aims to demonstrate – through partners, customers and profit – that it is a better form of business. The constitution identifies that the 'happiness of all its members relies on their worthwhile and satisfying employment in a successful business'. To achieve this, the partnership aims to give all partners a relevant, consistent and rewarding experience during their career. This experience is based on the partnership and partners themselves delivering three commitments: taking responsibility for the success of the business, building relationships powered by the principles, and creating real influence over their working lives. There is an implicit obligation for all the partners to improve the business in the knowledge that they all share the rewards of its success.

In recent years a number of organizations and academics have defined a conscious business as one that has the following principles: a higher purpose, a conscious culture, a win-win philosophy for all its stakeholders, and a leader who has high levels of self-awareness and responsibility towards the greater whole. The John Lewis Partnership seems to actively commit to and live out these principles. There are of course a number of other retailers who live out the principles of a conscious brand: Wholefoods, Patagonia, Tom's Shoes, Southwest Airlines, Unilever, IKEA and BMW, to name but a few, but the ownership model itself and the way it is brought to life in all facets of the business demonstrates why John Lewis was awarded the Brands with a Conscience award in 2005.

Humanity-based

Perhaps one of the most critical aspects of how the John Lewis brand lives out the principles of a conscious brand is the way in which it cares for its people. When Spedan Lewis set out the higher purpose for the business in 1929 as 'the happiness of all our members through their worthwhile and satisfying employment in a successful business' he also set in motion the development of a culture and an inherent set of values for the business. While the mantra for many businesses today is growth at all costs, John Lewis sets out its aim 'to make sufficient profit' to ensure the long-term growth of the business. Sufficient profit is informed by balancing three things: the well-being of the partners, the sharing of profits and the need to continually reinvest in the business. The business believes that this way of thinking results in greater engagement and, ultimately, a better customer experience. Andy Street, managing director of John Lewis says:

> We take a long-term approach, a lot of people are partners. Retail generally has a high staff turnover, but the level of turnover of staff in John Lewis is half the retail average and beyond five years it falls to a very low figure. Our perspective is: 'it makes good business sense to keep people who in turn benefit the customer with their knowledge and expertise'.

Agility and adaptability

Whilst today's management at John Lewis recognizes that its ownership model can be challenging, Andy Street cites one of the successes of the business model as '*not being a pure cooperative model*'. In his view:

> These tend to fail because they end up with paralysis of decision making or conflict within the group with no mechanism to solve it – in John Lewis the executives decide, allowing for clear, crisp, quick, decision making and agility (a key tenant of a conscious brand) but held accountable to all of the members. It's about not trying to have a perfect democracy.

Relevant and meaningful

Given today's challenging retail environment can the John Lewis brand, which holds true to a humanistic manifesto written in 1949, remain relevant, appealing and competitive? While the people in the John Lewis Partnership remain a key part of the business success, technology is playing an increasingly important role in the overall customer experience. Andy Street explains a simple but important equation for success: 'the ability to harness technology combined with great people equals a great experience for the customer'. While John Lewis has been known primarily for its white goods and food stores it has also managed to achieve brand stretch into the financial services market. In 2006 the strength of trust in the John Lewis brand resulted in a move into insurance and it also now offers phone and broadband packages. Retail experts in the sector expect 10 per cent of the John Lewis business to be in services outside of retail by 2017.

Integrity at the heart

One of the core tenants of the John Lewis Partnership brand has always been its integrity. It is summed up in the unique proposition of the business – '*Never knowingly undersold*'. As Andy Street comments:

> It remains a unique proposition – people always ask about differentiation and uniqueness, but it's in the way it's lived out, not in the words alone! Even in tough times we never lowered our standards.

To that very point, in the 2008 economic collapse the retail sales for John Lewis were down 14 per cent week on week and gearing to profit was very challenging. They were facing an uncertain and tough future ahead. Living up to their conscious principles and with no shareholders saying 'maximize profit for Christmas 2008' John Lewis stuck to the premise of '*Doing the right thing for the long term*' – and did not take short-term decisions, which ultimately manifested itself in: no compromise of proposition basics, maintaining quality and not de-specifying, not compromising over the number of people in shops, so the service remained exceptional, and holding their value proposition – their price match remained. While profits were down approximately 30 per cent that year, the brand's reputation remained intact. Brand reputation can be as much an indicator of future success as any other factor – in some cases more so. The reputation of a brand and the trust of its customers and stakeholders can be easily affected by one poor decision and, in turn, the performance and value of the brand can be diminished often to the point of collapse – as in the case of Enron's in 2001.

The difference – in action

There are many unique characteristics in an employee-owned or family-owned business. As Andy Street explains:

> An employee-owned business doesn't think about selling the business, they think about developing it. John Lewis can never be sold, so we have every interest in making it better, year after year.

But that doesn't mean the business doesn't have to make difficult decisions. Like any business, John Lewis has had to make difficult decisions to remain profitable, successful and sustainable. When it took the decision to close its key warehouse centres and open new distribution centres there were some casualties, but what set it apart was how it dealt with the human aspect of these changes – reconciling the well-being and happiness of their people with people losing their positions. The answer is in the conscious decisions they took and the way in which these were managed. An effective consultation process and good HR practices were put in place, which resulted in the redundancy management package being double the statutory minimum, 60 per cent of their people were redeployed and resources refocused on a growing part of the business – the online and catalogue business.

Win, win for all

In addition to the unique characteristics and conscious actions that the partnership takes the business model itself uniquely means a 'win-win' for all stakeholders – a core tenet of the conscious brands of today. Unlike other retailers, the business model is a closed and continuous circle of stakeholder relationships – partner – customer – profit – partner – customer – profit. In this way the cycle of win-win for all is played out.

This perspective on 'doing the right thing' also extends to John Lewis's relationships with its suppliers, as Andy Street explains:

> How we treat suppliers is a core principle of the business... it's about establishing long-term relationships so we benefit together working with our suppliers over time, for keen prices, but in a relationship of collaboration.

Stakeholder relationships are built on fairness and mutual trust, and a partnership rather than a purely transactional approach. This drives more innovation and better products, for example, chairman Charlie Mayfield says:

> We've worked with one bedding company for 30 years. They have come up with better, much lighter versions of synthetic duvets for us with similar characteristics to down equivalents. Because they have long-term confidence in their relationship with us, they are not afraid to invest in research and development. It's very difficult to get this if you just have a transactional relationship with your suppliers.

And finally, the relationship with employees can play a fundamental role in the John Lewis difference in action; because employees are co-owners, the business places trust in each partner, believing that as co-owners they naturally will do what is right for their business. Their people also have influence over decisions, and the culture empowers all levels of the business, delegating to the lowest level possible for decision making.

A culture of wholeness

The focus on its own people and their role as co-owners not employees has created a culture in John Lewis that ultimately seems to flow from the original purpose set by Spedan Lewis back in 1929. This is more about a way of being rather than purely a culture based on doing. As Charlie Mayfield says:

> We tend to focus on the people, the means and the ends in terms of the results coming out right.

Fundamentally this is a culture where people are 'asked rather than told' in an adult-to-adult relationship (although John Lewis has in the past been a paternalistic culture). In line with other conscious businesses it promotes two-way communication rather than a didactic culture. The culture is strongly based on fairness, respect and transparency, and balances ownership rights with responsibilities. There are three aspects of ownership that set the tone for the business: the right to knowledge, sharing power and sharing profits. The right to knowledge is an interesting one – John Lewis believes that it is a fundamental right for their people to know how the business is doing and that their people are more likely to buy into change when they understand why decisions are being taken and the implications of change. Sharing power means that as owners, partners are required to think more carefully and long-term in their decisions and actions. Leaders and managers are accountable to co-owners, and the chairman works for the partners not the other way around, as in most traditional organizations. Sharing profits is based on being 'fair not equal'. The bonus each year is distributed as a percentage of pay – therefore everyone gets the same percentage based on their salary and approximately 50 per cent of profits are distributed to the partners.

The responsibility that the partnership places on all of its partners is to 'do their job better every single day', which helps deliver strong competitive advantage. Charlie Mayfield sums up this approach as:

> We run the business for the people who own it and the people who own it are in the business.

The business can take decisions swiftly but often takes longer to execute decisions in order to take people with them, which they believe ultimately results in better business outcomes.

Current thinking around Teal businesses (introduced by Frederick LaLoux in his book *Reinventing Organizations*) explores the premise that in organizations that live out their higher purpose, people find greater meaning and fulfilment in their daily working lives.[2] These attributes are seemingly embedded within the culture of John Lewis. A business that lives out its higher purpose of focusing on the well-being of its people and being co-owned by its people is one that could potentially result in the partners (in Teal language) *'seeing each other not only as colleagues but as part of a common humanity'*. This results in them being more fulfilled, motivated and productive. It would seem that focusing on the means – means that the results will look after themselves.

Authentic leadership

Authentic leadership is an approach to leadership that emphasizes building the leader's legitimacy through honest relationships with followers, who value their input, and that are built on an ethical foundation. Generally, authentic leaders are positive people with truthful self-concepts who promote openness. A fundamental premise of leadership within John Lewis is around empowerment at all levels, openness of information, and *asking* for input not *telling* – and with accountability to fellow partners. 'I work for them they don't work for me,' says Charlie Mayfield, chairman of the John Lewis Partnership. John Lewis promotes four aspects of leadership:

- honest and consistent communication;
- prompt, visible and considered action;
- inspiring – providing hope for the future;
- emotional connection and reflective empathy – recognizing others suffering.

Holding management to account

Supporting this entire ethos is the Partnership Council, which among other things exists to hold the management to account (rather than in most organizations where the shareholders do this). The council has the ability to remove the chairman and chief executive if so required, and it can take key decisions that will impact the business financially. For example, the council impacted the pensions strategy by deciding to extend the pension age of employees from 60 to 65 and introduced a final salary non-contributory pension scheme, both of which demonstrate a philosophy that is away from self-interest and holds true to their purpose of looking out for the well-being of their people and the long-term health of the business.

And what of the challenge of executive salaries, which is one of the most controversial issues in the UK? The John Lewis Partnership has a guideline for the highest-paid employee – the chairman will be paid no more than 75 times the average pay of a non-management partner in Oxford Street (in the UK FTSE 100 the ratio is 145, and in the United States it is 240 times).

No external shareholders and no conflict of interest

The John Lewis Partnership is for the benefit of its people, so the business can make decisions for the long term in the best interests of its customers and partners. This can often work counter-intuitively. For example, in 2001 John Lewis went against the trend when the dot-com bubble burst and it set up John Lewis.com. The business lost millions of pounds during the first few years but it is now a thriving element of the business and a key to its long-term success. The most important thing here is that the business is not beholden to the financial community to drive short-term gains.

A social commitment

'The partnership manages to preserve its innate character while keeping abreast of the fast-moving needs of social change.'

Bernard Miller, chairman of John Lewis Partnership, 1964

John Lewis holds fast to Spedan's vision of the partnership being a 'new social organism' and 'working for common good'. This is reflected not just in its business model but also in its social responsibility activities. The company's commitment to the Cotton Connect programme has given 1,000 farmers in India training in sustainable working practices and brings skills to life. The programme also aims to inspire children and to develop their imagination.

Values-based brand building

One of the ways that John Lewis represents its values and philosophy so powerfully is through its advertising. Over the years, the business has demonstrated its philosophy and values in a number of highly popular and award-winning commercials.

In 2010 the 'She's always a woman' commercial reinforced the spirit of John Lewis as an enduring brand. It demonstrated its relevance for generations of women and their families, implicitly underpinning the brand values of relevancy, longevity, value and relationship – 'whatever your age we are a brand you can rely on'. The commercial has received 1.46 million views on YouTube, 440 blogs have been written about it and the soundtrack reached number seven in the music charts.

The more recent commercials have continued to underpin a brand in touch with people; a brand that has resonance as much when times are hard, as when they are good. John Lewis manages to resonate with how people are feeling at any give time, because its advertising links to a core human truth – it speaks to the humanity in all of us. The commercial 'For gifts you can't wait to give' in 2011 demonstrates John Lewis showing that it is in touch with the zeitgeist – the shift in human consciousness from a consumer-driven society where enough is never enough – to a society that values '*giving over wanting*'. All of these commercials speak to longevity, relevance and values – family, humility, democratization, caring, giving and thoughtfulness.

John Lewis's approach to advertising and values-based brand building is underpinned by a comment from Andy Street:

We have a different goal to our competitors and we go about achieving it in a different way, it pervades how we decide to do things, what we do in challenging times and how we express our values. This is not a soft business model – it's a better business model. It's a better way to do business.

The brand accolades

John Lewis was ranked second in the UK Business Thought Leaders Index for thought leadership – behind Apple and above Google and Amazon. It ranked sixth in the Centre for Brand Analysis Top Consumer Superbrands and ranked sixth in the UK's most meaningful brands by Havas Media.

Reframing for the present day

This can of course all sound very worthy – and a key question in all of this is: where is the focus on profitability? Perhaps in response to critics who questioned the viability of the John Lewis Partnership in today's challenging markets, the constitution was revised in 2009 stating:

> The partnership aims to make sufficient profit from its trading operations to sustain its commercial vitality, to finance its continued development, to distribute a share of those profits each year to members and to enable it to undertake other activities consistent with its ultimate purpose.

Again, we can see how purpose is driving a key reframing of the business.

Fit for the future

The challenges that face any retail brand in today's competitive environment – property costs, discounters, reputation, scandal, disintermediation, quality, new technology, cost to service and a new breed of supermarkets – remain top of mind for the John Lewis Partnership. Andy Street talks about never being complacent as key to remaining a successful business and building a brand relevant for the future. Not complacent means bringing customers the products they want, where and how they want them – the iPad 3 sold out faster in John Lewis than with any other retailer in Britain. With the emphasis on providing a convenient way to shop, John Lewis customers are voting with their feet – or in this case clicks – market share for John Lewis online is at around 21 per cent while key competitor Marks & Spencer is around

13 per cent. It is about investing behind the strategy: supply chain expertise and data science to help the business grow efficiently and profitably. And it is about consistently innovating and looking at opportunities to upgrade and stretch the brand: for example, overhauling the home department to compete with IKEA; the insurance offering; enhancing personalization versus a mass approach; and defending what John Lewis is famous for – discontinuous change.

What will ensure a leadership position for the brand?

John Lewis believes that technology is changing the nature of work and how the workplace operates. Today, one-third of John Lewis business is done online. About two-thirds of transactions include some kind of online and offline. So the business, in 'Andy Street's words, has to '*have the whole waterfront covered*'. Click and collect is an important part of the John Lewis offer – it takes approximately two hours to pick a product accurately, package it, take the payment, do the necessary checks and get it into the transport system to get it to the specified location. What the brand is delivering here is 'convenience and ease'. Over 50 per cent of online business is done via click and collect, which is approximately one-sixth of its total business numbers.

Andy Street talks about 'businesses needing to conduct themselves differently, from the kinds of jobs they create to the way they deploy technology to the way they collaborate'. John Lewis has identified four ways in which it is keeping ahead of the game:

- Create a point of difference – consistently focus on simple things such as high quality, innovative products at great prices and geared towards what clients really want.
- Build long-term sustainable relationships with suppliers.
- Maintain an exceptional service and recognize that the quality of online service is as important not less than in-store and provide an authentic and very knowledgeable service within store.
- Provide convenience through stores and online and ensure that click and collect 'gets their offer closer to the customer'.

Right up to date

The one area of the business that can demonstrate a business that is right up to date is its fashion. Today, John Lewis fashion is carving its own place in this sometimes fickle and certainly fast-moving world. Fashion has been a challenge in the past, but now its market share in fashion is growing faster than any other category – at double the rate of the market, says Paula Nickolds, buying and brand director. Here again, the principles of John Lewis come to the fore. It is focusing on the editing and curation of its choice of labels and products. It remains committed to the quality of the service of its people and to consistently innovate. Nickolds speaks about putting forward an 'authoritative view of fashion' – being 'fashionable and modern, not a fashion victim'. This is simply and powerfully reflected in the John Lewis campaign 'loved&found', which was rolled out in late 2015. The campaign speaks to the care and thought that buyers at John Lewis have put into their collections and choice of designers. John Lewis has recognized that what discerning fashion customers want today is curation. First, it is about making it easier for customers to make choices from a considered collection; second, giving greater meaning to the key pieces in the collection. These are fashion and lifestyle pieces that have been discovered, carefully put together and feel unique. And the innovation does not stop at fashion – a new spaceship-like store has opened in Birmingham with the first John Lewis day spa, juice bar and brands such as J Brand, AG, American Vintage and Alice Temperley. These are all part of demonstrating that John Lewis is not just ready for the future but sometimes leads the way.

The human factor

Three generations of people work in John Lewis and in many ways it is like a modern extended family. In the past it may have been paternalistic, but today its common humanity combined with commercial realism underpins its success. It has a purpose focused on the happiness of all its members that relies on their worthwhile and satisfying employment in a successful business, and a long-term ownership model that gives it the perspective it needs to continue to thrive. John Lewis blends knowledge and experience with new thinking to evaluate what needs to stay the same and what needs to change. It embraces change and innovation, because if it doesn't it will not stay relevant to the lives of its customers or its people. But it is a common humanity that underpins the affinity that exists between its people and its customers and makes it one of the most loved brands in the UK. Long may it continue.

John Lewis is more than a shop – it's a way of being 'an emotional state'.
Paula Nickolds, John Lewis buying and brand director

Reflective questions

- What are the key qualities of an ownership model that impact high performance?
- What are the five key challenges of adopting and executing an ownership model?
- How might the introduction of more ownership-led businesses impact the social, economic, environmental and spiritual well-being of our planet?

Notes

1 This chapter was written from sources in the public domain. When we talk about John Lewis we refer to the whole group or partnership, including the Waitrose business, because the John Lewis Partnership and its brands all work to the same constitution, higher purpose, principles and values.

2 Frederick LaLoux (2014) *Reinventing Organizations: A guide to creating organizations inspired by the next stage of human consciousness*, Nelson Parker, Brussels

Influence
at adidas

NICHOLAS IND

Brands with a conscience do more than just put their own house in order. They challenge the way that suppliers and partners work and are open to the influence of others. By inspiring employees to think about corporate responsibility, specifying labour standards in the supply chain, working to reduce the environmental impact of processes and practising transparency, a brand with a conscience has power beyond its organizational boundaries.

The global sportswear brand adidas, with more than 50,000 employees, 1,100 independent factories in 61 countries and millions of customers around the world, is one such organization. Its scale means that its influence on others is magnified as its choices impact on the networks of people and businesses linked directly and indirectly to its activities. Similarly, scale also means that adidas has to be responsive to the demands of those that connect with the brand. Frank Henke, global director of social and environmental affairs at adidas, observes that there 'has always been a lot of expectation from our different stakeholders – especially when it comes to raw materials and working conditions'.

Sustainable thinking is not new at adidas – back in 2001 the company was the first in the sporting goods industry to produce a sustainability report. It has also long been affiliated with the Fair Labour Association (FLA), committing to the FLA standards for itself and its suppliers. Yet as stakeholders continually demand more, so adidas has to be open-minded and develop more sustainable materials and processes.

Be open-minded and look towards the future[1]

Typical of adidas's approach is its participation in the Better Cotton Initiative (BCI), of which it is a founder member. The way in which most cotton is produced is highly degrading to the environment. To make 1 kilogramme of cotton requires as much as 20,000 litres of water. Cotton producers also account for 24 per cent of the insecticides and 11 per cent of the pesticides sold in the world.[2] The idea of BCI is to make global cotton production more sustainable by working throughout the supply chain to tackle the negative impacts of cotton farming – reducing pesticide and water use – while improving working conditions for farmers. In 2014, 30 per cent of adidas cotton was sustainable and the goal is 100 per cent sustainable cotton by 2018. Alongside the promotion of better cotton, adidas has also invested in new environmentally friendly production processes such as DryDye, which uses no water, 50 per cent fewer chemicals and 50 per cent less energy than traditional fabric dyeing. This technology was introduced by adidas in 2012 – by the end of 2014 it had produced 4 million yards of DryDye fabric, saving 100 million litres of water.

Innovation is at the heart of adidas and always has been. From the beginning, the company's founder, Adi Dassler, worked closely with athletes observing their needs and using new materials and designs to enhance performance.[3] The Dassler philosophy still pervades the company to this day, but increasingly there is an environmental focus to innovation. Partly this has been due to the company's growing commitment to sustainability, but it has also been influenced by its different stakeholders. Stella McCartney, adidas design partner, has a strong belief in the importance of the environment and refuses to use leather, fur or toxic materials in her ranges. As an outsider, McCartney is able to push the adidas brand further and to challenge it to change its practices, while at the same time learning from adidas's innovations in materials and technology, which she notes are 'essential to solving the sustainability conundrum'.[4] Similarly, Greenpeace has been an influence on adidas. Initially it criticized the company for its practices, but now it is working with adidas to phase out the use of polluting polyflourinated chemicals (PFCs) by 2020. While once a laggard, adidas is working towards the goal of 99 per cent PFC-free in its products by 2017 and is now lauded by Greenpeace as a fashion detox leader that acts as a role model for other businesses.

The move from a quiet participant in sustainability to active evangelist is particularly noticeable in the company's latest initiative: a shoe made from ocean plastic waste and illegal fishing nets. The shoe is a result of a partnership between adidas and Parley for the Oceans – an organization in which creators, thinkers and leaders come together to raise awareness about the state of the oceans and to collaborate on projects such as the Ocean Plastic Programme that aims to combat plastic pollution (something that DNV GL has also been working on through the development of innovative technologies: see Chapter 7). The shoe itself was designed and produced in just a few days using existing production processes and was then presented during a talk titled 'Oceans. Climate. Life', at the United Nations headquarters in New York. This is no mere vanity project but a step towards full production in 2016. Eric Liedtke, executive board member responsible for global brands, says of the relationship with Parley: 'Adidas has long been a leader in sustainability, but this partnership allows us to tap into new areas and create innovative materials and products for our athletes.'

A journey into the mainstream

With such a diverse range of stakeholders around the world, adidas has a tremendous opportunity to influence the behaviour of others. Yet to seize this opportunity requires transparency and openness, which can be challenging in the highly competitive world of sportswear. The company publishes its global supplier list and uses the economic, environmental, social and governance performance standards set by the Global Reporting Initiative (GRI) to inform its annual sustainability report; adidas also works with socially responsible investment (SRI) analysts to deliver the information they need to make informed decisions about the company and its sustainability performance.

However, there are two audiences that represent particular challenges for the company: consumers and government. The former is interesting because research consistently shows that consumers have strong concerns on environmental and ethical behaviour, but adidas finds (as does Unilever) that it is often hard to engage consumers with the issue of sustainability and particularly to influence consumer behaviour once a product is purchased. The actions of governments can also be passive – and it is adidas's experience that some step back from active measures and rely on corporations to take the lead. Henke says, 'that's hard for us to do. We can complement governments, but we cannot replace their duties.'

Where adidas does score is with its own employees. The profile of adidas employees is young with 64 per cent categorized as Generation Y. These individuals, born after the early 1980s, are attracted by companies that care about the way they impact on the world and contribute to society.[5] Generation Y seek out such companies and also demand more of them when they join. This is pushing adidas to become ever more engaged on its 'journey of integrating sustainability into the mainstream.'[6]

Notes

1 '*Den Blick voraus richten, möglichst weit voraus*'. Standard number nine from the Adi Dassler Standards (2009)
2 Source: WWF
3 Ind, N, Igesias, O and Schultz, M (2015) How adidas found its second wind, *Strategy+business*, Autumn
4 Amed, I (2015) Stella McCartney: change agent, *The Business of Fashion*, spring, pp 6–9
5 Meister, J (2012) Corporate social responsibility: a lever for employee attraction and engagement, *Forbes*, 7 June
6 Interview with Frank Henke, adidas, 25 June 2015

Healthy business

03

BRIGITTE STEPPUTTIS ON DR HAUSCHKA

○ *Vision and dedication are the building block for successful brands.*

○ *Understanding the social-human-ecological and business environment is key.*

○ *Success comes from innovation and profit, but only as a means to and end.*

Would you like to work for a leading company...

- that cannot be sold or bequeathed to anyone because the capital does not belong to any one individual or institution

- where profit is a means to an end and is used to further the developments of the company. It ensures that the firm will remain independent and be able to continue growing in the future

- where all employees share the profits in the form of cash and non-cash payouts:
  - This system encourages long-term thinking and sustainable practices and therefore a stronger focus on the customer's needs

- where your salary comes in three parts or four, depending on your personal needs:
  - The basic part, which is the minimum living wage
  - The additional part, depending on area, position and responsibility
  - The social part: subsidizing fees for children in kindergarten, school or private school
  - Plus additional social and childcare according to needs

- On top of that every employee gets a bonus at the end of the year, usually amounting to one or two months' wages.

- And when you leave the company, the company says thank you properly: you will get an additional 'goodbye' payment of another three or four months' wages for every year worked, paid on departure. This is not a pension, but is meant as an incentive to encourage people to invest in their future even after leaving the company.

So would you like to work for such a company? You would, wouldn't you? This is no start-up, hipster outfit, but a disciplined and value-based business, built by Rudolf Hauschka and Elisabeth Sigmund, a business founded in 1967 on the ideals of Rudolf Steiner (known as the creator of a new esoteric spiritual movement, called anthroposophy, at the beginning of the 20th century).

Dr Hauschka is one of the pioneers in the natural cosmetics sector. Started in Germany in the 1960s, these products can now be purchased all over the world in specialist outlets, wholefood shops and pharmacies, which ensures that consumers can obtain professional advice on their choices. In the 1970s, during times of social unrest in Germany and terrorist threats from Bader-Meinhoff, the sector's relatively small and health-conscious customer base was an eclectic mix of anthroposophical followers, hard-core bio fans, young hippies and other non-conformists with a mission to change the world and who were opposed to uncritical and uninformed consumerism. This tendency was followed in the 1980s by the global trend towards greater health awareness in food production, leading to the development of the organic and wholefood movement.

Together with this development of the natural cosmetic movement, Dr Hauschka grew into an international brand in the 1990s, mainly through word of mouth. Since it was awarded the Brand with a Conscience award by the Medinge Group in 2006, its turnover and number of employees have almost doubled. During this period the natural cosmetic market enjoyed stratospheric growth, attracting a lot more people, 'as now the organic movement no longer excluded hedonism, but actually embraced it and even became quite egoistic. To enjoy it, to comply with a certain lifestyle, the consumer of course still wanted to help the world, but also to consume an enjoyable product.'[1]

Nowadays the market is unregulated and overgrown and has become extremely fragmented. Marketing conventional cosmetics as 'natural' has become the norm, and that is confusing to customers. 'Naturally inspired' beauty products account for about 75 per cent of the 'natural' beauty market – three times the share held by 'truly natural' brands.

In this highly competitive and confusing cosmetic market, the question is whether the Dr Hauschka brand will survive. In order to answer this question, we need to explore the history of cosmetic chemistry, and the Dr Hauschka brand itself, both closely linked with the brand WALA.

Led by the rhythms of life

The chemist Rudolf Hauschka, along with Elisabeth Sigmund, co-founder of Dr Hauschka Skin Care (and obviously the brand's name giver), did not start off as a skin-care formulator. For over 30 years his sole focus was on developing medicine through the company he founded in 1935, under the name of WALA Heilmittel.

A few years earlier, in 1929 Hauschka was researching a technique using natural products for making medicine without the need for alcohol as a preservative. Hauschka had already described how he primarily used water as a solvent for his compounds. His reasons were that this had been 'severely neglected by studies to date' and later observations led Hauschka to conclude that, when used as a preservative, alcohol left behind a 'dead physical substrate' that reduced the effectiveness of the healing substances.

In 1924, at a congress in the Dutch town of Arnhem, he met with Rudolf Steiner, founder of the anthroposophical movement, who proved to be a great inspiration. Steiner advised Hauschka to 'study rhythm, as rhythm carries life'. And so he did, exploring the use of rhythm in pharmacological research. He went on to explore the rhythms of cold and warm, movement and rest, light and darkness.

Four years later he succeeded in preparing a water-based medicinal herb extract. It would keep for many years without the addition of alcohol or other preservatives, while at the same time retaining the healing powers of the plant. This was a great breakthrough, and a particular advantage for natural medicines used to treat children, as these should not be tainted with alcohol.

During his research Hauschka began to extract rose petals in water. One example was left untouched and soon rotted. Another was exposed to circadian rhythms – the rhythms of the rising and setting sun – and developed a stronger aroma that lasted for years. This unique approach continues to be used to this day.

Practising doctors were very enthusiastic about Hauschka's medicine, and in 1935 he founded the first WALA laboratory in Ludwigsburg in south Germany.

WALA is the abbreviation of warmth/ash light/ash and refers to the natural preservatives power created by using heating and cooling, exposure and darkening.

During this time the first basic corporate principles were established. In 1938 his enterprise moved into larger premises in Dresden to accommodate the rising demand and at the same time he opened a branch laboratory in south London. Three years late the WALA laboratory was forced to close by the Nazi regime, which did not tolerate the anthroposophical movement. Hauschka and his wife were arrested and imprisoned for four weeks.

The influence of Rudolf Steiner

After the war, Hauschka reopened on the grounds of a homeopathic hospital near Munich, where his wife, Margarethe Hauschka-Stavenhagen served as the doctor in charge. After some disagreements over the homeopathic philosophy ruling the hospital, they moved in 1950 to Eckwaelden, near Stuttgart. They opened a new laboratory, producing medicine for WALA Heilmittel, and the WALA team extended. Hauschka and his wife were joined by their friend, the businessman Max Kaplan. His partner, Maja Mewes, joined them as head of the laboratory, along with three lab assistants, each of whom brought specific knowledge and talents.

From the start, Rudolf Hauschka was anxious to be completely transparent with the people living in the area so that they would understand and support his enterprise. This was successful early on, and together they grew into a thriving community. The first WALA building was built in 1954, when Hauschka laid the first stone of a unique building using as few right angles as possible – compliant with the architectural rules of anthroposophy and with a medicinal herb garden laid out behind the building.

As well as seeing the concept of natural rhythms as the central theme of his scientific work, Hauschka was anxious to find a social structure for his entrepreneurial activities that would be compatible with human needs. From the very beginning he established his vision of a business to serve people rather than the other way round, with a pioneering commercial approach.

Hauschka did not want people to be motivated to work at WALA just because they received a salary, but also because they were dedicated to the company's ideals. One of the key factors shaping WALA's organizational structure was the social maxim formulated by Rudolf Steiner:

> The welfare of a group of people working together is all the greater when each person does not keep the achievements for himself, ie when each person shares the fruits of his achievements with his colleagues, and when his own needs are not satisfied by his own achievement but by those of others.[2]

Please bear in mind that when the company was founded Hauschka was already 62 years old and, having gone through two world wars with the associated upheavals, was still pursuing his ideals and finally manifesting them in a business.

All founding members had a deep understanding of how nature would be important for their success. But what was lacking was a clear vision for technology, since this was new for all of them. As advocates of the anthroposophy movement and a multidisciplined team of scientists, doctors, lab technicians and business people, they made up their own anthroposophical-influenced rules, which still form the basis for success of this leading organization. It led to the birth of the Dr Hauschka cosmetics brand.

The fundamental values of WALA

- The concept of natural rhythms as the central theme of the scientific work, as developed by Hauschka.

- Finding a social structure for his entrepreneurial activities that would be compatible with human needs. Not to view people and their work as 'commodities' but rather to help them to develop.

- The 'healing impulse' is not limited to WALA's patients or customers, but to its entire environment. This involves respect towards people and nature, and a company model that views commercial profit as a means to an end rather than as the end itself.

- Active environmental protection in all parts of the company. Later these points expanded to include:
  - Cultivation projects for producing raw materials in developing and emerging countries such as Afghanistan and Burkina Faso.

It is now a foundation-owned company, meaning it has 'donated' the company to its cause, so that employees would be committed only to serving the fundamental idea of WALA rather than the interests of owners or shareholders. This means that profits do not go to individual shareholders but instead are either reinvested directly in the company or distributed among employees.

From medicines to cosmetics

In 1960 Hauschka decided to extend WALA and develop a cosmetic range. In 1962 he sent letters to anthroposophical pharmacies and doctors and other clients of WALA medicines. Among others, he approached Elisabeth Sigmund who, from her beauty salon in the Swedish capital Stockholm, had regularly ordered preparations from WALA in Eckwaelden since 1950.

Sigmund, who had also been influenced by Rudolf Steiner, was surprised and pleased by Hauschka's interest. She herself had been searching for natural ingredients and experimenting with skin care and so she responded with a detailed 11-page letter, full of ideas. The enthusiastic Hauschka wrote back immediately to invite her to Eckwaelden, with the words: 'Since receiving your letter, I am already in love with you.'

During the summer of that year she travelled with her husband to Eckwaelden at the beginning of her holidays in order to present her skin-care concept in person. The doctors and scientists at WALA were so impressed by her presentations that she ended up spending her entire holiday with them.

Over the next two years she continued to travel frequently, spending weeks at a time working with the development team. Later, newly developed cosmetics were sent to Sweden, where Sigmund tested the new recipes and sent back her observations.

In 1964 the collaboration was made official and together with the WALA laboratory she developed natural cosmetics that could be mass produced in accordance with the technique based on natural rhythms, which already formed the cornerstone of the WALA medicines.

A name change, rebranding *avant la lettre*?

The cosmetic range was then launched in 1967 under the name Heilende Kosmetik nach Elisabeth Sigmund (Healing Cosmetics by Elisabeth Sigmund). In 1972 the name was changed to Dr Hauschka Skin Care Range by Elisabeth Sigmund. The words 'Healing Cosmetic' could no longer be used, as a result of newly implemented advertising laws, and neither could it be named 'WALA' because of the potential for confusion with Wella, a hair-care brand. In 1978 it evolved again and became Dr Hauschka Skin Care. For Elisabeth Sigmund this change of name was always secondary. It was important to her that the cosmetic preparations were marketable and that many people benefited.

Sigmund's road to success

Elisabeth Sigmund, originally from an upper-middle-class family in Austria, had always had a passion for cosmetics and beauty. She had studied medicine, herbs and natural cosmetic recipes from an early age. Being fascinated by her mother's toiletries she began to analyse the ingredients and at the same time gained a thorough introduction to cosmetics through her grandmother's herb garden.

Her father, Ludwig Rasch, had brought her up under the anthroposophic way of life, in contrast to her mother's strict Catholic background. Shortly before his death, when Elisabeth was just 14 years old, he asked his friend Hans Erhard Lauer (1899–1979) to look after the anthroposophic education of his daughter. His influence, in addition to books by Rudolf Steiner, were important factors in Elisabeth's decision to become a cosmetician.

During her youth it was not common for young women to wear make-up, except for special events such as a theatre visit. But as part of her research, Elisabeth bought a bright-red lipstick, which already showed her interest in decorative make-up, which she would later introduce to the Dr Hauschka cosmetic line. This continued throughout her life and, right up to her death in 2013 at the age of 99, she was never seen without lipstick.

She started to prepare her own cosmetic remedies in her early youth, studying recipes from varied sources, such as a pharmacist who was a friend of the family. Another source was her grandmother Anastasia, who had brought the recipe of the Crème Celeste, the 'heavenly cream' from Moravia. This face cream, containing almond oil and rose water, was one of the beauty secrets of the Empress Elisabeth of Austria-Hungary. Later, when she developed the cosmetic range for Dr Hauschka, the Crème Celeste was the foundation of the now famous Rose Cream, although as part of a much richer formulation. She was particularly interested in cosmetics not just for their decorative but also for their healing power, adding more herbs and extracts to achieve this.

After completing school she began training for nursing and studied medicine for two semesters, although this was disrupted by illness. During this time and after reading the book by Rudolf Steiner about his lecture on 'The artistic element in his world mission', she decided, against her mother's wishes, to study cosmetics. She was largely self-taught, attending selected lectures at university, visiting sources at large cosmetic firms and also working at the Vienna Cosmetic Institute.

She did not agree with the methods used at the institute so she decided to create her own cosmetics, based on plants and herbs. She travelled around the country on her motorbike and conducted intensive research in libraries and cloisters, reading old and forgotten medicine books.

In 1937 she married fiancé Karl Sigmund (1909–2007), who was aiming to have a diplomatic career within the Austrian Army. In March 1938 German troops marched into Austria and then in September invaded Poland, starting the Second World War.

The first cosmetic salon

After the war was over, following an invitation from a wealthy aunt, they both decided to immigrate to Stockholm. This proved to be a disappointment, as it turned out that the aunt's fortune had vanished. Penniless, they decided to stay, with Elisabeth learning the Swedish language and continuing her cosmetic studies.

After they established themselves in Stockholm, Elisabeth opened her own cosmetic salon and started to prepare her own cosmetic line, which was based solely on natural components. It was not easy to obtain good-quality components and she had to order most of them from organic shops in Germany or Austria. Because of the influence of Rudolf Steiner, these criteria were important to her. Fresh plants came from her Swedish garden supplier. And she ordered the WALA medicine components, which formed the basis for her cosmetic range, directly from Eckwaelden.

During this time Elisabeth, who observed that most women came to her salon with cold feet, developed her own holistic treatment method, starting with a warm foot bath, treatment, and relaxation during a face massage, which she believed helped to drain swollen lymph nodes.

Her husband was instrumental with the technicalities of producing the creams, which were only produced in small quantities. She developed her own products and invented her own holistic method of skin-care treatment, which she applied and refined in her cosmetic salon in Stockholm. Most of these used WALA products as a base. She was ahead of her peers in many ways. In 1961 she spent a year in India, travelling on her own, to study and discover new plants, herbs and ayurvedic medicine – a specific way to each individual's needs.

A new era of development

In 1969 Hauschka died at the age of 78. Elisabeth Sigmund had worked together with Hauschka for many years and they both appreciated each other highly. At this time, after 20 years in Sweden, Sigmund relocated to

Eckwaelden for good. She took care of customer enquiries, visited trade fairs, held representations and worked to develop additional products.

In 1971 she started to teach cosmeticians in a special treatment method, which she had developed in her beauty salon in Sweden. Even now, her influence and importance can still be seen in the Dr Hauschka cosmetic line.

The Dr Hauschka Skin Care line adopted the same holistic approach as the WALA medicines, but in this case applied to the skin with the aim of developing sustained dermatological health. Products were developed that respected and supported the skin's natural processes to cleanse, balance and renew.

Rudolf Hauschka and Elisabeth Sigmund drew on centuries of knowledge of botanical ingredients and combined this with modern science and technology to create natural skin-care products. Skin-care techniques were developed that treated the skin with reverence, safe-guarding lasting skin health against 'quick fixes' that subverted skin functions. Standards for natural cosmetics clearly defined which raw materials and processing methods can be used and which cannot.

The unique concept of Dr Hauschka cosmetics is the holistic approach. It does not target specific skin types or problems, but is based on the conviction that every individual skin has an innate power to care for itself and to regenerate. This concept remains unique today, even as the number of natural cosmetic brands and products has grown immensely over the last decades.

An anthroposophic business model

Karl Kossmann joined WALA in 1962 and was responsible for the business side of the company. He studied the foundation model of Ernst Abbe, who in 1889 set up and endowed the Carl Zeiss Foundation for research in science. The aim of the foundation was to secure its economic, scientific and technological future and improve the job security of their employees. The success of employees was based solely on their ability and performance, not on their background, religion or political views. In 1896, Abbe reorganized the Zeiss optical works into a cooperative with profit sharing.

Kossmann was very fond of this model. He was greatly influenced by it and founded the current business model of WALA and Dr Hauschka upon a comparable basis, where employees have a share in company profits and the social contract acknowledges the importance of employees and motivates them to have a stake in the outcome.

The social contract

- WALA encourages all its employees to take responsibility for their workplace and to bring their own suggestions and ideas for improvement. They also have freedom within their area for decision making.

- 80 per cent of the salary is paid at the beginning of the month to meet day-to-day living costs.

- Regular meetings are held to inform employees about internal developments, aims and the financial situation of the company.

- Share of profits with the employees.

- Voluntary social help such as additional money for childcare, private schools etc.

- Offers of further education for all employees, such as talks or 'Eurythmie', which is a form of performance art used in education and art therapy.

- Flexible work time based on 'time accounts', so that employees can balance work and life better.

This is a large part of the success of Dr Hauschka. People like to work there. In 1983 the company had about 175 employees and an annual turnover of about 17 million Deutschmarks. In 2009, there were approximately 700 employees and a turnover of €96 million. In 2015 the workforce has grown to 1,000 and the turnover of Dr Hauschka cosmetics is now €100 million – with WALA it comes to a total of €130 million.

Since 2000, a 'Green Letter Box' has been available for employees, encouraging them to get involved with their own ideas and suggestions for improving the environment and ecological security. Suggestions must also be relevant to the health and safety of all at WALA; they should be original and include suggested methods to realize the objective.

There are info and action days to raise employees' awareness regarding the environment, with lunchtime discussions about the meaning of sustainability.

For example, in response to the question 'Is saving energy complicated?' four WALA employees and their families found that without great sacrifices they could reduce energy spending by 10 per cent:

> We are also trying to reduce our CO_2 emission. There are no company cars that emit more than 115 gr. WALA pays 100 per cent of the transport costs to every member of staff who comes to work by public transport. This is even more relevant as WALA is based in the countryside, where a car is the normal means of transport, so that everybody is encouraged to come to work by bike or, failing that, via a car-sharing initiative.[3]

Catering in the cafeteria also takes account of sustainable requirements: preferably regional and seasonal produce; a long-term relationship with the suppliers who should be fair trade with fixed minimum prices; no child labour and no usage of genetically modified seeds. Demeter quality is 70 per cent (a strict biodynamic certification). Meat is organic and fish is from sustainable sources.

The WALA foundation ensures that the legacy of Rudolf Hauschka remains. The management reports to the Foundation Board. This board of directors has a veto or right of decision in significant business decisions. At the beginning of this case we described some of the conditions, the sum of which leads to a system that encourages long-term thinking and sustainable practices, and also a stronger focus on customer needs.

Environmentally healthy for all

The social contract is only one side of the business model. All WALA and Dr Hauschka's production activities are based on environmental principles that ensure responsible handling of natural resources, ideally from biodynamic sources; careful processing of raw materials, and always recycling or using substances or raw materials from sustainable sources; minimizing the amount of resources used and, if possible, using renewable energy. And WALA is actively negotiating participation in a biosphere project hoping to encourage exchange of knowledge about plants and their environment.

Since all medicines and cosmetic items such as creams and oils are free of preservatives it goes without saying that packaging is crucial to protect them from light and oxidization, to ensure they stay in peak condition as long as possible. Packaging is critical to the quality of the product. And still, all packaging at WALA comprises materials suitable for recycling such as glass and aluminium. The eco-colours are used for printing, and the paper for the packaging is made of PC certified material (from sustainable forests). All content literature is printed on recycled paper.

That is the legacy of Hauschka. A truly holistic way of aligning the interests of all stakeholders, customers, employees and society – with nature being a crucial stakeholder; and, of course, also suppliers to WALA.

Raw materials from Bulgaria, India, Iran and Afghanistan

The raw materials play an essential part in the quality of the WALA medicines and Dr Hauschka Skin Care products. The WALA medicines range consists of approximately 900 different remedies, including many medications for self-administration, while the Dr Hauschka cosmetic range consists of 150 products. This does not include the recently added Dr Hauschka Medical range. It is a constant challenge to produce more than 1,000 ingredients in sufficient quantities from high-quality raw materials that are all renewable natural products and are subject to natural fluctuations in availability.

WALA considers it an absolute priority to use raw material from biodynamic cultivation. If they are not available, they then draw on plants harvested in the wild or grown through certified organic cultivation in accordance with EU standards. As many raw materials as possible come from regional sources that are socially responsible in their production. Working conditions, wages and environmental protection measures are all important criteria, especially when purchased in developing and emerging nations. Imported goods are not only controlled through laboratory checks but also through stringent inspections and sensory quality control of each shipment. This is to ensure that all medicines and cosmetics are subject to regulations to keep strict chemical, physical and microbiological standards.

The thriving success of both the WALA Heilmittel and, to an even greater extent, the Dr Hauschka Skin Care range has increased the need for raw materials in the production. The supply of raw materials such as herbs and flowers comes from cultivation in WALA's medicinal herb garden, the company's Demeter Sonnenhof farm and from harvesting in the wild. Certified suppliers are also being called on when necessary.

Plants that cannot be cultivated in these gardens are harvested where they grow naturally. At all times, the gatherers take great care not to overharvest and permission is obtained from the responsible environmental protection authorities before harvesting. WALA also undertakes measures to care for and maintain the population of protected plants, which contribute to the biodiversity of the area.

The more demand there is for the products, the more need there is for the specific raw materials vital to the brand. This in itself is a significant challenge and is the main reason that Dr Hauschka tries to produce important raw materials in its own fields. This avoids dependence on other importers, who cannot guarantee the quantities or quality standards they put on their ingredients:

> It would not be a problem to increase the turnover by 10–15 per cent, if we go into the drug store markets. But then we would have to make compromises on the quality of their ingredients. For example, to use conventional almond oil instead of bio almond oil. We do not want to make these compromises.[4]

Driven by various factors, including the growth of the company, a number of other projects have been initiated in Bulgaria, India, Iran and Afghanistan, to establish project partners as independent suppliers to Dr Hauschka. The aim is to keep as much of the value chain in the region. In this way, WALA is profiting from the consistently high quality of the raw materials, but also the people and the environment in the growing regions are profiting from the avoidance of pesticides and the establishment of economically sustainable structures.

As far as possible, their sourcing policy complies with the demands of sustainability, the environment and its protection. It begins with the raw material through the complete supply chain until it is developed into the product and used in the bathroom. Every single step is important.

From nice to indispensable lifestyle brand

The breakthrough for Dr Hauschka cosmetics came in the late 1990s. One factor was the change of the packaging design in 1998. The products became a way of life, natural cosmetics were en vogue. Julia Roberts used Dr Hauschka cosmetics for her film *Erin Brockovich* in 1999 and spoke openly about it. They became Hollywood's favourite eco-friendly products. This led to an imitation effect with other Hollywood actresses and it snowballed from there, leading to endorsements from models and glossy fashion magazines worldwide.

But success does not always come easily. The history of the WALA and the Dr Hauschka brand is not without controversy. In 2009 the offices of WALA were searched by the Federal Cartel Office, who suspected that the company was dictating the retail prices. In July 2013 a company spokesperson denied the allegations of price fixing but subsequently they were fined €6.5 million.

In 2012 a story appeared in the *Sueddeutsche Zeitung* that WALA (together with WELEDA and three other natural medicine producers) were funding Claus Fritzsche, who on his numerous websites was dedicated to defaming critics of complementary medical practices and practitioners, for example the British researcher Edzard Ernst.

Despite these controversies, Dr Haushka continues to thrive.

The future of natural cosmetics

According to consultancy company Kline, as of 2015 the natural personal-care market has seen double-digit growth every year for the past six years. Today, natural cosmetics and skin care are estimated to be worth US$33 billion, accounting for 13 per cent of the overall global beauty market. Kline predicts that the market will hit $50 billion by 2019.

A primary driver of growth in the natural beauty market is the increase in customer awareness of the chemicals used in everyday cosmetics. There used to be very little information about the ingredients of natural cosmetics. Now, there are various websites that provide 'dictionaries' of ingredients or offer a comprehensive database of 'chemical free' beauty products. Apps such as 'Skin Deep' and 'Think Dirty' let customers scan products to reveal ratings on a scale of 1 to 10, from healthy to harmful. Digital and social media are supporting this awareness. Concerns around cosmetics are an inevitable part of a global awakening to the 'cocktail of chemicals and pollution' that people live in, and awareness of the effects on their physical well-being. Since 2014, the EU has banned more than 1,000 chemicals from being used in consumer products, including cosmetics and food.

The increase in the natural beauty market has put extra pressures on brands. Antal Adams, current press office at Dr Hauschka, says the brands that will survive will be those with the most financial power, coupled with the most innovative analytic technology for production of raw materials. Dr Hauschka's tradition is built on research and innovation. But the products are bought not only for what they do, but also for their ethical component.

Adams says that one problem with the natural cosmetics market is that there is no strict regulation. The terminology can be confusing for consumers. 'Most consumers think natural means bio but this is not true. Or they think natural cosmetics are automatically fair trade, which is also not true. Or that bio is synonomous with protection for the environment, which is not the case if the product is flown, say, from China.'

Conventional enterprises will only adopt the techniques used by Dr Hauschka when they become profitable; the general awakening of environmental consciousness has helped Dr Hauschka to expand: 'Dr Hauschka works for the clients and the firm. Profits are necessary for reinvestment.' As well as continued innovation and new products (such as the recently launched night serum based on apple), there are plans to build a new laboratory and logistics centre at their base in south Germany at a total cost of €70 million.

Adams stresses the importance of following the original message. With this in mind, the emphasis remains on innovation, new research and development centres. The increased market combines the environmental movement, ethical overseas projects (such as those in Ethiopia and Afghanistan) and the financial power of the foundation. And given that this is at the heart of the organization, it looks as though Dr Hauschka is here to stay.

Reflective questions

- Would you like to work in a place like this?
- If the market is growing and Dr Hauschka is too, how can they secure future growth and maintain their principles?
- What would a challenger brand to Dr Hauschka look like?

Notes

1 Quote from Antal Adam, press officer at Dr Hauschka
2 Rudolf Steiner
3 Quote from Antal Adam, press officer at Dr Hauschka
4 Quote from Antal Adam, press officer at Dr Hauschka

Alqvimia: the energy that will save the world

GUISEPPE CAVALLO

Some luxury brands concentrate on a female audience, serving busy and beautiful entrepreneurial woman. Some of them go further and choose to embrace a bigger mission, serving the feminine from a deeper perspective.

Alqvimia is a connoisseur's brand in the luxury cosmetics market. Its line includes body and skin-care products, pure essential oils, aromatherapy and more. Founded in 1984, it has always been a different type of player, pioneering natural luxury cosmetics and introducing alchemic processes in a market that concentrates on hedonism and appearance as driving forces for the business. Idili Lizcano, the founder, embodies – as normally happens in luxury – the essence of the brand. Born in Spain in the years when Spanish dictator Franco was at the peak of his power, Lizcano had to flee to Paris with his family when he was a young boy. In the city of lights, he developed a deep love for and knowledge of fragrances: a passion that he retained when he started studying philosophy at university. The image of a young philosophy student lost in a perfume shop in Paris has something of a romantic flavour, but that was Lizcanos's life.

Feminine energy and ancient wisdom

When Lizcano returned to his homeland at the end of the 1970s he was already a fine connoisseur of the power enshrined in the essence of plants and flowers, but his understanding of the botanical world became deeper when he was introduced to the ancient tradition of alchemy.

The 1980s were years of ostentatious materialism and power games. Lizcano felt that the world was running on a neurotic masculine energy – a man's world, with an economic system that did not serve people but, on the contrary, alienated the individual. In line with his spiritual training, Lizcano advocated a fairer world and a more ethical business system. But he felt that the true essence of the problem was of a higher nature and decided that he could help work on the system.

He made a resolution to empower feminine energy, the nurturing force that abides both in men and women, but is best expressed by a woman. An empowered woman, he reasoned, will bring a creative spirit to the world and will spread a sense of nurturance in the places where power is exercised. Lizcano created Alqvimia, natural cosmetics that were created according to the tradition of alchemy. The product line was built around the power of essential oils, treated with alchemic processes, and thus empowered with additional energetic benefits: a value proposition that was not for all, although understood by many.

In 30 years of business history Alqvimia has created a well-defined and loyal customer base. Its mostly female clients appreciate the excellent quality of its products and the exquisite finesse of its fragrances. 'Our products are our best ambassadors,' says Lizcano. Many among his clients report benefits that go beyond what is stated in the company's communication. A number of women, for instance, reported that an oil essence advertised to make the bust firmer not only delivered on the promise but also cured breast nodules. The people at Alqvimia report many stories of this type, and remind us that the essence of the brand is infused with the tradition of those alchemists who searched for higher knowledge and were driven by a sincere will to heal people and the world.

Showing the true face of Alqvimia: the art of speaking out

For years, the customer base of Alqvimia developed and grew through word of mouth. The company was somehow shy in expressing its alchemic essence and pushed the natural side of the brand more overtly. At the beginning of 2010, Lizcano felt that he should seek a deeper, more outspoken connection with his public. He sensed that the times were right for the brand to tell its story, to speak to women and invite them on a journey. Lizcano wanted to tell his clients that they could connect with their feminine energy, a source of creativity and the secret of their real beauty. There were two elements to this story. One was about the natural, mostly organic ingredients of the Alqvimia products. The other, arguably the most important since it is the key to the uniqueness of the brand, was related to the alchemic wisdom that inspires the creation of all Alqvimia's elixirs.

From 2010, the company and Idili Lizcano felt that a new stage had begun for the Alqvimia brand. He wanted to return to the original spark that ignited the Alqvimia story. It was time to invite women to come on a transformational journey, restore their confidence and summon the force of their feminine energy.

A new corporate campaign in 2014 made it clear that Alqvima was ready to speak out. With its claim 'Beauty is Pure Light', the brand shifted the attention of women to their inner self and put beauty at their service.[1] The initial response from the public showed that Idili was right. The market is calling for brands with a higher vision and a sure commitment.

A solid business with a feminine spirit

Today, Alqvimia is a brand that appeals to feminine energy. It is a brand with a higher mission, but with its feet well grounded in business reality and a solid economic performance.

Entering the new millennium, Lizcano initiated a growth strategy that involves both the sales performance of the brand and its impact in the world. New business agreements extended the distribution on a global scale. Alqvimia is now present in over 20 countries through independent distributors. A new flagship store was opened in Madrid, adding to the one in Barcelona's city centre to make sure the brand is visible in the two main cities of the domestic market in Spain. A new state-of-the-art factory was built near the headquarters, in the northern part of Catalonia. A breed of new highly talented employees has been brought into the company.

To ground Lizcano's vision of empowering feminine energy he created a new training centre in an ancient 14th-century mansion, which was renovated with respect for the environment and the heritage of the building. Every month the company's employees gather at the training centre to learn the secrets of the vegetal world and techniques for their personal growth. Here, key clients are invited and introduced to the wisdom that lies at the heart of the brand. New services are being added to the product line. To help women regain equilibrium and confidence and find the way to their inner beauty, Alqvimia is launching an energy-balancing treatment for customers and a course for spa operators. Alqvimia considers brand awareness to be more than a business goal – they consider it to be a service to society.

It is no wonder that Lizcano's vision is holistic. Because business is so important, he wants to contribute to the growth of a more humanistic economy. To spread the word that ethics and success can be merged together in business, Lizcano has launched a series of conferences that gather influential speakers in front of hundreds of entrepreneurs and consultants. The name of the conference speaks for itself: The Happiness Forum. It represents a new arena for Lizcano to advocate his principles and business ideas.

The considerable amount of investment that Alqvimia's growth requires is fully financed by the company. Lizcano likes to mention that one of his goals is to show that an ethical business can be successful and sustainable, so he constantly keeps the economic and financial ratios under strict control, and makes sure that the numbers speak for him.

Note

1 The campaign was built to respond to the spiritual needs of the Alqvimia public. For an illustration of the pyramid of needs used by Alqvimia, see G Cavallo (2015) *El Marketing de la Felicidad*, Codice, Madrid

Merci: Destination store

04

PHILIPPE MIHAILOVICH IN COLLABORATION WITH CAROLINE TAYLOR
ON MERCI PARIS

○ *You have to be courageous to make a difference.*
○ *Don't flaunt your cause to sell your luxury goods or environment.*
○ *You cannot be generous unless you are successful.*

What destiny for this lifestyle design concept store?

Merci was created to build schools in the world's fourth largest island, Madagascar, a beautiful country of exotic rare species, stunning nature and kind people, yet one of the poorest places on earth. The press have termed Merci a concept store or a charity shop, but to the owners, it is not. Although Merci received Medinge's Brands with a Conscience award in 2010, the house does not consider itself as a 'brand' either.

In reality, Merci sees itself as 'the story of a couple, a choice of well-being, a place with a sense of doing things, its own sense of being with its own story,'[1] and a one-of-a-kind loft-style village where visitors come to be inspired. It is a destination that offers internal and external journeys from the moment you arrive. Merci wants you to discover and enjoy yourself, and there is no pressure to buy – but the unusual design items are sure to tempt you!

The Merci store, Paris

SOURCE: Merci

Surprise!

When the Merci store opened in March 2009 it was a welcome surprise to those of us who appreciate design and design-related innovations. On the edge of the trendy Marais district in Paris, in a street best known for used-camera retailers and motorbike showrooms, Merci offered a super-loft design wonderland filled with 'wow' items and installations: a creative fusion of an urban market, exhibition space, art gallery and a home – a dream space you could relax in and simply imagine or reimagine as your home.

I brought visitors, architects, journalists and designer friends to Merci. I even invited the owner of Germany's design emporium Stilwerk to visit, to illustrate what he could do with their new Jean Nouvel-designed Stilwerk centre in Vienna. I challenged Stilwerk to create its own brand universe with soul, as Merci had done.

Merci started as a concept store. As with a glossy design magazine, the name represented a personality and a philosophy, and the content would change monthly in order to remain fresh and encourage regular visits. The founders did not consider it a brand, because they did not brand the items in the store as Ralph Lauren or Armani would have done, but nonetheless it was a brand in that it had its own unique position and personality. It quickly became popular with locals and tourists.

Unlike most famous brands, few knew who was behind Merci, why it was named Merci, or what its philosophy was all about. Merci did not want to use their cause as a marketing hook. The founders wanted to create an atmosphere for inspiration – a wonderful eclectic mix of fashion, design, household goods, a florist, a coffee shop with a used book library and a restaurant: 'A place where you wish to go, have a coffee and enjoy.'[2] It was simply called Merci, worded in exactly the same red typeface now found on the 18,000 street containers from the French fabric recycling project Les Relais[3] – and, in its courtyard entrance, a cute red vintage Fiat 500 with recycled clothing on its roof.

Merci took the press and public by surprise. The buzz spread fast across Paris – design professionals, bloggers and the general public loved it and, within a very short period of time, a large percentage of Asian tourists were visiting. Merci became a destination within the destination of Paris. 'The key is not to have visitors come for five minutes to shop but for two hours to stay and enjoy the new things,' explained co-founder Marie-France Cohen.[4]

Who thought of this in the first place?

Most leading brands begin as a surprise. After the surprise (assuming it is a pleasant one!) we naturally become curious to know who came up with the idea in the first place. This is especially true with art, design and luxury brands. We want to know the creative genius behind the concept. If there is a human face and personality behind it, we would expect their name to be the brand, eg Ralph Lauren. So, why is it called Merci, a generic word meaning 'thank you' in French, instead of the names of the founders – two well-known and successful Parisians, Marie-France and Bernard Cohen?

Marie-France and her husband Bernard Cohen started a children's fashion chain called Bonpoint in 1975. By the mid-2000s they had 40 boutiques worldwide with a turnover of around €50 million. They then decided to sell the business to Edmond de Rothschild's financial group, although they remained at the helm until 2007 when Christopher Descours, president of EPI and ex-LVMH senior manager, bought the brand outright in his quest to create yet another French luxury group.

Prior to receiving a healthy sum after 30 years of hard work, creating what had become France's first high-end retailer specializing in children's wear, Marie-France and Bernard understood that they would never again have to work to earn a living, or worry about debts, production and all the other factors involved in running celebrity-filled boutiques from St Germain

Marie-France and Bernard Cohen

SOURCE: Brodbeck & de Barbuat

in Paris to Madison Avenue in New York. However, selling Bonpoint left them with a sense of emptiness. They prepared to embark on a new adventure that would allow them to explore their creative and philanthropic passions to the full.

Bernard Cohen, the son of a leather entrepreneur in Tunisia, arrived in Paris in the 1960s to study architecture and went on to create a contemporary furniture boutique called Le Point, but his meeting with Marie-France Goutal, a Dior stylist and sister of the late perfume creator Annick, was to change his life forever. After seven years of marriage and three sons, he helped Marie-France and one of her eight siblings, Dominique, to open a children's clothing boutique called Bonbon – meaning candy in French but also encompassing her philosophy that things should always be 'bon' (good, happy, correct).

The loving couple eventually went on to merge their two businesses and names to create Bonpoint – a concept store offering effortlessly chic clothing for kids. Annick created their fragrance, an instant success, and the philosophy of family business permeated throughout. It was only a matter of time before Angelina Jolie, Claudia Schiffer, Katie Holmes and Michelle Obama would become clients.

On selling Bonpoint in 2007, the Cohens decided not to simply donate money to charity, and not to stop working either. They enjoyed working together and they certainly did not want to spend the rest of their lives living on a yacht while playing the stock market. Instead they would spread the love and embark on a project for pleasure rather than for wealth, where all proceeds after salaries and taxes would go to humanitarian causes. Their accountant thought they were crazy. 'Crazy about life, about family, about materials, about beautiful things with a million ideas per second, perhaps,' replied Marie-France.[5] And although money is freedom, there is no point in adding money to money. That's when Marie-France and Bernard decided to become volunteer shareholders. They set up an endowment fund from which to provide a sustainable income to a good cause while everyone and everything else in this new venture would be business-based.

Merci

It's about saying *thank you*

Marie-France explains that she was raised surrounded by love and that love is key – to love and to be loved. The couple decided to open up shop again – only this time, a totally new concept: Merci. Naming this venture Merci literally says *thank you*. 'Thank you for having the parents I had, thank you for the life I live and thank you to all the people who will join in this adventure,' says Marie-France, but she also likes to state that 'it was selfish at the beginning' because they did it for themselves. 'When you are creative, you stay creative, you cannot retire, you must at least share your knowledge and experiences and will always want to continue creating.'

Textile workers in Madagascar had produced Bonpoint clothing for 30 years, so the Cohens wanted to give back by donating 100 per cent of their profits towards couture workshops to help women and children in this desperately poor former French colony – geographically cut off from Africa and linguistically cut off from the world that communicates in English. With Merci, the Cohens wanted to say thank you to life and thank you to the talents and creators who had helped them to succeed: 'It is success that makes generosity possible.'

Digging deeper, I found that as a result of French tax laws, it wasn't 100 per cent of Merci's profits that could be donated, but rather 100 per cent of *the Cohen's profits*, who at the time owned 40 per cent of Merci. The chosen beneficiary was ABC Domino, a non-governmental organization (NGO) created by Yves Cohen (not related) and other wealthy retirees to create schools in a remote part of Madagascar. On its website, Merci says of its purpose: 'The medium-term aim is to do everything to integrate education into the heart of this micro-region of south-west Madagascar and to make school – the only solid and stable institution – the centre of a human ecosystem that ensures a real development, and not just one happy exception in the region.'[6] 'At last,' I thought, 'generosity will triumph over greed in the 21st century. Merci is a humanist model for the future.' As such, I nominated Merci for the Medinge Group's Brands with a Conscience award in 2010, and it won.

It is also about business

> We are very low-key. We don't want people to buy because it's a charity thing. This isn't a charity shop. The purpose here is to make money.[7]

The idea was to be both masculine and feminine, to mix luxury with affordability covering all price points and be a place for people to live in a creative dream world. In 2010, Merci offered a wide selection of prestigious fashion-designer labels that included Stella McCartney and Yves St Laurent – stock from earlier collections that the labels would donate for free, for Merci to sell. However, this this was not sustainable as the marques also had obligations to offer clearance items to their staff, press and key customers. Instead the company shifted its focus away from a reliance on end of lines from well-known designers to developing and curating its own unique offer, involving young designers and artists as well as their own internally designed items. This is how blogger Howard Sullivan describes it:

> Marie-France and Bernard Cohen have shown how philanthropy and luxury can mix with their new charity-boutique, Merci, in Paris. The Cohens have created a world of change where not only do you find designer clothes, all exhibited on the most interesting array of new and vintage props and pieces of furniture, but you will also find rotating art exhibitions, a central courtyard space that can host events and a series of changes to the various 'departments' of the shop... but its ability to combine understated luxury with philanthropy is what sets it apart from most of the world's other concept stores.[8]

With such a large space, it would take years, if ever, to be profitable, and therefore even longer before any schools would be built. Why were there no obvious in-store references to their cause? The Body Shop, for instance, used to paste their campaign 'Against Animal Testing' on windows and throughout their stores. To Merci, being explicit about the cause is unacceptable. As Jean-Luc explained:

In the store there is almost no advertising about the social cause. It is written, it's on our website so that people who want to know can know, but we don't use the charity thing as a hook or a communication thing. We simply do things, and by doing things we are able to give to society, so that is the Merci philosophy regarding the social problem. The majority of people shopping at Merci don't know what we are doing. We have a board at the till with information leaflets to give to the people who ask, and on our website there is one portrait of the company and just one portrait of the foundation showing each year the exact amount of money that we have been funding. So it's very honest and transparent but it's not ever in windows and never in pictures showing the situation because we find it's a kind of insanity to be showing what's happening there – showing it in this luxury environment! We are very comfortable about what we sell but we believe that the mix of images – their world and our world – is visually unacceptable for us. However, we feel good about obtaining a profit as a result, and with this profit being able to be generous.[9]

Exceptional people, objects and events

'Merci is really happy to serve as a platform to present and promote young designers to numerous clients and international personalities who visit Merci,' Marie-France explained. 'Merci is seen as a happy project, with a wonderful team, an amazing space, a refreshing and eclectic choice of products with a touch of luxury and simplicity. My husband, Bernard, and I are totally unpaid,' she added.[10] 'All the proceeds of Merci go to the charity we created to help, among others, the children from Madagascar, the poorest of the poor.' Merci had indeed been working with the aim to do good, to treat staff like family and to provide customers with endless pleasure and excitement, and ultimately build schools for poor Malagasy children. It was a dream project for everyone.

The 'wonderful team' that Marie-France refers to is key. I was most surprised to discover the amazing pedigree of the team behind Merci. It is truly a collective of experienced, committed creative people from 20 to 70-something years of age, with a shared conscience, passion and cause. Although some are direct members of the Cohen family, all are seen and treated as family. The team included the artistic director of *Marie Claire Maison* magazine, Daniel Rozensztroch, and Jean-Luc Colonna D'Istria, who has a strong pedigree in eco design gained while working with Bien Joué, Nature & Découvertes and later, Résonances, a high-end eco-design concept store where he worked with Rozensztroch. Together, they often curated 'improbable meetings' of objects and unique pieces animated and signed by living creators or connected to cult industrial items.

'They would always do major research to find artists,' an architect told me:

They travel around the world and bring back amazing things, very avant garde. The team always looks for purity and authenticity because there are so many things that are déjà vu. 'It's not because things are made by hand that they are *bon*,' they would say. They need things to surprise them – that are aesthetically pleasing – and as they have seen so much, not much is new to them, so they need something to really touch them. That's why they always choose exceptional items. For Merci's celebrated *Matiers Premier* event, they found things in very noble materials such as untreated wood or in unusual blends such as raw concrete mixed with silicone.

Merci believes there should always be things linked to daily life as well as exceptional objects, and always presents very well chosen items. It was 'wow!' Before you knew it, you were buying something you didn't need, expensive but so gorgeous you couldn't resist.

Exhibitions and events are key success factors. One reason for this is that Merci will purchase many items for an event but only some will become part of their permanent collection. As they never know beforehand which, and can often be surprised, it provides a good occasion to test them. The business structure consists primarily of two divisions, Fashion and Home, each section headed by a buyer with a dedicated scenographer (the word 'merchandising' is not in their vocabulary). Within each division there is a permanent collection and a temporary theme collection, some of which are also sold online. They even have two dedicated press offices, one for fashion, one for design.

The Merci store at Christmas

SOURCE: Merci

As with many showrooms, art galleries and concept stores, much of the stock is purely exhibited before being bought or sold. At least half of everything sold is on consignment. This allows lower inventory overheads, promotes constant change, encourages pop-ups elsewhere and keeps the store fresh with an endless flow of 'wow!' products. 'Merci has this saying,' the online team explained, 'We don't buy what we sell, we sell what we buy'.' Merci is a place where they sell what they like to sell, things that they find on their travels. Some sofas are kept in order to solicit bespoke orders but many are one-off pieces that cannot be remade. The permanent collection mixes famous brands and young designers. Merci has discovered many young French creators who have used local fabrics and garments that cannot be found elsewhere.

The Merci space is considered a nomad area because everything is moveable and changeable, as one would expect in an art gallery. There are no fixed furnishings. Each presentation stand is different and can be easily moved. In the fashion area, poles and clothing rails are attached to the ceiling on pulleys to allow for quick changes. Even the changing rooms may easily be moved to optimize space. The wall hooks for hanging handbags are magnetic, allowing changes in position in any direction along a metallic wall.

As in a theatre, the 'coupole' or atrium space acts as an impactful performance stage – an exhibition/installation art space serving to surprise and introduce visitors to the store's key themes of the month (or sometimes three days only). Merci tends to host at least 12 themes per year. They like to speak about the past: past habits, attitudes, ways of doing things, a return to source or roots, things that are more pure and natural (even if industrial – such as Savon de Marseille), always something linked to nature or very sophisticated or ecological. If the theme of the moment is home-orientated, they will seek ways for the fashion side to complement that home theme.

A foundation of friends and family

Although Merci came to life in the minds of Marie-France and Bernard, the success of it largely depends on the pedigree of talented friends and family members.

Swildens, a fashion brand sold in Merci, is owned by Marie France's niece. Merci's fashion buyer, the Cohen's daughter-in-law, instigated the production of their own 'Merci-Merci' collection, as most branded retailers do. Annick Goutal's (Marie-France's sister) fragrance collection is unique to Merci. The children's section upstairs was dissolved after the Cohen's son and daughter-in-law launched their Bonton children's fashion store less than 100 metres from Merci and in its place came bedroom linen – now one of the most popular categories, offering fantastic colours that tend to change every six months. It has proven extremely popular with airbnb hosts and bed-and-breakfast owners – not only in France. Due to their tremendous success in this category, the house has now introduced a 'cotton' section. A few doors down, one Cohen son opened a pizza restaurant called Grazie (thank you), with similar signage to Merci.

The big shock came in September 2010 when Bernard Cohen passed away unexpectedly as a result of cancer. Marie-France was devastated, as were staff, the customers who knew him and the press. Her creativity and his sense of commerce, glued together by their love, passion and strong sense of family, had come to an abrupt end. Marie-France remained strong but was distraught. Her role at Merci became more demanding, yet it no longer had the same meaning for her.

On 25 January 2014, I attended a three-day Merci event called 'Bon Voyage' and took the opportunity to interview the founders. I was not at all expecting what came out: 'The big news is that Marie-France has decided to sell the company so we have changed ownership,' Jean-Luc Colonna D'Istria informed me:

> Marie-France will give all the profits that she has made from the company to the charity programme, so the cycle is complete. We have made a success and the result is to build a strong charity programme and the new owners are committed to continue to feed the system for years to come, so that's a very nice story and very unique to go that far. Already just to make profits with a space like this... and because it has been a success... she adds value and the value is going back to where she wanted it to go, so it's a very exciting cycle.[11]

FashionUnited wrote: 'It was a change of management by default. None of the Cohen children – not Thomas who had created Bonton, nor Julien who runs his own chic pizzeria, or Benoît who works in cinema – were interested in taking over the reins.'[12] The business transfer between the Cohen family and the new owners, the Gerbi family, seems a good fit and could be considered as a happy extended family.

Laurent Gerbi-Darel is the son of Daniele Darel, co-founder with her husband Gérard of one of the most successful French family fashion businesses in its sector, Gerard Darel. Established in 1971, the label enjoyed an exceptional boost in 1996 after the Darels purchased a fake pearl necklace worn by Jackie Kennedy and replicated it to sell in-store. Over 35,000 were sold and the American market was successfully penetrated. 'Today, the brand is sported by all, from toddlers with the children's collection (designed by

Valérie Gerbi, Laurent's wife and friend of Marie-France), to adolescents, young women and trendy middle-aged women.'[13] This includes famous models and actresses, singers and politicians, notably Susan Sarandon, Meryl Streep, Charlize Theron, Hillary Clinton, Charlotte Gainsbourg, Nastassja Kinski, Brooke Shields, Angelina Jolie and Eva Longoria.[14]

The change of ownership was not seen as a disruption to Merci. Laurent told me that his main concern is to retain the soul of the place and Marie-France added that her philanthropic plans for Madagascar will be continued under the new family. 'Because it is part of the DNA of Merci,' Laurent added. Clearly Laurent faces an interesting challenge. How will this young business manage to continue to pay staff well, host amazing exhibitions regularly, support a charitable cause as well as afford to invest in its growth?

Destination London

On 24 January 2015, I was back at Merci, this time for a prearranged video interview with Jean-Luc for the purpose of this book. By now Merci had done pop-up stores in Liberty's of London, Tokyo's Ginza, Amsterdam, Milan and even The Gap in New York and they had worked exceptionally well, giving the store global exposure: 'So far we are happy that what we had imagined from scratch seven years ago was possible,' Colonna informed me:

> We don't pretend that it's a business model to follow. It's a way that small companies can also think differently. Its not only big banks and foundations, and this is what we are proud of. Common sense on the business side and common sense on the social side and not mixing.
>
> Merci, as a business, is growing very fast. Now it's about $20 million here in Paris, which is a lot for one retail operation. The internet is growing very fast – we now have online shopping doing very well and the next project is London – a flagship opening at the end of 2016 in the area of Kings Cross next to St Martin's, which is a new neighbourhood, like the way we started a new neighbourhood in Paris – and there's a new block of London that will be a kind of creative and cultural environment. We found a fantastic brick building that used to be a coal factory and it will be very exciting – different in terms of shape, but the same philosophy of being smart but not a luxury building. So that's a big project for the company. I think we have to succeed in London first. We don't want to grow too fast. We want to keep the human side of the business, and make the right decisions.
>
> If this concept is multiplied too fast, there is a risk that it loses its identity and, for me, the identity is very, very crucial – that we try to manage every detail and know the partners and the customers and the designers we work with well.

If you go too fast, you lose this, so that is the reason why we try to slow down rather than accelerate.[15]

'My idea at the outset was never to expand beyond one store,' Marie-France admitted, 'but, like Colette, to stick to one shop that is desirable, found only in one place, a unique destination.' This is exactly what the traditional luxury 'maison' used to be too.

Comment

Merci is definitely not a conventional brand story. Merci is a destination store, a concept store, a home, a living magazine, a marketplace, a design gallery, and a truly unique lifestyle. Merci is a commercial enterprise 'like the others' in that it is founded by shareholders, but 'not like the others' as it can be considered a social entrepreneurial brand, or perhaps more a concept than a brand. The author would like to believe that Merci perfectly represents the 21st-century brand, founded from a conscience and a cause, and not simply out of a desire to accumulate wealth. Merci, Merci.

ABC Domino Madagascar receives funding from Merci, the SLJ Cohen Restaurant Group, Groupe Rothschild, European Homes and others. So far, five schools have been built in Madagascar and 16,000 children are being fed daily. A high school is now being built for kids who have outgrown the primary schools and Julian Cohen, son of the Merci founders, and who is now in charge of the foundation, has recently purchased a small hotel to transform into an 'école atelier' or workshop school.

Reflective questions

- What key story-building factors should Merci consider in order to succeed in London?
- Is Merci a brand?
- To what extent should Merci develop its private-label brand?
- What lessons could Merci learn from luxury brands and concept stores, if any?
- Can a brand afford to be charitable while in a growth phase?

Notes

1 Interview with Merci Communications Director Benedicte Colpin, Paris, 5 June 2015

2 Telephone interview with Marie-France Cohen, 21 September 2015

3 lesrelais.org

4 Telephone interview with Marie-France Cohen, 21 September 2015

5 Marine Trévillot, M, [accessed 22 September 2010] Bernard Cohen, le créateur de la maison Bonpoint, nous a quittés [Online] purepeople.com

6 Merci-merci.com

7 Colman, D (2010) [accessed 5 January 2010] High and Low, with a French Twist, *New York Times* [Online] nytimes.com, 5 January

8 Sullivan, H (2009) [accessed 17 August 2009] The Retail Curators [Online] yourstudio.wordpress.com

9 Mihailovich, P [accessed 25 January 2015] Merci Jean Luc [Online] https://www.youtube.com/watch?v=cHiar9xPVtU

10 Moodstep, J (2012) [accessed 4 November 2012] Happyview*72:Marie-France Cohen – Bonpoint – Merci [Online] Moodstep.com

11 Mihailovich, P (2014) [accessed 29 January 2014] Merci, The Paris Concept Store has been Sold by Owner Marie-France Cohen [Online] vimeo.com

12 FashionUnited (2014) [accessed 9 January 2014] Merci Change de Mains [Online] FashionUnited.fr

13 Sacastar [accessed 29 October 2010] Connaissez-vous Gérard Darel? The Blog! [Online] Sacastar.com

14 Toli [accessed 1 December 2015] Gérard Darel: Histoire de Cette Grande Enseigne de Prêt-à-porter Feminin' [Online] web-libre.org

15 Mihailovich, P (2015) [accessed 25 January 2015] Merci Jean Luc [Online] https://www.youtube.com/watch?v=cHiar9xPVtU

Sustainable fashion at H&M

THOMAS GAD AND BRIGITTE STEPPUTTIS

In Paris, January 2008, Ingrid Sundström of H&M stepped up to receive the Medinge Group's Brands with a Conscience award. However, granting the award to H&M was a contentious decision within the group – the result of an intense discussion among the members as to the appropriateness of honouring one of the world's largest fashion retailers that was known best for selling fast fashion and promoting consumption. Finally, a small majority of the members voted for H&M to get the award, mainly because the company had an ambitious programme to tackle some of the complex sustainability issues in fashion retailing.

H&M had started its sustainability programme back in 1995 with a code of conduct and regular audits and it was really the only fashion retailer that had a structured programme to deal with sustainability issues in fashion. Also, given the scale of H&M, it was in a position to have a significant impact on the market and to become a role model. It was this that really swayed the decision within the Medinge Group.

Seven years on from the award and the attitude within the fashion industry to sustainability has changed significantly. H&M has continued its work along the lines established in 1995 and has continued to innovate. Many of their competitors have followed. Sustainability has since become an important part of corporate investors' relations with business and H&M argues that it also influences some consumers. H&M's research shows that around half of consumers mention that 'they are actively looking for fashion with the added value of sustainability'. Still, for many, it is fashion and price that are the most important factors.

Now in 2015, H&M has, for the first time since the brand was founded in 1947, updated its business concept to include sustainability: *fashion and quality at the best price in a sustainable way.* In addition, H&M has also developed a *sustainability vision* as part of its overall corporate vision:

> We believe in a better fashion future – one that makes fair and sustainable fashion affordable and desirable for all. Our vision is that all our operations are run in a way that is economically, socially and environmentally sustainable, which will mean our business is helping to meet the needs of both present and future generations. We believe that quality, affordable fashion can be made and sold in a way that is also good for people and the environment. With this in mind, our business concept is simply to offer quality fashion at the best price.[1]

Karl-Johan Persson, CEO of H&M, represents the new, younger generation of the family business. Persson is compassionate and personally very active in sustainability issues and has made them an important integral part of the corporate business strategy. In the company's sustainability report from 2014, he expresses what sustainability means for him:

> My grandfather founded H&M in 1947. He often spoke about the importance of long-term thinking, not just about maximizing short-term profits. He wanted to look at our customers and colleagues and feel good about the business – that it was run the right way. As CEO, I have a long-term perspective on H&M. And just like my grandfather, when one day looking back at my time at H&M, I want to feel proud of what we achieved. That we offer our customers great value for money, but also that we have a positive impact on the world.

When talking about the challenges the company faces, Persson says:

> We want to go from a linear production model to a circular one. And we have to do it at scale. At the same time, we need to make sure that our growth helps the millions of people along our entire value chain to better lives and further improves their working conditions. Promoting fair living wages in our industry is an important part of this. Just as creating transparency, so that we can know exactly where each part of our products comes from, as well as for our customers to be able to make truly informed choices.

Together with the Sustainable Apparel Coalition, H&M is driving the development of the Higg Index, one of the most important new tools to communicate a product's sustainability score. The Higg Index allows a comparison with other brands by measuring apparel and footwear products, brands and suppliers on their sustainability performance. The hope is that this will result in consumer labelling that will allow customers to compare products, even from different brands, based on the same standards in an easily accessible way. H&M believe that this kind of transparency will ultimately make sustainability a key driver in the industry. Helena Helmersson, H&M's former head of sustainability says:

> We can offer our customers a more sustainable choice. We can make a difference to hundreds of thousands of people working in our supply chain and to the environment and communities around us. We work hard to make this difference bigger every day.[2]

For the Medinge Group, given our original concerns as a group about consumption we also wanted to know how the company sees the sustainability issue – and the implications it has for workers making clothes in places such as Bangladesh. Catarina Midby, who is responsible for sustainability in the UK and Ireland, argues that H&M has taken positive steps to tackle these challenges:

> We have started to educate consumers and give them the possibility to recycle their unwanted clothes, from any brand and in any condition, in our stores. The idea of the circular economy is to recycle old garments into new ones, closing the loop. And we recycle as much as 97 per cent of the clothes we collect. Since 2008 we have not only introduced fashion recycling to the high street but also developed a long list of new sustainable materials: recycled polyester chiffon, crepe and tulle, all kinds of organic cotton fabrics, organic hemp sateen, organic silk, organic leather, Tencel and Monocel (FSC certified or organic cellulose produced in a climate smart way). The design process determines 80 per cent of a garment's sustainability value, so it's all about designing for the complete life cycle of the garment. As an example of this full life-cycle perspective we have also worked on solutions for how to reduce climate impact in the user phase. We have developed a new wash care label 'Clevercare' (**www.clevercare.info**), which shows you how you can wash and care for your garments with a reduced environmental impact. It's great to work for a company with such a wholehearted commitment and that puts so much time and resources into sustainability.
>
> H&M is a major buyer in poor countries like Bangladesh where poverty levels have decreased thanks to the textile industry. We have introduced a fair living-wage programme with a goal that all our strategic suppliers' employees should earn a fair living wage by 2018.
>
> It also helps that fashion is changing, and is becoming more about personal style than fast-changing trends. Fashion now has greater longevity, especially since 2007–08 when we began introducing sustainability thinking into the design process. Today everyone at H&M has a shared responsibility for sustainability. We have a total internal awareness and that's why sustainability effectiveness has increased a lot over the last seven years.

Though the choice to give the award to H&M was a contentious one back in 2008, the company has since demonstrated it was prescient. H&M has worked hard to embed sustainable practices in its own operations and perhaps more importantly has encouraged suppliers, other retailers and consumers to be conscientious as well as fashionable. As part of this process in 2015 H&M became a Global Partner of the Ellen MacArthur Foundation, accelerating the transition to the Circular Economy.

Notes

1 H&M (2015) [accessed 23 October 2015] Our Sustainability Vision [Online] http://about.hm.com/en/About/sustainability/hm-conscious/sustainability-vision.html
2 ibid.

Crazy about chocolate, serious about people

05

SANDRA HORLINGS ON TONY'S CHOCOLONELY

○ *Ideals and business go hand in hand (and beat competition).*
○ *Tell the cause story over and over again.*
○ *Journalism × repetition beats marketing.*

This is a story about a fast-growing niche chocolate brand in a sector dominated by a small group of multinationals. A story that shows the power of a cause to both motivate owners and employees and generate commitment from customers. A story that demonstrates how an idealist brand can begin to change the world for the better. It is also a story that illustrates the challenges that a brand can face as it grows and develops from a founder's principled idea into a larger business concept. Finally, it is a story about journalism, or 'the marketing of truth', as Maurice Dekker, founder of the brand, will explain.[1]

But beware: the story of Tony's Chocolonely has been carefully crafted. Not intentionally at first, but it was due to the wilful involvement of a journalist – a wonderful storyteller and great observer – that the brand moved from being an idea to a business, one might even say a flourishing business. However, because this business is based on ideals, it is hard for category leaders to compete. The crafting of the brand story starts in 2003...

Driven by a cause

... when Dekker read *The Black Book of Marks*. Written by Klaus Werner and Hans Weiss, the book gives insight into the unscrupulous practices of leading global brands, including leading global chocolate brands. Werner and Weiss claim that the vast majority of chocolate, if not all of it, is made using slave labour. However, there was little or no public response to the book. There was also no response to a small article that appeared around the same time in the newspapers reporting on kids who had gone missing in Mali, probably taken and put to work on cacao plantations in Côte D'Ivoire.

Does modern slavery still exist?

Tony's team found that approximately 5.5 million cacao farmers produce about 4 million tons of cacao globally every year, with 60 per cent of all cacao coming from Ghana and Côte d'Ivoire. They also found that 2,300,000 children work on cocoa plantations. And 90% of them work under illegal and very dangerous circumstances. Tony's refers to slavery as any form of forced labour or exploitation. In the annual Fairyear Report 2014/2015 they report 90,000 people in West Africa to be victims of human trafficking and forced labour. 90,000 people in this sector are victims of modern slavery.[2]

Dekker was upset. How could such a big problem get so little attention? We would all be horrified if this was closer to home, he figured. He knew about the strong connection between the Western-world people and cacao – we eat, dream about and love chocolate – so he set out to bring the problem closer to his Dutch home. Now, it would be good to get acquainted with Dekker: a TV producer, journalist by heart and developer of a Dutch television programme, *Keuringsdienst van Waarde* (broadcast in the UK as *Food Unwrapped*), a consumer watchdog programme that investigates the claims made by brands. This television programme is his communication platform, and it is the birthplace of Tony's Chocolonely.

In addition, Dekker thought that this might well be the long-term story he had been looking for to repeat over and over again. For Dekker, journalism equals marketing and the key to success in marketing is repetition. In order to spread an ideal with the power of marketing, a journalist + repetition would be key.

Slavery in chocolate: modern slavery and child trafficking

CHILD LABOUR AND SLAVERY IN COCOA

In Ghana and Ivory Coast 2.300.000 children
work on cocoa plantations

at least

90%

of these children work under illegal and very
dangerous circumstances

90.000

people in West Africa are victim
of human trafficking and forced
labour. Children are taken from their
families and/or are forced to work,
denied an education and often work
under dangerous circumstances

SOURCE: Tony's Chocolonely

Slavery in chocolate: cocoa from Ghana and Ivory Coast

SLAVERY IN CHOCOLATE
cocoa from Ghana and Ivory Coast

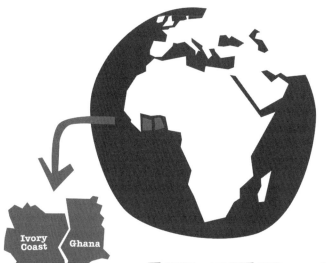

Ivory Coast
and Ghana
are the largest
cocoa producers
world wide

60%
of all cocoa
comes from
here

2,500,000 farmers
produce this
cocoa

SOURCE: Tony's Chocolonely

However, that's a step ahead of the story. In 2003, the concept of sustainable brands had not yet been launched, sustainability as a business strategy was still in its early days, and interest in the predictions of the Club of Rome, outlined in 'An end to growth', was far from what it is now. At that time, Dekker started by simply asking questions about chocolate production and the amount of slavery involved in making a regular chocolate bar.

The Club of Rome was founded in 1968 as an informal association of independent leading personalities from politics, business and science, men and women who are long-term thinkers interested in contributing in a systemic interdisciplinary and holistic manner to a better world. The Club of Rome members share a common concern for the future of humanity and the planet.[3]

Meet Teun van de Keuken, who was the leading journalist reporting on this chocolate item in the television programme. He not only became the face of the research into slavery in chocolate production, he later gave his name to the brand that had its origins in attentiveness to unethical practices; Tony's Chocolonely. Teun is the Dutch equivalent of Tony, and 'lonely' refers to his lonely quest for slave-free chocolate. His research led to the launch of a brand and a new company, with a mission to achieve 100 per cent slave-free chocolate. Twelve years later, the brand has a convincing market share in the Netherlands and is on its way to crossing borders and gaining a market share in the UK and the United States. The aim is to directly influence the home markets of the leading brands in the chocolate industry and bring the problem of child slavery closer to the homes of consumers in the UK, the United States and elsewhere.

Where marketing meets journalism

In 2003, the cacao sector was not ignorant of the issue; two years earlier the CEOs of the leading global chocolate brands had personally signed the Harkin Engel Protocol, an international agreement to eliminate 'the worst forms of child labour' (in accordance with the International Labour Organization's Convention 29) within 10 years. You could have expected that an action plan – a programme for improvement – would come from this agreement, in order to achieve the desired goals. However, the reality was less rosy. The 2010 final annual report of a study by Tulane University's Payson Centre revealed that none of the six stated objectives in the protocol had been fully achieved. Moreover, there was no evidence early on that the protocol had done anything to reduce child labour in the cacao sector.

However, in 2003 hopes were high at the Amsterdam office of Keuringsdienst van Waarde, and Nestlé was an easy target. All that a television journalist needs is a telephone and a camera. You start calling, you find a product manager, a marketing manager or even just a customer service representative, and you start asking questions.

The questions asked at Nestlé exposed a weak spot in the marketing policy of this leading giant. This reveals another method of journalism; first they start asking questions through the channels provided by the organizations, and when the answers make them wonder, or are inconsistent or don't sound genuine, they start asking more questions through other channels and sources. In short, the journalist starts digging to find the reality behind what looks like a smokescreen.

Being Dutch, Van de Keuken's questions are pretty direct and straightforward.

'So if you say child slavery is too big a word, do you agree that child labour exists on a large scale in the industry?'

'Yes,' answers Nestlé's head of PR, 'let's say that slavery exists... because they are so desperately poor.'

Van de Keuken is flabbergasted by the confession and his response, thinking out loud, is too straightforward for Nestlé: 'Because they don't get paid enough by Nestlé or by the companies they work for.'

The head of PR ends the conversation by hanging up the phone.

In retrospect, solving the slavery problem is not as simple as just paying more at the start of the supply chain. At least, that's what everyone keeps telling Van de Keuken and the other members of the team. Although Van de Keuken is the face of the programme for this item, the real drive behind the research comes from Dekker, the owner of the production company and the developer of the television concept. Dekker has long been a television journalist, but has always been highly interested in the field of marketing. It is his conviction that 'journalism = marketing' that led to the birth of Tony's Chocolonely in November 2005. This principle turned out to be the Trojan horse for competing with enormous multinationals with their overwhelming market power and marketing budgets.

The multinationals made a big mistake: they simply never imagined that a journalist would play them at their own game.

Make the story stick

Tony's team's aim was to raise awareness about slavery in the cacao industry. The vehicle was their television programme. In order to be able to tell the same story over and over again, they needed new angles to bring the problem closer to consumers.

The team wondered about a legal angle, and they consulted a Dutch professor in criminal law, asking him to compare buying a chocolate bar to the offence of purchasing a stolen bike. (In 2003, it was common practice to sell and buy stolen bikes in the famous Vondelpark in Amsterdam, but this is now an offence that can even lead to jail time.) The professor liked the concept, reasoning that, strictly speaking, you commit a criminal act when you buy a chocolate bar that you know was made by committing an illegal act. And slavery is undoubtedly an illegal act.

Van de Keuken decided to prosecute himself for eating and buying chocolate bars, and turned himself in. At this point, the attention really took off. His action created a storm of publicity and public response throughout the Netherlands, with thousands of people signing a petition for Van de Keuken to be taken to court. Van de Keuken and the team travelled to Burkina Faso, to the border with Côte D'Ivoire, in order to collect evidence. Several children testified, sharing their stories and the heartbreaking, humiliating details of their lives. It was a long haul, and the legal case was finally closed in 2007 when the court decided that Van de Keuken could not be trialled in the Netherlands since the criminal act was committed in Africa. However, the idea that eating chocolate was a criminal act was a catalyst for debate. It was time to return to Nestlé.

First, however, a little about Dekker's personality. It is useful to know that Dekker is no sour, seasoned campaigner, but a bon vivant, a light-hearted epicurean. He is definitely no cynic, but a playful television producer looking for clever ways to stay ahead of the game. In his view, journalists and corporates play a game of chess. Move, countermove, put someone in check or checkmate, which is a shame – but then you begin another game.

So Dekker opened a new game. His approach was in no way meant to be rancorous, rather slightly confrontational, and he tried to entice the multinationals to play along. By this time in 2005, the promotion for the new *Charlie and the Chocolate Factory* film had started, a US$150 million production, in which Felicity Dahl, the widow of Roald Dahl, was involved as executive producer. The team had a simple idea: could they create awareness by launching the first slave-free Willy Wonka chocolate bar at the premiere of the film? At this point, the team crossed paths with Nestlé again, as Nestlé held the rights to the chocolate bar. This time, the brand manager for the Willy Wonka bars received a phone call, but when he realized it was a sensitive issue, the conversation reached a dead end.

Annoyed to the max

By this stage it was two years on since van de Keuken prosecuted himself in 2003 and the team had gained extensive knowledge of the problems in the cacao sector. However, the persistence with which the market players denied the slavery problem (and, in the same breath, the team researching it) annoyed them to the max. It was time for a new angle to fire up the story. Dekker decided to launch a chocolate bar, as proof that it is possible to produce a slave-free chocolate bar. The continuous attention from Van de Keuken, Dekker and their team on this injustice finally roused the multi-nationals in the sector.

However, the team had to invest, and this revealed the gap between journalism and business practices. Once again, Dekker, owner of the production company and initiator of the story, led the initiative. The first bar was launched as a joke, as a new storyline. It made great television, with Van de Keuken following the whole supply chain from bean to bar, negotiating and demanding insight into the production process as a direct customer of the chocolate producers, the commissioning company. The wrapper for the bar was made overnight and challenged the usual colour codes used in the industry.

'How was I to know that red is the code for pure chocolate and blue for milk?' Dekker laughs. 'I was ignorant of the whole industry and red to me is a colour to raise awareness, a signal. And that's what the first Tony's Chocolonely milk chocolate bar was about. Raising the signal, a red flag. But I am not naive; our success today is based on the conviction that to really make multinationals listen, we had to play their game. And I realized I wasn't playing with them on a level playing field. But the idea of a chocolate bar at the supermarkets, giving consumers a choice, competing on price and shelf position and delivering proof that you can build a business on ideals; that turned out to become the game changer.'

When the first bars sold out within an hour of coming onto the market, Dekker decided on the spot to start a chocolate company.

From ideal to business, from a business perspective

Between **2003 and 2005** a market survey was conducted. There were in-depth insights into the challenges of the supply chain, a major competitive analysis was conducted, and the team knew all about the strengths and weaknesses of their competitors.

In 2005 the brand purpose became clear, the brand name was invented, and the ideal behind the brand became visible in the product claim: 100 per cent slave-free chocolate. This immediately put the competitors in arrears.

In 2006 the company was launched, production started and field experience was gained.

In 2007 and 2008 the team made some rookie mistakes. Costly mistakes.

'For which we forgave ourselves,' Dekker explains, 'because what did we know about this market? We ordered too much, too late and had no focus on a one-product strategy. We enthusiastically extended our portfolio and were diverting our time and energy. The financial risks we took were large and boomeranged back on us. We were investing in a volatile market, we were fined €20,000 by the Dutch Media Commission due to impermissible advertising in our TV programme and we lost money on melting chocolate into bars again, when a product extension failed. But how proud we were to be awarded the Brands with a Conscience award in January 2008. We were seen, acknowledged, and the boost helped us keep faith in everything we were doing.'

However, being on the same playing field, the competition only saw the chocolate company, the new kid on the block. They had fierce competition in their blood, and this competition raised its head when Tony's was taken to court by Bellissimo, a Swiss chocolate brand that challenged the claim of '100 per cent slave-free chocolate'. However, it appears that they may have forgotten that the roots of the brand were in journalism, and that the purpose of the brand was to raise awareness for a problem, not necessarily to sell chocolate bars. Imagine the smile on the faces of Tony and his team when they gracefully embraced this law suit, seeing it as another opportunity to tell the story to the world.

On 2 June 2007 the Amsterdam courts delivered a decision denying the claim by Bellissimo.

Bellissimo asked for a ban on Tony's promotion of Tony's Chocolonely in the television programme and the statement that it's '100 per cent slave-free guaranteed'. The claim was denied since this assertion cannot be considered misleading (and therefore illegal).

However, Tony's adjusted their claim to 'on our way to 100 per cent slave-free chocolate', because there is still so much improvement needed in the cacao sector.

Verkade, originally a Dutch brand and now owned by United Biscuits, didn't understand that difference either. A major chocolate brand in the Netherlands, Verkade approached Tony's to learn more about the sector, the system and the solutions. After several conversations, Verkade decided to become fair trade, the first step towards paying a fairer price to farmers in the cacao sector. The team at Tony's were proud. By sharing their knowledge and network they were able to set something in action, something bigger. Feeling positive, the team waited for Verkade's press release, but disappointment soon followed. There was no reference whatsoever to Tony's Chocolonely in the release. So, in turn, the team thanked Verkade at the auction they had organized to give their sustainable policy some weight. The first fair trade chocolate bar (5 kilogrammes) was auctioned, and Tony's bought this at a price of €15,800, making the headlines the next day, thanks to Verkade.

In 2009 and 2010 they finally made some money. In collaboration with the Dutch postcode lottery, a fundraiser for a greener and fairer world, they became visible in millions of Dutch households. Tony's expanded its points of purchase and was sold through large supermarket chains. But Dekker had to acknowledge that the stakes were high, and every time he placed another mortgage on his house it reflected on his role and competencies. It was then that Tony's was faced with its own malpractice suit; the hazelnuts sourced in Turkey involved child labour.

'So our principles were challenged. We changed to a Dutch supplier. That was no tough decision. But to be honest; I felt we were at a crossroad,' Dekker sighs. 'Yes, we were a brand with a clear purpose, great storytellers and promising market perspectives. But the brand was also at a turning point; there was the risk of losing momentum, the story about slavery had been told and no product innovation was planned.'

From small business to market challenger

Now meet Henk Jan Beltman, who came into the picture at that time. On paper he looked like a good candidate to help grow the business of Tony's Chocolonely, being a marketer by heart, tried and tested in the multinational world and somewhat experienced in the world of sustainable brands (leading the Benelux division of innocent, the drinks company). Dekker knew that the brand might fizzle out if nothing substantial changed. However, Beltman represented everything that annoyed Dekker: a 'would-be' sales manager without many principles.

Dekker's initial aversion and distrust was hard for Beltman to swallow, but he did.[4] He is now self-declared Chief Chocolate Officer and major shareholder of Tony's Chocolonely. He is responsible for an annual growth of 50 per cent since stepping into this small but promising enterprise. For Beltman, Tony's became the platform for seeking more pride in his work and leading the change he wanted to see in the world. He saw the opportunity to help Tony's Chocolonely grow and he knew how to play the game, both within the Netherlands and in the rest of the world. Dekker's distrust did not hold him back. He pursued Dekker and was able to convince him that he was the best man for the job. Dekker made room for Beltman and now openly compliments him on a job well done, saying that Beltman turned out to be 'the best sales manager of principles'.

Beltman's contribution to the brand is broader than just sales and revenue growth. Beltman established the brand. Together with the team he has formalized all of the previously unwritten brand attributes: its purpose, values, identity and strategy, just so that everyone knows what Tony's Chocolonely stands for.

> ## Tony's vision: on our way to 100 per cent slave-free chocolate
>
> For Tony's this means all the chocolate in the world, and no more slavery in the chocolate industry. Tony's is *leading by example* with their strong will and outspokenness, ensuring that 'cannot' does not exist, and 'because' is not a solid reason. Tony's team members are entrepreneurial in their own fields, meaning that they are not afraid to try to learn from mistakes. There is also room for a little fun along the way, because although the goal is serious, working in the chocolate business definitely beats working in financial services, for example.
>
> *Crazy about chocolate.*
> *Serious about people.*

He publishes an annual 'FAIR~~Year~~ Report' [*sic* – we will refer to them as FAIR reports in the rest of this book] and is very proud that Tony's has received a Great Place to Work award in the Netherlands, supporting his conviction that pride in your work is a great driver for growth. This goes both for him and for the team, many of whom were involved with Tony's from the very beginning. Those who have since left still feel strongly attached to Tony's – having worked there is an invaluable asset on their CV.

Being in charge of the brand from 2010 on, Beltman constantly looks both backwards and forwards, and at the end of 2014 his annual reflection was put under pressure by a comment from Van de Keuken, who had entered the stage again.

Here it is helpful to know that Van de Keuken has never been a shareholder. As a journalist he values his independence and nowadays he has moved on to other assignments. However, he was the face of the brand and his name is forever attached to it, so the outside world still considers Van de Keuken to be the founder of the brand. Therefore, it is only logical that when a Dutch newspaper interviewed Beltman about the fair trade system (about which they wrote a critical review) they also asked Van de Keuken for his opinion. His opinion still carries weight in the company and among consumers. In this specific article Van de Keuken made a puzzling comment about the brand, quoted as saying that, 'The attention is now too often on happy faces and success stories, which sometimes gives the company a high, happy-clappy calibre.'[5]

Beltman has carefully reread and reflected on the comment, wondering whether it unbalanced the brand promise. One aspect of this is the 'crazy about chocolate' theme, which stresses happiness and is designed to make people smile. Perhaps this undermines the other aspect, 'serious about people', which really does connect back to the company's roots.

Beltman also reflected on another point about brands. He and his team may have influence over sourcing, production and packaging, but Tony's Chocolonely is a brand that lots of people identify with. There is a network of stakeholders who are connected to a greater or lesser extent to the brand and its origin and purpose: 100 per cent slave-free chocolate throughout the whole supply chain. These people are very happy to express their views – sometimes volubly. This involvement is a powerful driver for the brand but it also makes the brand hard to manage.

However, Beltman is fully aware that being the biggest shareholder does not mean that he owns the brand. The value of Tony's Chocolonely is created by a complex group of stakeholders, all involved in one way or another. In their annual FAIR report, Tony's literally states that 'together we realize the future of a fair industry', as an employer together with the team, the farmers and their cooperative, consumers and fans, customers and suppliers. 'The biggest impact Tony's can have is by making all consumers aware that slave-free chocolate is still a distant reality. Tony's is a vehicle, a messenger, a way to really speed up the change we all want to see in the world (but don't all live up to yet).'

So for Beltman, the serious part of the brand promise is non-negotiable. Anything that directly benefits the labour conditions of workers at the beginning of the supply chain comes first.

'We will only accept straight As on this topic,' Beltman says. 'However, being who we are – wilful, committed, ambitious and outspoken – we will not stay down on other topics, such as quality, taste and fun. And in the field of quality, dilemmas are the order of the day.'

Leading a brand with a conscience brings a constant debate over dilemmas:

- What if you have fought 10 years to trace the whole supply chain from bean to bar and you run out of traceable cacao? Will you shut down operations and wait until there is new stock, or do you amend your principles a little bit?

- What if you want to launch a stunning new taste, cherry meringue, and then you find out that there is no meringue from free-range eggs on the market?

- What if you want to stretch the brand to other categories, and the former owner comes up with an idea for a fair trade cigarette?
- What if you are personally convinced that trusting people is the basis for equality and that checking up on them brings back memories of imperialistic inequality?

Beltman has faced all and more of these challenges in the past five years. He has sometimes held on to his initial beliefs, and at other times has been convinced by someone involved in Tony's to make a tough decision. Whichever scenario he chose, it was always based on Tony's principles: Tell it like it is. Lead by example. Inspire to act.

The Tony's website has a detailed explanation of the solutions for the problem of limited stock. The meringue cherry was not launched until a baker was found who was willing to change the ingredients in his meringue recipe. Tony's will also remain a chocolate brand, because chocolate also means pleasure, when produced in a proper, economically viable way for everyone involved. In this regard, Beltman found that, contrary to the market belief, it is very simple to solve the slavery problem; simply start by paying a better price at the beginning of the value chain (and stop calculating in a percentage topping this price).

However, his personal dilemma has not yet been resolved. In order to deliver proof of Tony's efforts, the world wants tangible results, which means that Beltman has to check and trace all beans to bar. In 2013, Tony's could fully trace the cacao mass contained in the chocolate bars. They buy cacao directly from Aponoapono in Ghana and Blaiskero in Sud Côte d'Ivoire. Because of the personal relationship that has been built over time, the farmers are certain that they can sell their cacao to Tony's over the long term for better prices. Furthermore, Tony's measures and publishes data on the percentage of products without artificial additives, the number of instances of modern slavery found in the chain, the number of cases of illegal child labour, the percentage of families of Tony's farmers who have enough resources to go the doctor if necessary, and the percentage of Tony's farmers' children up to the age of 15 who go to school. Actually, Beltman uses 17 long-term business goals and 53 variables to measure these goals, but it still feels awkward and out of balance.

And still, Beltman continues the storytelling. Having lost the platform of the television programme (due to the fine for illegal brand promotion), Beltman took to the core product of Tony's Chocolonely.

In the industry there is not a lot of tangible difference between chocolate bars. The colour code is strong with red for pure and blue for milk, the bars are more or less the same weight, and definitely divisible into equal parts. That equality, of course, was a perfect narrative hook for the team at Tony's. In 2012, Tony's introduced their unequally divided bar, and now every product tells in an instant the story about the unevenly divided chocolate industry.

If you look closely you can see the West African countries hidden in the chocolate bar. From left to right you can see: Côte d'Ivoire, Ghana, Togo and Benin, Nigeria and Cameroon. It is not quite politically correct, as Togo and Benin have since merged, but this was the only way they could fit a whole hazelnut into this piece of chocolate.

Consumers didn't like this change, with a lot of comments being received after this major adjustment and complaints still coming in. Customers complain that it is not so easy to break off an equal piece of the bar, or that they don't know how much an individual piece of chocolate weighs. This is exactly what Tony's is after – to make consumers rethink the unequal distribution in the chocolate supply chain. The chocolate bar itself has become the platform for storytelling.

To make sure Tony's stays ahead in the market, Beltman involves his stakeholders both in the progress they have made and the pitfalls they have encountered. Tony's openly shares their insights and mistakes in their FAIR report, which gives the brand a head start in this social era. Open up, don't pretend to be perfect, but be real. Make a difference for customers, suppliers, farmers and employers – that's what Tony's stands for.

For Beltman, being real, being human equals being 'serious about people', and this brand claim counts for everyone involved with the brand. He proudly shows off the small kitchen in Amsterdam where the surprising combinations and scrumptious chocolate bars are developed under the supervision of Eva, chocolatier. Arjen, responsible for Tony's design, enthu-siastically describes the development of the visual identity, how he carefully cut out the logo of the first wrapper by hand, because he couldn't find the right font to express Tony's identity: open, honest, optimistic, adventurous, resolute and, of course, experts in chocolate. Arjen is still the gatekeeper for Tony's style guide, now a full-time job in which he interacts with a variety of stakeholders, telling the story of Tony's Chocolonely over and over again. Arjen may well stay on board, because Tony's is about to cross some borders.

Tony's Chocolonely Title Net Revenues

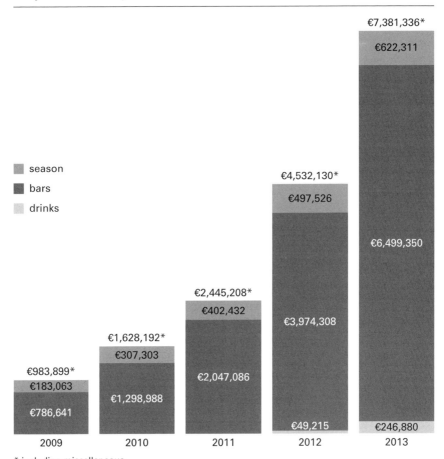

▨	season	
■	bars	
▫	drinks	

2009: €983,899* — €183,063 / €786,641
2010: €1,628,192* — €307,303 / €1,298,988
2011: €2,445,208* — €402,432 / €2,047,086
2012: €4,532,130* — €497,526 / €3,974,308 / €49,215
2013: €7,381,336* — €622,311 / €6,499,350 / €246,880

* including miscellaneous

SOURCE: Tony's Chocolonely

Beltman's focus is still on 50 per cent annual growth, year after year, and 4 per cent net profit. With a market share of 7 per cent, Tony's beat Verkade in the Dutch market and, with 33 per cent brand awareness, there is still room to grow in the Netherlands.

However, Beltman's ambition reaches far beyond the Netherlands. He shares with Dekker the conviction that if you want the multinationals to change the way they play, you have to challenge them at their own (chess) game. To help them bring out the best in them and use their scale and marketing power for the benefit of the cacao supply chain.

So, when confronted with the happy-clappy comment publicly made by Van de Keuken, Beltman proudly answers, 'We move beyond the discussion; at Tony's we have developed great taste and we focus on shelf position, thus gaining a strong position in the level playing field. We have a growing fan base, our story gets told by every bar we sell. It is crystal clear that we are crazy about chocolate. But in doing so we have delivered proof of concept, based on a non-negotiable principle: we are serious about people. And that's a pretty serious brand promise that we live up to. Every day. With every chocolate bar.'

Reflective questions

- How could Tony's Chocolonely create awareness in your country?
- What other brands are great at storytelling?
- What other non-traditional brand-building strategies do you know of?

Notes

1 Interview Maurice Dekkers, 2015
2 Tony's FAIR Reports 2013–
3 www.Club of Rome.org
4 Interview Henk-Jan Beltman, 2015
5 *NRC Handelsblad*, 6 December 2014

Lovechock happiness inside

SANDRA HORLINGS

Brief encounter

When Laura de Nooijer and Jan-Bas Reijners met on a bus in 2008, neither of them knew that they would share a future together.

Don't think this is a love story between Laura and Jan-Bas. Although there is definitely a lot of shared affection at the heart of Lovechock – the business that grew from their first encounter on the bus as they returned from a seminar given by Raw Food guru David Wolfe in Antwerp, Belgium.

Now, seven years later, Lovechock, officially born in the Netherlands in 2009, is the largest grower in the organic segment in Europe. It is sold in 18 countries throughout Europe, mainly organic retail outlets and supermarkets. By the end of 2015 Lovechock has 40 people and its own chocolate factory.

Let's go back to the bus. Visualize Jan-Bas, early forties, with a previous career at a leading coffee and tea multinational, recovering from burnout and seeking inspiration. He is mulling over a new business idea: how to start a juice and tea bar. Unfortunately the seminar has been no help, because it zoomed in on the power of cacao. But it was intriguing – especially something that David Wolfe had said about the best way to prepare and eat chocolate: 'You don't roast cacao. You cold grind it. And you eat it. Raw.' He rethinks his experience in coffee and, as he sits on the bus next to Laura, intuitively knows that this is the right way to go forward.

Lovechock is organic raw chocolate, available in tablets, bars and rocks. The bar was the launch product. It looks like a collection of four bonbons rather than a solid chocolate bar (and has a tiny personal message included – from the maker to you). Visualize the rocks as small crunchy and crispy chocolate snacks, stuffed with fruits, nuts, spices and herbs, proven to have a positive effect on your health. And with distinctive taste combinations and superb flavours.

In the regular chocolate production process, the cacao beans are roasted and ground at very high temperatures whereby much of the cacao's beneficial qualities are destroyed. But raw chocolate is different. The raw cacao beans are not roasted but cold ground and the beautiful ingredients in cacao (such as antioxidants and two so-called love-chemicals: tryptophane and PEA) remain intact. In the Lovechock process, from the cacao bean through to the end product, the temperature is kept below 49°C.

Laura had been travelling the world, soul searching and learning from other cultures. In Mexico and Brazil she had discovered the power of eating raw cacao and on her return to Amsterdam she starts experimenting with chocolate recipes, making them ever more tasty, delicious and healthy. She is in Antwerp to promote her recipes. She invites Jan-Bas to taste one of her home-made small chocolates – raw, heart-shaped and filled with superfoods. Jan-Bas is more than interested. After a full day of presentations on the subject he is extremely curious about the taste of raw chocolate. So for Jan-Bas proof is in the chocolate; the taste is nice, rich, interesting. As a brand marketer at heart he immediately thinks of the intrinsic product value and the extrinsic emotional value of raw chocolate. The opportunity is exciting, so he offers to write a business plan.

One thing leads to another. The business plan becomes reality. Throughout 2009 several meetings and brainstorms lead to a descriptive brand name – Lovechock – and a brand promise that tells it like it is: happiness inside – based on the fact that the more flavonoids (antioxidants) and 'love chemicals' that stay intact, the bigger the effect on your mood.

Purpose, perseverance and possibilities

In mid-2010, a new partner joins them: Franziska (Fran) Rosario. Alongside Laura's sense of purpose and Jan-Bas's perseverance, Fran is good at turning possibilities into opportunities. The three are a great mix. They share a love for a healthy way of living and challenge each other on brand and business decisions.

For example, they talk about making functional claims in the German market, where the market demands vegan and sugar-free products. And although Lovechock can deliver proof for both claims, they decide to hold on to the overall brand promise; bring happiness to people's lives. For Fran it is not about products and sales; 'Lovechock is a life's mission. It is far more rewarding for me to reach for a higher goal; to help people live a healthy lifestyle and belong to a group of like-minded people, who share the same philosophy.'

Laura, who is the spiritual compass of the company, believes that happiness inside comes from love for yourself, love for others and love for mother Nature. Laura's holistic vision on life and food is reflected in the products, the flavours and also in the consumption moment. Looking pure and honest on the outside, the experience of the product is supposed to add to a loving and happy feeling. The key experience definitely lies in the chocolates, but Laura also adds little personal messages; some 250 quotes that make you reflective and happy.

I master the inner alchemy of body, mind and soul

I wake up to my sacred truth

True to the heart of the business

Lovechock is growing. Rapidly. This leaves Jan-Bas, Laura and Fran with numerous decisions to make, every day. On finance, sales, operations, supply, product development, marketing, personnel and more. Next to daily concerns there are questions about the future. Is raw food here to stay? Will people really change their food and eating behaviours? Will the strict separation between organic and conventional supermarkets remain or will a hybrid concept emerge? And how will this affect the value chain of Lovechock?

With all these challenges, there is little time for reflection. And it is hard to prioritize. To choose.

Still they have to. And their brand manifesto is key: love for yourself, for others and Mother Nature is at the heart of Lovechock. Laura says: 'Open people's hearts by making them more conscious about food, whilst respecting people, profit and Mother Nature.'

And they are realistic. Being a small Dutch company, a start-up not so long ago, the focus is on manageable growth. They challenge the status quo by delivering healthy, tasty, attainable, delicious, superb chocolate. Convenient and home-made.

Along the way, business decisions are being made in line with a shared set of values: wisdom, freedom, balance, honesty. The final check: is Lovechock bringing happiness to the world? Because that is what Lovechock is about. And that's a tasty promise.

The case for eco-gastronomy: why we should all have access to food that is good, clean and fair

06

PETER BROWN ON SLOW FOOD

- ○ *Local autonomy derives from a strong, shared central philosophy.*
- ○ *Leading by example is the way to go.*
- ○ *Powerful brands take positive action, have a sense of humour and provide pleasure.*

Evolving from oenophilia and gastronomy in Italy, to a major international movement promoting eco-gastronomy and food that is good, clean and fair for all, the Slow Food movement (headquartered in the little town of Bra in Piemonte) has become one of the leading international movements in the arena of food production and consumption. You will learn in this chapter how local autonomy, and a clear core set of values and principles, has allowed Slow Food to become a highly respected and influential international brand. How have clearly enunciated philosophy and values, combined with a determination not to become 'corporatist' as the brand internationalizes, allowed for flexibility, speed and local relevance, in the context of an international movement? I will consider this question and also look at the specific attributes of the brand that make it an exemplary 'brand with a conscience'.

Slow Food Manifesto, 1989

Born and nurtured under the sign of industrialization, this century first invented the machine and then modelled its lifestyle after it. Speed became our shackles. We fell prey to the same virus: 'the fast life' that fractures our customs and assails us even in our own homes, forcing us to ingest 'fast food'.

Homo sapiens must regain wisdom and liberate itself from the 'velocity' that is propelling it on the road to extinction. Let us defend ourselves against the universal madness of 'the fast life' with tranquil material pleasure. Against those – or, rather, the vast majority – who confuse efficiency with frenzy, we propose the vaccine of an adequate portion of sensual gourmandize pleasures, to be taken with slow and prolonged enjoyment.

Appropriately, we will start in the kitchen, with Slow Food. To escape the tediousness of 'fast food', let us rediscover the rich varieties and aromas of local cuisines. In the name of productivity, the 'fast life' has changed our lifestyle and now threatens our environment and our land (and city) scapes. Slow Food is now the only truly progressive answer.

Real culture is here to be found. First of all, we can begin by cultivating taste, rather than impoverishing it; by stimulating progress, by encouraging international exchange programmes, by endorsing worthwhile projects, by advocating historical food culture and by defending old-fashioned food traditions.

Slow Food assures us of a better-quality lifestyle. With a snail purposely chosen as its patron and symbol, it is an idea and a way of life that needs much sure but steady support.

Good, clean and fair: the evolution of Slow Food

The story of Slow Food is the story of evolution, adaptation and progress... but always rooted in a central core philosophy and values. For readers who are not familiar with the brand, I will give a brief summary of the origins of this movement and their key moments of evolution.[1]

The story has its origins in the 'anni di piombo' in Italy, the 1970s and early 1980s when factions of the militant left and right engaged in a cycle of violence and terrorism. In the midst of this social unrest, many young communist activists sought non-violent and practical causes they could adopt in line with their political beliefs, often occasioned by some social 'spark' (as in Germany with the anti-nuclear movement).

For a young Carlo Petrini (born 1949) the 'spark' was the Festival of the Thrush in Montalcino in 1982, which he was visiting with fellow members of the Arci (popular social and cultural clubs sponsored by the Italian Socialist and Communist parties). Despite his young age, Petrini was already a long-time communist activist and publicist, the founder of the 'free and meritorious association of the friends of the Barolo' – a cultural group focused on oenology, which promoted a democratic and 'healthy' lifestyle; plus a founding member of a local cooperative centred on wine and restaurants.

Petrini was horrified by the quality of the food offered at the festival and engaged in an angry exchange of letters with the host. He was invited to argue his case the following year at a debate in Montalcino on 'The *Case del popolo* and their tradition of festivals and gastronomy'. He convinced his sceptical audience that quality and taste were as much a concern – and a right – of the 'democratic' left and its cultural clubs and groups as the more familiar centre-right proponents of traditional 'gastronomy'. Petrini was on his way.

Inspired by the Milanese food culture magazine *La Gola*, to which he contributed, Petrini went on to found Arci Gola in 1983, a national oeno-gastronomical league under the auspices of the Arci, with the aim of creating a market for goods of indisputable quality, to be sold at fair prices. This culminated in 1986 with a conference to promulgate a philosophy of taste, combining pleasure and knowledge/education, coupled with awareness of food culture and preserving local food products.

Having consolidated a name for both himself and his group in Italy by the mid-1980s, Petrini was then presented with two opportunities to galvanize the movement. First was the scandal of methanol-tainted wine in Cuneo, which killed 23 people, forcing the Italian wine industry thereafter to focus on quality, control and distribution of stock. Petrini remained close to this movement, eventually co-publishing the now famous *Vini d'Italia* in 1988. Second, and the reason for a new name for the movement, was the opening of a McDonald's in Piazza di Spagna in Rome in March 1986, which caused much distress to Arci Gola (and many other Italian commentators). Arci Gola responded with a manifesto, extolling the virtues of 'eating slowly' and placing pleasure and quality above the needs of production for profit. It was a response not only to the quality of food available in the fast-food culture, but also the environment of eating quickly and efficiently, rather than for taste and pleasure, which was entirely against the Arci Gola philosophy. As Petrini put it, an environment full of 'inducements to eating quickly, without chatting; it is like a visit to a protein-filling station'.[2]

With Arci Gola enjoying a fast-growing membership in Italy, and with a clear concept now of 'Slow Food' within a wider 'Slow' philosophy, Petrini decided to make the cause international with a meeting in Paris in late 1989 at which international delegates signed a 'Slow Food manifesto' (see boxed text). This emphasized Slow Food as a political response to the fast pace of modern life and globalization; the first Slow Food Congress took place in Venice in 1990. The brand Slow Food, and the visual identifier of a snail, became the international (trademarked) brand identity of the movement, and were adopted also in Italy in 1991.

The intervening 25 years have seen an extraordinary expansion and development of the activities of Slow Food. To list but the highlights:

The first **Salone del Gusto** in Turin in 1996, a now biennial event showcasing artisanal, sustainable food and the small-scale producers that safeguard local traditions and high-quality products. At this event, Petrini articulated the need for an **Ark of Taste** (*Arca del Gusto per salvare la pianeta dei sapori*), one of the most important and long-running Slow Food initiatives. This is a type of alimentary 'Noah's Ark', a catalogue of both animal and plant species that are of 'excellent quality', indigenous or long adapted to a particular territory, linked to a specific area, made in limited quantities amongst smaller firms or are rare/in danger of extinction. Oriented to food consumption, not just survival, Slow Food provides resources for growing or breeding these species in order for them to be consumed in a sustainable way. The Ark of Taste now runs to some 800 and more species across 50 countries.

In support of the burgeoning ark project, in 1999 Petrini launched the concept of the **Presidia**, whereby the production of a product – of high quality, highly localized and relevant to the local community, available in small quantities and potentially endangered – receives the direct support of Slow Food. Active involvement by Slow Food includes direct expert help to local farmers or fishermen, helping to form a cooperative of small-scale producers, providing rights to the Slow Food Presidium brand and extensive communication for the product.

In 2003, as a natural development of the Ark of Taste and Presidia, the **Slow Food Foundation for Biodiversity** was founded, to supervise and coordinate Slow Food's efforts across the span of its biodiversity-related activities. These now include not only the Ark and Presidia, but a project to launch 10,000 good, clean and fair food gardens in Africa, a global network of farmers' markets and the Slow Food Chefs' Alliance (an international network of chefs who support small, local producers and the use of local produce). The foundation states that its object is to 'support and disseminate the culture of biodiversity as a factor of human, civil and democratic growth... it shall work to safeguard the personal right to pleasure and to taste, thus establishing a harmonious relationship with nature in compliance with the traditions and the economic, gastronomic and agroindustrial identity of the terroirs'.

A year later, 2004, Slow Food helped inaugurate the **University of Gastronomic Sciences** in Pollenzo near Bra, to give an academic foundation to Petrini's vision of gastronomy and educated 'gusto' by offering a master's programme.

In the same year, a decade of work on the Salone, Ark of Taste and Presidia culminated in the launch of the **Terra Madre** network, which is now pivotal to the Slow Food movement. Terra Madre connects food communities that are centred on small-scale, sustainable and local production, from across the world, both remotely and physically, through a biennial gathering. An 'offshoot' of this network is the Indigenous Terra Madre network, emphasizing the role of food production and consumption in the culture and sustainability of indigenous communities. Specific Indigenous Terra Madre network gatherings are now organized. The first Terra Madre Giovani event in 2015, during Milan Expo, was specifically for younger members of the network.

The organization continues to develop and expand, having launched Slow Food Germany in 1992, Switzerland in 1993, United States in 2000, Japan in 2004, the UK in 2006 and the Netherlands in 2008, with Terra Madre communities worldwide. It is now active in more than 150 countries and counts 100,000 members and 2,000 Terra Madre communities.

What is the conscience of the Slow Food brand?

Articulating the conscience and purpose of Slow Food simply is easier said than done. Here are three ways of describing what Slow Food is actually about.

First, from the Slow Food International website:

> Slow Food envisions a world in which all people can access and enjoy food that is good for them, good for those who grow it and good for the planet. Our approach is based on a concept of food that is defined by three interconnected principles: good, clean and fair. GOOD: quality, flavoursome and healthy food; CLEAN: production that does not harm the environment; FAIR: accessible prices for consumers and fair conditions and pay for producers.[3]

Second, from the Slow Food UK website:

> Slow Food is a global, grass-roots organization... that links the pleasure of food with a commitment to the community and the environment... In over two decades of history, the movement has evolved to embrace a comprehensive approach to food that recognizes the strong connections between plate, planet, people, politics and culture.[4]

Finally, from the Slow Food Youth Network website:

> Slow Food is an international organization that stands at the crossroads of ecology, gastronomy, ethics and pleasure. The organization was founded in 1989 as a reaction against the upcoming fast-food chains. It opposes the standardization of taste and the growth and unrestrained power of multinationals in the food industry. Slow Food strives for high-quality food, produced in a sustainable way... and, of course, food that tastes good! It is essential, not only for us, but also for the future of the earth to change the present food system. Slow Food promotes small-scale agriculture, protects biodiversity and fights the food industry's politics of endless growth.[5]

Note the different language, and the different emphases of each description. One of the successes of Slow Food has been to encompass a range of descriptions of its brand philosophy with different emphases (at different times, for different audiences), while at the same time finding a way of summarizing and encapsulating a complex movement in three easy-to-remember simple guiding principles: that everyone should have access to food that is *good, clean and fair*:

- *Good* is understood by Petrini to require two conditions: that a product can be linked with a certain naturalness, respecting the original characteristics as much as possible; and second that it produces recognizable and pleasant sensations, which are understood to be culturally relative and specific, in short 'good to the palate and good according to the mind'.

- *Clean* is understood as less relative than good; that a product should respect the earth and the environment, not pollute, waste or overuse natural resources in the journey from field to the table. In short, it should be 'sustainable' in its entire production, distribution and consumption journey.

- *Fair* is the most political by far as it relates to social justice and social and economic sustainability. A new 'fair' system of food production and consumption would allow producing communities to flourish and deliver 'a worldwide network that is capable of opposing the dominant system'.[6] This involves 'quality of life through dignified jobs that guarantee sustenance and fair remuneration',[7] as well as economic sustainability through fair pricing and an investment model suited to agricultural production.

These three concepts encapsulate and summarize a broader, and still more radical brand philosophy, the philosophy of the 'Slow Movement', not just for food, but for society. It is beautifully encapsulated by Petrini as follows:

> In a world that appears ineluctably condemned to the standardization of all products and the flattening out of flavours, a world whose resources have been harnessed to the interests and profits of a few, Slow Food sees its international vocation as a proposal for an alternative model of development... the first objective is to spread knowledge and awareness; starting from there we can give dignity and economic value to every territory... offering to the world the hope of a future different from the polluted and tasteless one that the lords of the earth have programmed for all of us.[8]

The Slow Food philosophy has specific tenets, which Petrini articulates.

First, Petrini has always insisted on the right to pleasure: 'pleasure is a human right because it is physiological. We cannot fail to feel pleasure when we eat'.[9] This has always set Slow Food apart from other food-related non-government organizations (NGOs) that focus on food largely or purely as nutrition.

Second, Petrini argues that gastronomy is not just a science of food,[10] but is related closely to several other scientific disciplines with which it must be analysed holistically.[11] This allows the 'gastronome' to analyse and comment on other academic fields to which Slow will relate.

Next, Petrini argues that it is vital to link eating for pleasure and the environment, and that this has been a pivotal development in Slow thinking: 'a gastronome who has no environmental sensibility is a fool; but an ecologist who has no gastronomic sensibility is a sad figure, unable to understand the cultures in which he wants to work. What we need then is eco-gastronomy.'[12]

Petrini argues strongly that local populations are the best guardians of their eco-gastronomical environment through sustainable agriculture that targets quality of life not profit:

> By confusing development with growth, one confuses quality of life with material accumulation and the frantic pursuit of greater profits, which do not necessarily produce improvement in quality. We thus need to strongly support the rights of every population to provide its own nutrition and to choose freely and democratically the kind of agriculture they prefer. Rural agriculture is fundamental both in the battle against genetically modified organisms (GMOs), the big conglomerates of agrichemistry and agrifood, and in the defence of biodiversity and the sovereignty of food and farmers.[13]

The social significance of a local ecosystem of food production and consumption was spelt out in Petrini's opening address to the first Terra Madre gathering in Turin in October 2004:

> We are firmly convinced that food communities, founded on sentiment, fraternity, and the rejection of egotism, will have a strategic importance in the emergence of a new society, a society based on fair trade. Through their labour they bind together the destinies of women and men pledged to defend their own traditions, cultures and crops... they are an important and strategic factor in human nutrition, in the delicate balance between nature and culture that underpins our very existence.

Petrini asks that 'consumers' should redefine themselves as 'co-producers' with a fundamental role in sustainable food production, understanding their social and political role in this process. These 'co-producers' therefore become part of a community of food production, and these food communities coalesce in a network of communities which Petrini describes as 'community of destiny', and a 'worldwide network of gastronomes', who are all equal by virtue of being gastronomes in equal measure.[14]

Finally, Petrini argues strongly the case for 'natural limits' to production and consumption... 'But in order to achieve this we must renounce economic growth as the sole criterion for human progress.' He argues for a replacement of traditional measures of success such as gross national product (GNP) with more balanced measures such as gross national happiness.[15]

In summary, Petrini argues that 'the basis of a strategy that leads back to quality must be the recovery of another dimension, the adoption of slowness as a value external to the prevailing system, as a creative space and a meeting point of those values that are excluded from the system'.[16] If ever there was a statement of 21st-century counter-culture, this surely is it!

Slow Food as an *evolving* conscience with practical application

It is important to recognize that Slow Food has an *evolving* conscience, based on *consistent* values, but adapting as the environment around it changes.

There has been a real evolution of the movement from a largely Italian-based and Italian-modelled gastronomic food and wine association, preserving traditions at peril in Italy and emphasizing the right to food as pleasure, first to an international proponent of biodiversity and then the more political network of Terra Madre small-scale local farming and fishing across the world; an evolution from a focus on gastronomy and 'taste' to the cultures and traditions of food consumption and production, from 'fork to fork'.

Terra Madre represents an evolution of focus from the *product* (inherent in the Ark of Taste) to the *people* connected to the product, their culture, context and techniques, which also need to be preserved; from the taste and quality of food to the ecosystem of food, encompassing culture, employment and skills. It marks a refocusing from 'gastronome' to the food community of producers and 'co-producers' who buy the product. It also marks a clear evolution from a focus on First World gastronomical concerns to food 'justice' in developing countries.

These evolutions could be understood as a shifting balance between objective and subjective: from an early phase of insisting on 'gusto', the more subjective taste and quality of food, to a very scientific focus in the 'mid-period' of the movement (exemplified by the Ark of Taste and Foundation for Biodiversity); then to a new balance: a continued reliance on solid science, data and empirical evidence coupled with a support for culture and tradition.

As Shane Holland, chair of Slow Food in the UK, puts it succinctly: 'our science gives us an intro... it must be from the head, as well as the heart'.[17] But science without culture and empathy would, in Petrini's words, be very sad.

Slow Food: a brand with deep political conscience, but political independence

Slow Food even at its simplest level of 'gastronomy' is inherently political as well as social. The concluding chapters of 'Slow Food Nation', which set out a new 'slow' way of living and a 'holistic vision of the world of gastronomes', promote what appear to be a dismantling of capitalism and return to a rurally focused, almost pre-industrial landscape of food, culture and tradition. Petrini has sometimes been accused of Ludditism in his rejection of modern food production and consumption. So is Slow Food an inherently left-wing movement?

Whilst the movement has indeed become more political in recent years (especially in the UK, United States and Australia), and the focus on Terra Madre has given Slow Food a distinct political edge, the politics cannot be simply understood as 'left' or 'right'.

As early as 2002, Petrini said that 'the problems of poverty, hunger and mass agriculture as practised by big conglomerates belong neither to the left nor to the right'[18] (he also claimed, perhaps less convincingly, that it is 'not my intention to denounce the capitalist system in itself')[19]. The modern generation of activists agree. As Elisa Demichelis, one of the International Area Coordinators at Slow Food International, observed to me: 'I don't think Slow Food can be associated with a political organization, food has gone beyond these traditional political borders.'[20] As Shane Holland points out, the very farming communities of the UK or the United States that Slow Food supports are generally among the most conservative elements of society and are by no means natural supporters of left-wing parties. To engage with these communities therefore requires specific focus on the issues to which Slow Food chooses to focus and campaign, collaborating with the communities that it promotes and helps to sustain, rather than aligning itself with a political movement – let alone endorsing a political party. In this, Slow Food is different from other eco-environmental organizations with which it often collaborates, many of which have aligned with the local Green Party or local left-wing parties.

This non-partisan, politically engaged approach has won Slow Food many friends... and a place at the tables of numerous local, regional, national and international administrations, of different political persuasions. These administrations in turn have actively supported Slow Food's programmes.

The Salone de Torino has always been supported by the City of Turin and Region of Piemonte, for example, while the November 2015 Indigenous

Terra Madre event in Meghalaya, India was supported by the regional government and the United Nations (UN). Slow Food in the UK is regularly consulted by working parties in UK government and is a trusted source of advice, opinion and data for the Department of the Environment, Food and Rural Affairs and the Food Standards Agency.

Slow Food continues to have a strong, robust relationship with the European Union (it opposes many of the EU's efforts at homogenization), where it has a permanent office. Slow Food is the only food-related NGO that has a role at the UN, and Petrini himself has won the accolade of UN 'Champion of the Earth', the highest environmental award.

Slow Food is willing to partner with an array of NGO partners on specific campaigning issues, such as Oxfam or Friends of the Earth, regardless of that partner's political stance, but will hold its own position. Slow Food is adamant in maintaining its independence. It does not rule out support by companies, but carefully vets them (eg how much does the company pay its workers? Are production processes, where applicable, good, clean and fair?).

Of course, a politically motivated organization with a clear agenda, rather than a network of middle-aged 'gastronomes', has more chance of attracting the energies of the politically engaged youth. Much focus is now being given at Slow Food to ensuring that the membership and leadership are rejuvenated. To this end, there is a specific Slow Food Youth Network (SFYN) – not based in Bra but in Amsterdam, a clear signal of the internationalization of the organization. It claims that 'we are the world's future leaders, entrepreneurs, farmers and consumers,[21] a robust self-awareness that Petrini clearly endorses, having been a successful young activist in his time. As he has said of the SFYN: 'For any association it is absolutely mandatory to be able to always collect the spirit of time and "our" youngsters are the ones that better than others can succeed in that... SFYN is an incredible resource for our association: it's a think tank of ideas and activities that sometimes almost overwhelms us but that we will always support.'[22]

The language and rhetoric of SFYN is more politically charged than that of the main organization, without in any way diverging from the central values or ethos of Slow Food. As Joris Lohman, who runs the network, expressed to me: 'my generation, the millennials, we rediscovered food as something to explore the political implications of what we eat. So we balance pleasure and gastronomy with the serious issues we focus on.'[23] The activities of the youth network mirror the main movement, including Terra Madre Giovani, but also focus on issues with which urban young people often can engage, for example, food waste.

Slow Food in practice: a global conscience with local autonomy

Petrini has always maintained that an internationalized Slow Food community must not become corporatist, not a BINGO as he puts it (big international non-governmental organization) reflecting of the type of global organizations he likes to attack in his writing. So how then to run 'an ethical franchise' (to quote Shane Holland)[24] that is present in 150 countries and currently counts some 100,000 members?

The answer is one well suited to a brand with a conscience. Not by central dictat, not with an overarching bureaucracy, not a list of strict guidelines as to what can and cannot be done. Rather, by a strong central philosophy made available by Petrini and Slow Food internationally, to which individuals, grouped in what in Italian are referred to as 'convivia', voluntarily subscribe. Slow Food is self-selecting: there is no test for entry, no qualification to represent the movement. Rather it is assumed that anyone wishing to join the movement actively shares the values and beliefs of the movement. Therefore any potential disagreements that might emerge would not be at the level of belief or philosophy (that is, 'strategy') but about a specific course of action (that is, 'tactic').

This allows for maximum autonomy and self-governance at the local level, perfectly reflective of a brand that preaches the supremacy of locality. Groups are encouraged to establish themselves locally in 'convivia', which can be as small as 10 members. A convivium represents a 'territory' and organizes events for members, such as sampling, courses on taste and producer visits. Each is headed by a leader who maintains a link with the formal associations in that country. There is an international committee to oversee the activities, expansion and coordination of Slow Food, and any leader has the right to (self-) nominate themselves for the international committee, which is selected by ballot at the annual general meeting. All in all, the organization can be described as 'Sellotape and string'.[25]

As an example of this 'subsidiarity', Slow Food UK is being redefined as 'Slow Food in the UK', a political and lobbying organization at national level providing 'local and economic central support' on behalf of the various groups in the UK. This is including Slow Food England, Wales and Scotland, as well as the more localized groups such as Slow Food Cornwall, using a 'spiderweb principle'.[26]

Slow Food has a particularly interesting way of dealing with conflict in its network. If a member, expert or convivium does not agree with a positioning or a course of action, a dialogue is opened. It is quickly established if the disagreement pertains to a matter of values and philosophy or potentially wrong facts, statistics or poor argumentation.

The former apparently is very rare indeed, because of the self-selecting nature of Slow Food. In the words of Elisa Demichelis: 'We are happy to have an open discussion with people... on certain issues that are part of the philosophy of Slow Food, our cause is clear from the beginning. If you no longer feel you are part of the movement... we do not oblige anyone to be part of the network'.[27] The underlying principle of the relationship of the headquarters with convivia is the 'right to use' the trademarked brand and collateral. While Slow Food International would therefore find it difficult to stop a local activity, it can revoke the right to use the brand, as an ultimate sanction.

Two footnotes to this collaborative approach: first, the very open, non-hierarchical, non-confrontational and democratic governance is attractive equally to women and men, with 50 per cent of the base now female. Second, 'Italian-ness' and the Italian brand language have become a point of concern for the international community (where local communities may not speak Italian and communicate internationally mostly in English). There is a movement to 'de-Italianize': words such as 'convivium' and 'presidium' drawn from Latin have no particular meaning in English, so 'convivium' has become in the UK simply 'group', or 'chapter' in the United States.

This is symptomatic of a wider concern as to how an internationalizing Slow Food deals with its Italian heritage – 'our Italian roots are our heritage but also our Achilles heel; we are global and we are de-Italianizing'.[28] This in turn has caused concern in Italy that something fundamentally 'Italian' in the conscience of the brand is being lost. As Barbara Santoro, author of *The Italian Factor*, pointed out to me, the 'Italian factor' behind Slow Food has been eroded; the natural emphasis on communal, 'slow' eating that is so traditionally Italian and is still preserved in Slow Food in Italy does not translate so easily to an international audience, and it has not been given the same emphasis internationally as the focus on biodiversity and 'food science'.[29]

Slow Food and personal leadership: leading by personal example

All contributors to this chapter agree that the presence of Carlo Petrini as founder and president of Slow Food is essential for the movement; but all agree that the Slow Food movement is no longer dependent on him for its survival and growth and that the movement will continue after such time as Petrini steps down from his role. In the words of the 29-year-old Joris Lohman, head of the youth network and youngest member of the International Executive Committee, 'life after Petrini is a difficult topic. It is difficult to imagine Slow Food without him. But I am not afraid of this.'[30]

Petrini will be a very hard act to follow: a *Time* magazine 'hero' in 2004, and a UN 'champion of the earth' in 2013, he is intrinsically connected to the Slow Food movement. Hence, the task of capturing the 'conscience' and preparing for 'life after Petrini' rests on the writing, speeches and many videoed interviews that are helping to immortalize Petrini's philosophy... not to mention his charm and enthusiasm, which helps set Slow Food apart from other movements in the eco-environmental sector.

These written and videoed publications are vital to a movement emphasizing local autonomy: the Slow Food brand discourse evolves through discussion, dialogue and rumination, leading to yet another essay, presentation or book by Petrini. Each of these new publications acts as another chapter in the 'story' of the movement as a whole. Through his writing particularly, Petrini signals to the movement (and to his critics and press) the various evolutions in his own thinking and the further direction he would like the movement to take, or new foci he would suggest for the movement.

Three things mark out Petrini as an exceptional leader: an ability to engage and entertain; a sense of humour and genuine pleasure in his activities; and a sense of humility that not all things are always clear, or straightforward or always right first time. Interviewers emphasize how approachable he remains: neither austere, nor violent in his views, but passionate, warm and willing to engage.[31] His writing and dialogues are marked by a sense of humour, affability and sheer pleasure in food and eating.

This is reflected in the movement as a whole: there is no hectoring, no demonstrations with placards outside the gates of hated multinationals, but rather, an insistence on the right to pleasure, to enjoy the food that is produced, provided it is good, clean, and fair. There is a preference for positive, local, 'small' action over posturing or grandstanding, through leading by example. In Petrini's own words 'the path of the guerrilla fighter, that we prefer not to take. That is not the slow style. Our choice is to focus our energies on saving things that are headed for extinction instead of hounding the new ones we dislike... concrete actions and feasible projects are more congenial to us than denial and protest'.[32] Joris Lohman argues that this may be very much in the zeitgeist of the millennial generation, who seek positive action not just demonstration, an important appeal to a younger generation of activists.

Slow Food: demonstrating the features of a brand with a conscience

Brands with a conscience demonstrate certain behaviours, which are easily observable in Slow Food:

Acting in line with values

For a values and principles-based organization that is essentially 'self-selecting' for its members, acting according to values is a primary duty.

As Shane Holland emphatically points out: 'We are completely value-driven. We must always be "good, clean and fair" and we think long-term.' He also points to the inevitable focus on one or more values for a particular issue: 'We may place greater emphasis on one or more value so, for example, free school meals was about fair more than clean and good; whilst opposition to genetically modified food is first and foremost about "clean". All the dials must be on, but sometimes one may be set higher than the others.'[33]

Acknowledging that we are all fundamentally equal

This is fundamental to the philosophy of Slow Food. Petrini has answered the not infrequent accusation of 'gastronomic elitism' by reminding his critics that his aim is that ALL should have access to food that is good, clean and fair. Unsurprisingly for a former active communist, Petrini holds to equality of opportunity. The principle is also reflected in the movement's organization: Petrini is 'first among equals' in his role as president, he may be the public face but has always maintained the humility to listen to and learn from others in the movement. The organization is not per se hierarchical, being a grass-roots movement assembled into 'convivia'. What hierarchy does exist is, in the words of Shane Holland, 'for support, not for command or control'.[34]

Investing time and energy in relationship building

Unsurprisingly, Slow Food invests an enormous amount of time in relationship building. As Elisa Demichelis emphasizes: 'We are building mutual trust; 80 per cent of our time in Bra is working with people.'[35] Headquarters at Bra organizes Skype calls with the local leaders once a month, the SFYN uses Skype, Facebook and other social media, whilst local 'convivia' organize a range of local events for members. Via e-mail and telephone, leaders and members are constantly informing and sharing with each other, which allows ideas to evolve and change organically. Terra Madre provides the physical meeting platform for the international food community leaders to meet and get to know one another.

Taking responsibility when things go wrong

Things generally do not go wrong for Slow Food, because it is a movement of ideas. However, contributors pointed to the fact that ideas do evolve and they acknowledged there is always the possibility of factual error in scientific data or the availability of better data at a later point in time. Slow Food is open to journalists and academics alike, and is happy to acknowledge when such a case exists and to publicize the fact, and to acknowledge when it might make a difference to its often very nuanced positions. In fact, at the time of writing, Slow food International was in discussion with members in France and Poland regarding data and views on the use of gavage (force-feeding) in the production of foie gras, which is a very traditional dish in these parts of Europe (and arguably part of the cultural patrimony of France particularly), but one on which Slow Food had initially taken a very negative view.

Visibly accountable for its actions

While Slow Food is clear in its literature, websites and press releases about who they are and what they do, and while not afraid to put its name to its actions and initiatives, if anything Slow Food does not celebrate its account-ability. It is influential in informing and helping to steer decision making in local, governmental and intergovernmental authorities. But this is not trumpeted. As Elisa Demichelis ruefully observed in her interview with me: 'We should improve visibility of our success. Not in a self-congratulatory way, but we should collect and disseminate, communicate to the outside world more and better, particularly to influential people.'[36] The reason, as Shane Holland emphasized, is that 'we are part of a movement, a collective, but we do have our own unique voice. But we rarely say "we are uniquely responsible for that".'[37]

What next? Slow Food in the 2020s

Let's finish with a view to the future.

According to the contributors to this chapter, the future of Slow Food is likely to focus on:

- maintaining the guiding principles of access for all to good, clean and fair food;

- a continued insistence on taste and gastronomic quality;
- the continuation of the existing projects of Ark of Taste and the Presidia; but above all...
- a continued and increasing focus on the work of Terra Madre.

In other words, we may expect to see a more politically active movement, with Terra Madre as the basis of a powerful 'lobby' of producers and consumers. The coming years may see a new balancing between scientific protection, which is easier to campaign internationally, and the cultural and emotional attachment to food as human capital, which may be harder... but also deeply rewarding. We are what we eat, and how we eat.

This future will be played out less in Italy, or indeed Europe, but increasingly in Africa, Latin America and Asia. It will be reflected in the leadership of the movement after Petrini (the next president is likely to be African or American), the types of issues, especially in social justice, which the movement will embrace, and in the variety and types of intergovernmental organizations (IGOs) and NGOs that Slow Food will increasingly engage with. There will be also be 'rejuvenation', a focus on issues that affect young farmers and consumers.

Whether the wider 'Slow' movement, encompassing urban living and the 'umbilical' reconnection of consumers with the land, will become a powerful international force remains to be seen.

Medinge will certainly be playing close attention.

Reflective questions

- How can Slow Food remain practical in the 2020s and beyond (and not become utopian)?
- Draw a circular value chain for food brands and position Slow Food in it.
- How would you bring the principles of Slow Food alive in your own local community?

Notes

1 For an expansive, highly entertaining and insightful history of the movement, the reader is invited to read Carlo Petrini and Gigi Padovani (2005) *Slow Food Revolution: A new culture for eating and living*, Rizzoli, New York

2 Petrini, G (2001) *Slow Food: The case for taste*, Columbia University Press, New York

3 www.slowfood.com

4 www.slowfood.org.uk

5 www.slowfoodyouthnetwork.org

6 Petrini, G (2005) *Slow Food Nation: Why our food should be good, clean and fair*, Rizzoli, New York

7 Ibid

8 Petrini (2001) *Slow Food: The case for taste*

9 Petrini (2005) *Slow Food Nation: Why our food should be good, clean and fair*

10 Gastronomy is defined by Petrini as 'a science that studies food, or rather the culture of food in every sense'

11 Petrini (2005) *Slow Food Nation: Why our food should be good, clean and fair*

12 Petrini (2005) *Slow Food Nation: Why our food should be good, clean and fair*

13 Speech at the Suor Orsola Benincasa Institute, Naples, July 2003

14 Petrini (2005) *Slow Food Nation: Why our food should be good, clean and fair*

15 Petrini (2005) *Slow Food Nation: Why our food should be good, clean and fair*

16 Speech at the Suor Orsola Benincasa Institute, Naples, July 2003

17 Petrini (2005) *Slow Food Nation: Why our food should be good, clean and fair*

18 Interview with Shane Holland, 19 June 2015

19 Speech at the fifth national congress of Slow Food, Riva del Garda, June 2002

20 Petrini (2005) *Slow Food Nation: Why our food should be good, clean and fair*

21 Interview with Elisa Demichelis, July 2015

22 www.slowfoodyouthnetwork.org

23 http://www.slowfoodyouthnetwork.org/blog/carlo-petrini-about-sfyn/#.VdT8sPlViko

24 Interview with Joris Lohman, August 2015

25 Interview with Shane Holland, June 2015

26 Interview with Shane Holland, June 2015

27 Interview with Shane Holland, June 2015

28 Interview with Elisa Demichelis, July 2015

29 Interview with Shane Holland, June 2015

30 Interview with Barbara Santoro, July 2015

31 Interview with Joris Lohman, August 2015

32 See http://www.independent.co.uk/life-style/food-and-drink/features/carlo-petrini-the-slow-food-gourmet-who-started-a-revolution-1837223.html and http://www.theguardian.com/environment/2009/feb/04/slow-food-carlo-petrini [accessed 2 December 2015] as examples, and Petrini (2001) *Slow Food: The case for taste*

33 Interview with Shane Holland, June 2015

34 Interview with Shane Holland, June 2015

35 Interview with Elisa Demichelis, July 2015

36 Interview with Elisa Demichelis, July 2015

37 Interview with Shane Holland, June 2015

Vegetalia: nourishing life

GUISEPPE CAVALLO

Like some of the best value-based companies, Vegetalia was created in response to a personal challenge faced by its founder. In the early 1980s Salvador Sala was doing well. His gambling business, after a start-up phase, was finally successful and growing at a steady pace. But he felt something was wrong. His life was not in balance and he needed to make changes. He felt that he needed to find peace and a sense of purpose. Salvador understood that the nature of the business he was running had to do with his discomfort. This convinced him to sell his shares to his partners, who learned of his decision with wonder. 'How can you sell your stocks right now that our business is at its peak performance?' asked a colleague.

In his quest for peace and a balanced life, Salvador embarked on a personal journey that took him around the world. He met sages and experts who helped him on a path to greater stability and spiritual growth. Along the way, he learned that a healthy lifestyle can change your life. He adopted a vegetarian diet and experienced great benefits from it. If it was so good for him, he thought, perhaps he could persuade others to adopt a healthier lifestyle. It was 1986. Salvador started a company producing tofu and personally distributed it using a little red Renault van. This is the story of the birth of Vegetalia, a company that produces and distributes organic vegetarian food in Spain.

After almost 30 years, Vegetalia has developed into a solid and sustainable business. The company played a pioneering role in introducing vegetal-protein-based products in Spain and has stayed loyal to its core offer. Tofu, seitan and tempeh are still at the centre of their product line, but are now supplemented by a large variety of vegetarian and vegan products. The headquarters, built in a peaceful valley around an ancient mansion, is run on eco-friendly principles. Minimizing waste and recycling are key guidelines of the house. In their 70 hectares of land, Vegetalia grow organic vegetables that feed the production line. At the heart of the company site is a little hill. Here, expert gardeners plant aromatic and medicinal herbs. Some of them are grown as part of the company's research programme, others are there for their value to the local ecosystem and culture. The place is called 'The Hill of the Senses' and the employees have adopted it as the sacred heart of the company – an identity totem.

Vegetalia is not the only organic food brand to have grown in the Spanish market. A visitor to Biocultura, a fair dedicated to sustainable products and services in Spain, would find a number of well-established organic food brands. But the seasoned marketer understands immediately that most have a problem. Their identity is built around the mere fact that their products are organic. There is very little differentiation and most brands fail to connect with their public on the basis of their values. It is a lost opportunity, because many of the entrepreneurs and top managers in this market have a deep connection with their values and are inspired by visions of love and their contribution to the society.

The Vegetalia management understood this in 2012 and decided to embark on a journey that would empower them to share the value-based essence of their brand with the public. After one year of intense work, Vegetalia had developed a new brand strategy, connecting their values with the deep needs of their public. The brand was now able to speak at a functional level, addressing the need for organic, high-quality, tasty food – as well as at a higher level, where the vision of a better world, a connection with nature and the commitment to a healthy lifestyle is shared with the public. A new brand tagline summarized the new times for Vegetalia. *Alimenta la Vida* (Nurturing Life) represented both a commitment of the company and an exhortation to the public to flourish with the vibrant energy that a healthy lifestyle offers.

With clear views about its identity, a focused marketing strategy and a rampant organic food market, Vegetalia is now growing at an abundant double-digit rate. But a new challenge is forming.

Some of the brands in the organic food market did not do their homework and their management had to decide between chasing the leaders in a rush for identity or selling to wealthier and more financially powerful players. Capital funds and other professional investors are buying majority stakes in some of the historical brands and are still shopping. A phase of consolidation is to be expected in the organic food market and hard choices have to be made in the boardrooms of many of the companies. Confidently established on its brand path, Vegetalia is already responding to the new challenges.

The answers from the company's management seem simple at first glance, but they come after much consideration and the decision to stick to the mission and values of the brand. A steady vertical integration, to reinforce the control of the value chain at all levels and a stronger affirmation of the vegetarian and organic nature of the offer, will help Vegetalia. On a subtler level, the brand is reinforcing its commitment to its vision and to sharing it with the public. 'Not only do we offer high-quality healthy choices to our clients,' says Enric Barbany, the managing director of Vegetalia, 'our main role is to inspire them with the vision of a life in harmony with nature.' Enric's eyes brighten when he says these words: it is clear that the key to the brand's success is a true, deep and authentic commitment to delivering a higher vision.

Back to the future: sustainability at DNV GL

07

NICHOLAS IND ON DNV GL

○ *What you say and do makes sense when backed up by sustainable thinking.*

○ *An engaging vision and valueds help unify employee behaviour.*

○ *Success helps influence how others think about sustainability.*

In 2014, DNV GL celebrated its 150th anniversary with a series of events around the world, attended by some 16,000 employees, customers and guests. I was one of them. On a floating pontoon by the head office in Høvik, Norway, 2,000 of those people had dinner, listened to speeches and danced to Norwegian hip hop. My impression was of an organization with committed and engaged employees and a culture with a love of systems and a pride in a clear and distinctive vision rooted in the idea of sustainability.

Unless you work in the maritime sector, energy or oil and gas, DNV GL is not a name you are likely to be familiar with. Det Norske Veritas (DNV) is a foundation that was established in 1864 by Norwegian insurance companies as a certification and classification organization with the purpose of safeguarding life, property and the environment; Germanischer Lloyd (GL) was founded in 1867 in Hamburg by a group of 600 shipowners, shipbuilders and insurers. The two organizations merged in 2013 to form the world's largest entity of its kind with a turnover of 21,623 million kroner. So even though DNV GL is new – and its two component parts have had distinctive cultural attributes – research shows that a remarkable degree of oneness has been achieved in a short space of time. This unity has come about because DNV GL has worked hard at bringing the two cultures together, but also because there is a strong historical basis to the purpose of these organizations – a sense that their role is to benefit society and a broad range of stakeholders.

Sustainability as a perspective

Sustainability has become a widely used (and ill-defined) term, yet the underlying thought is hardly new. In the 1860s, when Det Norske Veritas and Germanischer Lloyd were established, purpose-driven organizations existed to generate value for all. This is not to ignore the 'dark satanic mills' and the poverty that so energized Friedrich Engels and Charles Dickens, but to argue that business, then and now, has to do more than generate returns to shareholders. As Svensson and Wood note, business is 'allowed to exist because in capitalist societies it is deemed to have a central and pivotal role in the betterment of society'.[1] The implication of this thought is that a business should reject a narrow and short-term approach in favour of what Freeman calls a stakeholder view, which he says is an ethical perspective that recognizes the need to meet the different but linked needs of a diverse set of stakeholders.[2] The rationale for this line of thought is that the business organization and its various stakeholder groups are not independent of each other. Rather the impact of employee perceptions affects the delivery of service standards to external audiences, while external reputation impacts back on the sense of self of employees. This idea of linkage suggests that organizations should not promote one stakeholder group over another, but rather meet the mutual interests of all stakeholders.

Sustainability also implies a longer-term view and the connectivity of current and future generations. This obligation to posterity was something that the economist (and one-time president of the National Conservation Council) Irving Fisher argued in 1912, was the essence of conservation. It was a theme that echoes in the Brundtland Report (1987), which defined sustainable development as 'development that meets the needs of the present without compromising the ability of future generations to meet their own needs'. Sustainability encourages people to think of both the present and the future; of individual needs and those of others; of the nature of business organizations and their purpose.

For DNV GL the sense of continuity with its historic purpose has encouraged sustainable thinking down through the generations, but as sustainability has become more widely discussed and debated, so in turn it has become core to the organization's thinking. Whereas before sustainability was considered as being concerned with the sensible management of risk, from 2006 it became the centrepiece of the corporate vision: 'global impact for a safe and sustainable future'. In this way, sustainability guides DNV GL and its decision making and forms the way it influences the attitude and behaviour of its customers.

Bringing sustainability to life

It is one thing to express a commitment to sustainability in a vision statement, but quite another to bring it to life. It means driving the idea through everyday decisions. DNV GL's approach here is to engage with diverse stakeholders, such as civil society, governments, researchers and academia, but to focus on two: employees and customers. Bjørn K Haugland, chief sustainability officer for the DNV GL group and evangelist for the idea that business play a significant role in delivering change, makes the point that sustainability is not something just for a small group of employees working on the strategic agenda, but something that everyone can engage with. 'You need to bring it (sustainability) to all your employees, you need to bring it into your core offering and you need to use it as a driver to develop and transform your core offering.' To realize this approach in turn requires a specific managerial attitude that is rooted in a questioning, participatory culture – one that is willing to engage in a dialogue with all its stakeholders. In practice, this means recognizing the diversity within an organization of 16,000 employees in more than 100 countries.

DNV GL encourages people to have their say both by nurturing a culture that encourages expressivity and in creating the mechanisms, including social media, roundtables and events that prompt discussion. Balanced alongside this freedom is structure – not surprising for a certification organization that lives by standards. Haugland says, 'the end result is a very uniform protocol, but the inspiration and development of new things – and the existing things we redevelop or improve, is very much informed by our local networks'.

What also gives unity to the organization is the commitment to the vision and the values. DNV GL's five values represent a statement of how individuals should behave in their relationships with each other and with external stakeholders:

- We build trust and confidence.

- We never compromise on quality or integrity.

- We are committed to teamwork and innovation.

- We care for our customers and each other.

- We embrace change and deliver results.

As we see with other *brands with a conscience*, it is impossible to mandate adherence to standards from the centre. There will always be situations and dilemmas, where individuals have to make their own choices. When the values guide those choices, the greater the likelihood that an organization will be conscientious. Of course the challenge here is that values are imprecise – they are subject to interpretation by individuals. So while values can steer, they can never determine specific behaviours. This looseness is particularly unsettling for a scientifically oriented organization with lots of engineers who work daily with precision. To try to overcome this, DNV GL focuses on both a top-down commitment and a bottom-up involvement. The former is concerned with communicating the values to employees, but also trying to stimulate thought and discussion about the meaning of the vision and the value words.

For example, in 2014 the organization launched an employee initiative based around Ernest Hemingway's shortest, short story: 'For sale: baby shoes, never worn'. The point of Hemingway's story (although his authorship of it is disputed) is that we can infer meaning from the slenderest of clues. Telling a story is as much what we leave out as what we put in – and in this compressed story, much is left out. Nonetheless, in the age of Twitter with its 140 characters and Vine with its six seconds of video airtime, people are used to compressing their thoughts. For DNV GL employees, the challenge was to emulate Hemingway and create a meaningful six-word story (or less) about what a sustainable future might be. The constraint of six words was powerful because it meant that would-be writers had to focus on the core of sustainability and be creative in firing the imagination of others. Overall 1,225 people provided contributions, including examples that expressed the connectivity to the future, those that evoked the beauty of the natural world and those that recognized the role that people can play. For example:

- A future proud of our contributions.

- Let our children reap our efforts.

- Blue skies, green leaves, clean seas.

- Saving nature with people.

By encouraging employees to engage with the vision and values, DNV GL enables people to live them in their day-to-day decisions. For example, the value that states 'We never compromise on quality or integrity' has the potential to empower employees to do the right thing when they come under pressure from customers to do the expedient thing. It explicitly directs employees to say 'no' if they encounter inappropriate behaviour or unacceptable working conditions.

Engaging customers

One of the core businesses of DNV GL is certification – ensuring that companies meet internationally defined standards of safety and performance such as ISO 9000, 9001, 14000 and 18000. Historically this was a checklist approach whereby companies would be evaluated to determine whether they complied with the standard. However, employing a sustainability perspective, DNV GL has moved towards focusing more on a dialogue with its customers not only to talk about standards but also to help future-proof an organization and assess its risks in terms of sustainability. Haugland says: 'We use every opening meeting and every certification we have with customers to engage in a dialogue about what sustainability means. We ask them, how do you see sustainability and how does it impact on your business?'

For DNV GL, sustainability is simply a better way to conduct business. It recognizes the importance of a long-term perspective, the interdependence of different stakeholders and the opportunity that it provides companies to improve performance. DNV GL's argument is that the identification of risk implies the creation of opportunities – a spur to seek out new ways of working. Trine Kopperud, assessment services manager in the Business Assurance division of DNV GL, notes that while many customers are receptive to discussions about sustainability, they do not always immediately appreciate the benefits: 'You have to listen to your customers, but you also have to challenge them because they cannot always see the reason to do something.' Inevitably, organizations are at different points in the development of their approach, but the prevalence of sustainability in governmental discussions, in the media and international organizations such as the United Nations (UN), means there is a widespread awareness of the importance of the issue and receptivity to the idea. For example, the airplane manufacturer Boeing is a certification customer of DNV GL. Haugland argues that while Boeing went into the certification process as something that they had to do, they came out of it with an appreciation that a sustainability perspective could also improve performance and make their processes more efficient. In particular with ISO 14001, which was used to environmentally certify Boeing's 787 airplane, one of the requirements was for Boeing employees to understand and integrate environmental practices into their day-to-day behaviour. While Boeing already had a clear commitment to environmentalism (with the 787 labelled as the world's most eco-friendly airplane), ensuring the engagement of employees has helped to ensure continued momentum towards sustainable thinking.

At illycaffè – the Italian coffee roasters – sustainable thinking is second nature. The company has spent two decades building direct relationships with coffee growers in Brazil, Central America, India and Africa and is committed to creating value for all its stakeholders, including paying growers above market prices in recognition of the product quality. Yet the company felt the need to validate its model and to see where the opportunities were for improvement. In 2011, DNV GL developed a bespoke supply chain certification standard to analyse the company's processes and strategies, and its relations with stakeholders. The process was designed to ensure congruence between stated goals and actions in terms of governance, personnel management, marketing, research and development, production and the management of the supply chain. Could illycaffè demonstrate a robust approach to environmental management, product safety and the human rights management of its suppliers? DNV GL's assessment validated that the company had incorporated sustainability into every aspect of its supply chain, from coffee sourcing to a perfect cup of espresso.

Given that DNV GL has 80,000 customers its influence on business practice is significant, not least because it has an independent status that prevents accusations of bias. It holds sway over others' attitudes and behaviour, because it is scientifically rigorous in its approach. Without this objectivity its influence would be diminished. To maintain this position and to realize the vision of having a 'global impact for a safe and sustainable future' the company is committed to ongoing research both in its own right and together with others. It spends 5 per cent of annual revenues on research and innovation – of which one-fifth is allocated to longer-term strategic research into future technologies and risk management trends. The important thing to note here is the 'global impact' aspect of the vision, because it speaks to the opportunity not only to develop ideas of direct relevance to DNV GL's operations but also to transfer the knowledge generated through research to partners and customers. It is this willingness to share that makes the global impact realizable.

Creating new narratives

While customers and employees are the core audiences for sustainability activity within DNV GL, there are also other stakeholders who are important for an organization that sees itself as having a broad social responsibility. This means being connected into the wider world of sustainability thinking and contributing to how sustainability is seen by governments, NGOs and international organizations. DNV GL has been a signatory to the United Nations Global Compact since 2003 and is committed to integrating into the core of its practices the principles linked to human rights, labour standards, environmental performance and anti-corruption. Also, together with the UN Global Compact Office and the Scandinavian think tank, Monday Morning, it researched and produced a Global Opportunity Report to identify the key risks (lack of fresh water, unsustainable urbanization, continued lock-in to fossil fuels, the rise in communicable diseases and extreme weather) and the opportunities in the transition to a safer and more sustainable future.[3]

Having a voice in these type of fora contributes to making an impact, but Haugland argues that even though DNV GL is a scientific company that likes to find solutions to difficult problems, the scale and diversity of the challenge connected to sustainability requires a more questioning approach. This connects to what has been previously described as an organic-based view that requires a different style of leadership 'that is more humble, open and participatory'.[4] The role of leaders in this approach is to initiate dialogue and to pose the right questions. It means that organizations should contribute their knowledge but they should also be open to learn from the practices of others. Here, managers have to think about how to build networks that involve and embrace their stakeholders.[5] One of the mechanisms used by DNV GL to facilitate this is the creation of roundtables that bring together activists, business people, scientists, thinkers and government to debate the dilemmas that make sustainability a challenge. For example, in June 2014, DNV GL hosted a two-day event with 25 participants from around the world, with the goal of exploring the pathways towards realizing the vision of a safe and sustainable future. Announcing the event, the then CEO Henrik O Madsen noted, 'sustainability is about letting creativity, ingenuity and entrepreneurship flourish'. The roundtable was a transformative process because it brought together participants from diverse viewpoints and enabled them to move beyond the possibilities dictated by precedent and to empathize with others – something that Richard Rorty regards as essential to an ethical perspective.[6] This bringing together of diverse minds is particularly vital when the nature of the debate around sustainability moves at speed, challenging many of the old ideas about what it means.

Within the framework of the need to preserve for future generations, the relative importance of different strands of thinking about managing consumption effectively, energy policy, management of waste, natural resources and biodiversity – and how to tackle the problems they imply – is continually shifting. As new initiatives and technologies change the possibilities, so organizations need to think different. For 2014, the roundtable focused on how to deliver the large-scale change needed to deliver the emergence of a new regenerative economy – a theme developed by one of the participants, John Fullerton, a former JPMorgan managing director and the founder of Capital Institute, which argues for 'putting finance and the economy back in the service of life by mimicking living systems that sustain the natural world'.[7] What this means more specifically is achieving a balance between the needs of people and the needs of the environment such that the economy is designed to be circular rather than extractive and wasteful. It will require a movement away from fossil fuel consumption (in this context it is noteworthy that Japan has a vision of being a carbon-neutral hydrogen society by 2040) and a restoration of the carbon sinks such as forests and grasslands.

For DNV GL the roundtables represent a journey to move beyond current thinking and develop new narratives. Fullerton couches this in terms of a new story: 'Until we have a new, enticing and hopeful story of how the human economy can and must work, I fear all the discussions about sustainability-related policy will continue to be bogged down in debates over free market versus regulation, left versus right and so forth.' Haugland echoes this belief: 'It is so important to stimulate our narratives, because a lot of our priorities are based on old narratives, and now we see that these old narratives are being challenged. New narratives are coming up, and we need to understand those new narratives as quickly as possible in order to allocate our resources, our research and our priorities towards those narratives.'

The role of business: influences

When it comes down to it, the core debate is whether business is a force for good or bad. As Dax Lovegrove of WWF once observed: 'Corporate brands are hugely influential on society and can either be part of the problem in fuelling excessive and high-impact consumption or part of the solution in driving consumers towards sustainable living.'[8] In reality, corporates are both good and bad. Most of the examples we have looked at in this book – while overwhelmingly positive in their intentions – stimulate consumption in one way or another. The point here is to recognize the dangers of 'high-impact consumption' and to design from a sustainability perspective at the outset. Haugland notes that leaders such as Paul Polman of Unilever and Richard Branson of Virgin have moved to make sustainability core to their businesses. Indeed, Polman and Branson now articulate their position as environmental non-governmental organizations (NGOs) would have done a decade ago – something that indicates how far some businesses have moved, but also something that raises a question mark as to the changing role of NGOs.

Adopting a leadership position, based on the requirement to meet the needs of all stakeholders, creates the opportunity to have considerable influence over others. For example, the sportswear business Patagonia whose purpose statement is 'to use business to inspire and implement solutions to the environmental crisis' has long argued that its impact derives not only from the relationships it builds with its evangelistic employees and customers, but more so from its position as a role model.[9] Through lobbying, initiatives and partnerships, Patagonia challenges the corporate world to do things differently; to act more responsibly. Similarly, DNV GL is inspired by the actions of others, whether it be the UN and its commitment to responsible action, companies such as Tesla that have built businesses with new technology or WWF, which it sees as a critical voice that challenges the way it works. And just as DNV GL is inspired, so it inspires. It too is able to use its independent, scientific position to persuade governments and businesses to do things in new ways, not as acts of altruism but rather based on two fundamental premises. First, businesses are integral parts of society with a responsibility to employ with integrity, deliver services and products that meet needs and expectations and nurture the development of local communities.[10] Leaders have to ensure that companies, 'live in harmony with society rather than clash with it'.[11] Second, adopting a sustainability perspective is good business. It can improve processes, reduce risk and generate efficiencies – these are the arguments that DNV GL uses directly to persuade its 80,000 customers to change and to influence other organizations by its sharing of knowledge with other stakeholders.

DNV GL's slogan is *Smarter, Safer, Greener*. These are good words, but the question is whether the organization really lives up to them. The key issue here is to translate words into actions. DNV GL has an advantage in this respect, connected to its status. It is owned 63.5 per cent by a foundation and 36.5 per cent by the previous owners of Germanischer Lloyd. Therefore it is not accountable to a broader shareholder base who might question the core responsibility it has defined of serving the needs of society. This societal orientation that comes from the roots of the two bodies that make up DNV GL empowers the organization to do the right thing – whether it is engaging employees to act with integrity or encouraging customers to integrate sustainability into their businesses. Therefore the support of its owners is an important element in enabling DNV GL to deliver on the promises it makes and to wield its influence over others. Notably, DNV GL was commissioned by the UN to provide an in-depth review of the impact of business and the UN Global Compact on sustainable development. The resulting report, 'Transforming Business, Changing the World', was presented by DNV GL to Ban Ki Moon at a meeting of the UN General Assembly in June 2015. The report welcomed the shift in understanding and commitment of senior business leaders and the move to position sustainability as a strategic issue, but it also made the point about the gap between intent and delivery.

DNV GL argues that business can have a profound impact on sustainability thinking if organizations are prepared to seize the opportunity and 'fully embed sustainability into their corporate DNA through strategy, management systems, day-to-day operations and by disclosing sustainability performance in a transparent manner'. This way of thinking will involve some fundamental re-thinks on issues such as accountability, taxation and equality – but as some business leaders are already demonstrating, this can help to re-establish the legitimacy of organizations and contribute to the well-being of people.

For Jon Woodhead, regional assessment services manager, DNV GL – Business Assurance, the challenge for business is about how we understand trends, critical risks and opportunities, and seize the initiative to make changes. 'For those willing to take the journey and that are able to navigate the map, the road to a sustainable and inclusive economy is paved with opportunities for sustainability business success. It is naive to think that the challenges we face today are marginal or only long term. They are not. Our response must be to trust in science and innovation, embrace change and show leadership to turn challenges into opportunities.'

Reflective questions

- If DNV GL were to be quoted on a stock exchange how might this impact on its approach?
- What would your six-word story be for a sustainable future?

- When organizations such as DNV GL, Unilever and Virgin adopt the perspective of NGOs, what does this mean for the way that WWF, Greenpeace and others work?

Notes

1 Svensson, G and Wood, G (2008) A model of business ethics, *Journal of Business Ethics*, **77**, p 305

2 Freeman, R E (1984) *Strategic Management: A stakeholder approach*, Pitman, Boston

3 DNV GL (2015) Global Opportunity Report, Høvik, Norway

4 Iglesias, O, Ind, N and Alfaro, M (2013) The organic view of the brand: a brand value co-creation model, *Journal of Brand Management*, **20** (8), pp 670-88

5 Gouillart, F J (2014) The race to implement co-creation of value with stakeholders: five approaches to competitive advantage, *Strategy & Leadership*, **42** (1), pp 2–8; Kornberger, M (2010) *Brand Society: How brands transform management and lifestyle*, Cambridge University Press, Cambridge

6 Rorty, R (2006) Is philosophy relevant to applied ethics?, *Business Ethics Quarterly*, **16** (3), pp. 369–80

7 DNV GL (2014) The Road Less Travelled: Pathways to transformation, Roundtable Outcome Document (Reflections by the Moderator, Jo Confino p 14) Høvik, Norway

8 Gowland, S (2010) The power of brands to create better futures, *Oxford Leadership Journal*, **1** (3), pp 1–6

9 Ind, N (2001) *Living the Brand: How to transform every member of your organization into a brand champion*, Kogan Page, London

10 Anholt, S and van Gelder, S (2003) Branding for good?, in *Beyond Branding: How the new values of transparency and integrity are changing the world of brands*, ed N Ind, pp 56–68, Kogan Page, London

11 Nonaka, I and Takeuchi, H (2011) The wise leader, *Harvard Business Review*, **89** (5), pp 58–67

Unilever and
the green bond

NICHOLAS IND

While there is a view that publicly quoted companies can struggle to meet the needs of shareholders and their wider social responsibilities, the Anglo-Dutch, fast-moving consumer goods (FMCG) company Unilever believes that both are essential for a business. When the company's CEO Paul Polman announced Unilever's sustainable living plan – its long-term strategy – in 2010, he set a target of doubling its sales while halving environmental impact by 2020. He also set out goals for improving the health of 1 billion people around the world and the livelihoods of 800,000 farmers who provide the raw ingredients for Unilever products. Polman has a clear view of the role of the company: 'If a business wants to be around for a long time, the best guarantee is to serve society. These notions have been lost in recent years, but we want to bring them back – for the greater good.'[1]

Unilever's plan is ambitious – and, for some investors who do not see the point of long-term thinking and sustainability, questionable. Polman's riposte to those who disagree is simple, 'don't put your money in our company'. As testament to those who do see the point and as a signal to the financial community of the central role of sustainability in the company, in 2014 Unilever issued a £250 million green bond – the first company to do so in the British sterling market and the first to be issued by an FMCG company. Green bonds is a new concept that has grown rapidly. The first bond issued by a corporate entity was in 2013. In the first half of 2015 green bonds were issued to the value of US$18.3 billion. The idea behind green bonds is to build on the ideals set out in the UN Principles for Responsible Investment, to fund projects with an explicit environmental orientation.

Unilever's intention with its green bond was to improve the environmental performance of plants in South Africa, the United States, China and Turkey in terms of areas such as rainwater harvesting, water recycling, LED lighting, building certification and solar water heating. The goal was to reduce by 30 per cent the greenhouse gas emissions, water and waste in existing plants and to use less than half the current performance in new plants. To ensure that the funding was being used in the proper way, Unilever asked DNV GL to validate the process. To do this DNV GL reviewed greenhouse gas emission, water and waste projections and evaluated the quality of the systems and controls that prepare projections and that also record them. The projects will then be evaluated every year by DNV GL against the established criteria.

The real question is: has the sustainable living plan been successful? Against the measures it set for itself, so far it mostly has been – although in some sense the easy part has been done – driving out inefficiency and waste in its factories and delivery systems and engaging partners in its supply chain, but by its own figures Unilever reckons that 70 per cent of environmental impacts come when the consumer uses a product. Unilever can have some impact there through lowering washing temperatures, for example, but much of the change will need to be driven by consumers behaving differently – a big ask.

Note

1 Pearce, F (2013) Unilever plans to double its turnover while halving its environmental impact, *Daily Telegraph*, 23 July

Conversations carved in stone

08

CRISTIÁN SARACCO ON COSENTINO

○ *Real success is achieved with others.*
○ *Through behaviour and demonstration a conscience becomes visible.*
○ *Products are for clients, while brands are for people.*

For the unfamiliar reader, Cosentino is a multinational Spanish company that manufactures and distributes surfaces in quartz, recycled stone, porcelain, granite and marble for use in architectural and design projects. Top-quality and state-of-the-art surfaces, they are used by well-known leading brands such as Silestone, Dekton, Eco and SenSa.

For those digging deeper, Cosentino is a role model. It is a family-owned and family-led company that has discovered a way to develop itself based on a conscientious approach and to achieve long-lasting business results. From Cosentino we can learn to be wise and authentic, to build meaning, to be open to hear and act accordingly, and to go beyond profits to support society and the environment.

Cosentino humanizes its business by listening and talking. The brand goes far beyond marketing by rounding out the brand's meaning – they leverage their brand awareness to build up others' businesses from the communities that they, as a company, support. In the words of the chairman, Francisco Martínez-Cosentino:

Be honourable, be good people, that is what will make us a great company.

The company ethos can be summarized in four big ideas, as Santiago Alfonso, Cosentino's marketing director, states:

● We have become a multinational corporation that at the same time continues to be a family business with visible and active owners, who are proud of what they do and act as an example for the entire organization. When the chairman, Francisco Martínez-Cosentino talks about consistency, perseverance, humility and honesty he does so based on his beliefs and he demonstrates them in all of his actions.

- We always talk with others, we always have something new to learn and we are open to that. In the end, this way we all win – the results always arrive.

- The exercise of co-creating together with our external stakeholders helps us to see the people who have certain expectations about our products and services and their quality; however, and perhaps more importantly, it helps us to be seen for our humanity and passion. What else could we ask for?

- The strength of our relationships with those who surround us comes from our conversations with them about things that interest us both, and about things we do that they recognize as valuable, both for them and for future generations.

This wisdom derives from lots of mistakes along the way, learning from failure, reflecting on what really matters and letting this speak through the follow-up actions. Cosentino's is a proud company, strongly rooted in the community, whether it is in their home town or elsewhere in the world. Since its creation, in both good times and bad, the company has done significant work focused on the well-being of individuals, both from a social, as well as an environmental standpoint.

Despite being a business to business (B2B) company, Cosentino's forward integration means that it holds conversations and acts with a scope that goes beyond that of its clients. The backbone of this close relationship with society is the organization's permanent alignment and commitment, through various initiatives, to the communities that surround it.

Over the years the company has formalized what was initially done intuitively:

Socially, Cosentino knows what to do and afterwards, perhaps, it will talk about it.

What makes me want to share this story is the commitment of Cosentino's people and its partners to live and share their social, institutional and environmental values. I have been privileged to have been able to experience this over the last 12 years, during which time I have seen the company grow, become more international and launch new products. At different times we have worked in tandem on various challenges, and the company has been virtuous since the very first day.

Cosentino's brand architecture

Corporate
Brand

Commercial Brands		Social Brands

SILESTONE
by COSENTINO

THE ORIGINAL QUARTZ

DEKTON
by COSENTINO

ULTRACOMPACT SURFACES

 Silestone Institute

SENSA
by COSENTINO

PROTECTED GRANITE

SOURCE: Cosentino

Marble extraction in Macael

Mining operations in the Sierra de Macael are on open-cast descending terraces.

Open-cast mining does not need tunnels, which means lower costs and greater efficiency. Pits can be tens of kilometres wide and thousands of metres deep, increasing in size until the minerals are exhausted or the cost of extraction becomes excessive.

Due to the characteristics of these quarries covering large areas, they can be cut away to discover marble. This cutting is performed by drilling and blasting, using large machines to take away this surface layer.

Currently, the degree of mechanization is high in quality and quantity, meaning that the Macael quarries are the most advanced in terms of the extraction and elaboration of ornamental rocks. However, this type of mining has a high environmental impact as a result of its waste production and the alteration of the natural surface layer. Nearby waterways can also be affected.

As we will see throughout this chapter, Cosentino carries out environmental actions to preserve and restore this environment.

'Stone people' with a great sense of compassion

In the beginning, the stones shook

The story of the Cosentino family and their relationship with the world of stone began with Eduardo Cosentino in the early 1940s, shortly after the end of the Spanish Civil War (1936–39). Eduardo, the father of the company's current owners, began quarrying and manufacturing basic products from the marble of Macael in south-eastern Spain.

His wife, Eduarda Justo, ran her own grocery. Together with her husband and sons they led a humble life in this small village in the middle of the mountains, located in one of the most depressed areas of Spain, living off the income produced by the shop and the small marble company.

In the early 1970s, Eduardo and Eduarda transferred the company to the second generation who ended up creating Mármoles Cosentino, S.A., an initiative of Francisco Martínez-Cosentino and his brother, Eduardo.

Eduardo went to Barcelona to distribute the marble and Francisco, who was the younger of the two, remained in Almeria to manage the company. Later, a third brother, José, joined the project.

Even then, the region of Almeria was still one of the most backward and inaccessible places in the country, having grown very little since the 1940s. Its sources of wealth creation were limited to the agricultural and mining sector, both creating low added value.

In the late 1970s, due to a large wave of immigration from the centre of Europe, Almeria's agriculture started to move towards production in greenhouses. Meanwhile, the extraction of marble flattened out due to the lack of technological resources. The brothers tried to make the business work, but the quarry yielded little. They would open up the hill and if they found the marble vein during the day then it would fall down at night, and vice versa; and so on, day after day. By the early 1980s, the quarry was finally sold.

It was a painful process but they learned from it. Even without the quarry they persisted in this line of business, and Francisco Cosentino began to build a reputation for himself in the region. But he soon made another error of judgement. He decided to create a marble derivative for home interiors known as '*Marmolstone*'. The product had the beauty of marble but, of course, it also had its flaws: it stained, it scratched and it lacked the proper durability. Not surprisingly, it tarnished his standing in the business community.

Far from giving up, the Cosentino brothers tried again, not just out of pride, but also because they recognized that many people already depended on the company's success, including their parents who were quite elderly.

Real success is achieved with others

This time, failure was not an option. Chairman Francisco Martínez-Cosentino said: 'I discovered, among other things, that to be successful you must surround yourself with people who are better than you and create a team who will stick it out with you until the bitter end. You also have to believe in what you are doing, no matter what, and be aware that your project has to change over time.'

This 'painful' growth process, both on a personal and business level, led Cosentino to promote and put more thought behind the conversations he was having with the company's various stakeholders. He realized that the company had to bring in good people and had to learn to listen actively and act accordingly.

Innovation as the cornerstone to success

Bringing in the experts paid off. In the 1980s, Cosentino's began expanding the geographic reach of its business within Europe.

And, shortly after, they diversified their offering – based on research and innovation. The company began the ambitious project to construct a revolutionary industrial plant, which in 1990 began to manufacture a surface composed of more than 90 per cent natural quartz, making it extraordinarily strong and durable. It was named '*Silestone*' – and is still an important pillar of Cosentino's success.

This was no easy task as an economic and financial crisis was taking hold, triggered by the rising price of oil, the Gulf War and the bursting of the Japanese property bubble. The effect in Spain was magnified as a result of the volume of public investment in the Universal Exhibition in Seville and the Olympic Games in Barcelona. The country then suffered a market contraction and went into a deep recession.

Faced with this situation, Cosentino did not lose their nerve and, possibly as a result of the committed relationships, they kept going.

And it paid off. Five years later, in 1995, *Silestone* was a success worldwide in the kitchen countertop industry. It evolved over time to become the leading brand in quartz countertops for residential kitchens and bathrooms. And, it was the first and only one with antibacterial protection, which in turn allowed Cosentino to reach institutions such as laboratories, hospitals, hotels and restaurants with its product.

Thanks to its ongoing research and development, other materials were subsequently created and became leaders in their respective sectors, such as ECO, Cosentino's recycled surface; SenSa, the company's granite line, which has an exclusive stain protection treatment; and the most recent, Dekton,

Cosentino – from the 1980s to today

1980

2014

SOURCE: Cosentino

an innovative ultra-compact surface that aims to revolutionize the global architectural and design world.

The company's firm commitment to creating high-value materials and solutions for the architectural and design world has always gone hand-in-hand with its dedication to promoting the company's international presence.

Today, the Cosentino Group and its products and brands are present in more than 80 countries. It has seven production factories and 15 that make kitchen and bathroom countertops, besides an intelligent logistics platform and two distribution hubs in the United States.

In addition, there are more than 90 Cosentino centres throughout the world. These are spaces that allow marble customers, and leading architects and designers, to obtain training and work with their end clients, together with Cosentino's teams of experts. In general, it is also a place to meet and hold conversations about hygiene and health, gastronomy, sustainability and/or architectural trends. It is here that the future success of Cosentino is formed and safeguarded. Here, Cosentino shows its sensitivity through active listening and their proximity – they maintain an inclusive and constant dialogue between the organization, clients, opinion leaders and end consumers. This enables the company to create beautifully, aesthetically pleasing products whilst at the same time responding to social and environmental demands.

As a result of those effective conversations, the products and their evolution respond to people's needs with regard to:

● Their use – as is the case with the one-piece sink.

● Health and hygiene – as is the case with Silestone's silver-based antibacterial protection.

Cosentino Centre, Israel

SOURCE: Cosentino

- Aesthetics in terms of shapes and colours – as is the case with Silestone, which is available in more than 60 colours.

- Respect for the environment in its production process, logistics (to the extent possible) and the product itself. For example, Cosentino's ECO line is composed of more than 75 per cent recycled material.

Social and environmental issues with the weight of stone

Throughout its history, Cosentino has recognized that both its international expansion, as well as its research and development programme, have been able to move forward thanks to a balance between economics, environment and society.

Again, conversations are key. The company seeks to understand the perspectives of stakeholders and to build a better future together for everyone related to the company. The company's relationships are a result of sharing its values. Products are for customers, and the company is for people – both based on a strong belief system within Cosentino.

Through their actions, the company and the people who comprise it demonstrate the values together and on a consistent basis, and this strengthens their long-term commitments. The values that Cosentino lives by and that are understood by all of its stakeholders are:

- *Accessibility*: interacting with people whatever their role or relationship to the company.

- *Entrepreneurship*: focusing on constant improvement and innovation in order to continue to grow.

- *Sensitivity*: promoting dialogue between collaborators, customers, suppliers and markets.

- *Flexibility*: adapting to the particularities of each region where Cosentino is present.

- *Modesty*: accepting that all of the company's actions should be guided by a sense of humility.

Interestingly enough, innovation and commitment are not made explicit in these values – but they are and have been very present in Cosentino's actions and its relationships. For Cosentino, naming these two values would be to state the obvious. They are values that are expected of such a company.

Cosentino's history

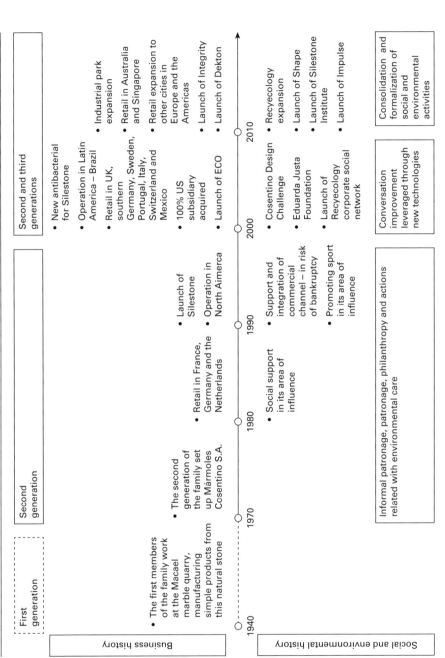

SOURCE: Cosentino

Although Cosentino believes that innovation is a prerequisite as a leader, it is unnecessary to explicitly state this. As is the same with commitment, which is a leader's duty – and stating it simply reduces credibility. It should be evident through actions rather than words.

Cosentino is built upon the efforts of people who are passionate about what they do, who dare to be part of the future, who are capable of reinventing themselves each and every day. The company demonstrates its compassion through its accessible and attentive nature, its ability to listen and by maintaining the spirit of the family business – because it considers itself one big family.

It is from this that the company's awareness arises and, as a result, we can talk about a brand, which as part of its strategic platform is also a *brand with a conscience*. A conscience demonstrates quality in the just and difficult balance between business, people and the environment. 'We have been on the edge of bankruptcy three times and that is what has made us strong,' says Pilar Cosentino, deputy general manager, part of the third generation.

Conversations with people etched in stone

Cosentino is committed to people. The company is clearly focused on creating value in society, particularly for those who live in the proximity of the company's facilities, whether they are industrial, logistical or commercial facilities.

> 'I remember that, in our period of growth, our distributor in the Basque Country was going to close their business due to retirement. We absorbed the company together with their employees and one of them is now the manager of operations there.
>
> 'Whatever the reason was, as far as we could, we always kept those companies running that made up our value chain.'
>
> Santiago Alfonso, marketing director

From an economic standpoint, when one of the players in the system needs help, Cosentino comes to the rescue. It may be a distributor or a marble worker who has a problem and it will be resolved by considering the business they have with them, whatever the length and depth of the relationship. For example, what are now distribution centres – Cosentino Centres – at one moment in time were independent companies on the verge of disappearing. Recognizing them as part of their network, Cosentino helped them to survive.

It could be argued that these actions could be classed as paternalistic. Yet rescuing such businesses ensures the success of the Cosentino distribution system. Being accessible to the customer, and their customers, helps them to perform better and grow. Based on an altruistic approach: if Cosentino's customers are successful, Cosentino will also be successful. It is a self-evident truth and, although it is often forgotten, it is sustained by relationships between people. By focusing on these facts, and paying attention to looking after people, the company brings its values of sensitivity and modesty into play.

In relation to protecting the environment, the aim is to preserve people's health. It is about manufacturing in an ecological manner, as well as manufacturing sustainable products and promoting dialogue between people about subjects related to architecture, gastronomy, design and fashion.

With regard to strictly social matters, the company focuses on safety and hygiene, issues related to its business and that are critical for people, and developing society through education, culture and sport.

Two-way communication

Cosentino maintains conversations with its various stakeholders on matters of mutual interest and based on what the company does with them. Internally, conversations flow between employees, management and owners.

It is worth noting that some employees are part owners; however, due to family protocols, they occupy positions in accordance with their knowledge and experience. It is common to see family members of the third generation responding to and accepting the authority of direct managers who are not related to the family.

Externally, in different ways and with different emphasis, the company converses with customers, marble workers, industry leaders, kitchen and bathroom architects and studios, consumers, families and companies, suppliers and strategic partners, opinion leaders, architects, world-renowned chefs and society in general.

It applies its know-how as a socially responsible business to three areas that complement one another:

- The Silestone Institute, which is dedicated to researching and promoting healthy lifestyles through hygiene in spaces where the company's products are usually found.

- The Eduarda Justo Foundation, which collaborates in the economic, social, educational and cultural development of Almeria, the Spanish province where the company was founded and where its headquarters are located today.

- At its core Cosentino, as a corporation, champions a certain number of social and environmental activities, generally those with the greatest implications and that are least promoted.

Silestone Institute

The Silestone Institute is an international platform dedicated to researching and creating awareness about hygiene in the kitchen and bathroom, both in public and private spaces, the objective of which is to promote a healthy lifestyle.

Its areas of activity are mainly the kitchen, both residential and professional, and in others related to the food industry and hospital sector. Its activities are focused on supporting and promoting research on antibacterial technology, and analysing and disseminating current health and hygiene laws.

Through its institute, the company aims to provide a broader view of the concept of hygiene by focusing on food safety, as well as other matters such as selecting materials and furniture, the distribution of space, habits, relationships and technologies.

Eduarda Justo Foundation

The foundation was created with the goal of promoting the social environment surrounding the Cosentino Group and, more specifically, to collaborate in the economic, social, educational and cultural development of Almeria, Spain, with a particular focus on people with limited economic resources.

It aims to identify local youth who have the potential to become future leaders. To do so, it has agreements with MIT, Harvard, Stanford, Colombia and Singularity University, among others.

Cosentino at a corporate level

In the social sphere

The company's activities in the social sphere are based on Cosentino's values. As a multinational company it assumes, voluntarily and truly, the responsibility of providing ongoing support to society through education

Cosentino's relationship with each stakeholder

COSENTINO®

Audiences		Economic	Social	Environment
Internal		• Compensation system • Corporate university	• Sports • Cultural	• Sustainability and management of natural resources, energy and waste
External	Clients	• Business support • Design support • Learning programmes	• Culinary art • Contemporary art • Research and awareness raising of hygiene in kitchens and bathrooms • Social network	• Resources utilization • Eco-architecture
	Prescribers	• Design support • Learning programmes		
	Consumers, strategic partners	• Design support		
	Young people	• Employment	• Leadership programmes • R&D programmes	
	People with different needs		• Professional and craft training • Improvement in life quality	
	Society		• Culinary art • Contemporary art • Sports • Social network	• Landscape restoration

and training in various areas, equality policies, initiatives for the benefit of the community and sponsorship of a wide array of cultural, educational and sporting activities.

All of these initiatives are in line with the goal of becoming more respectful of society every day – to be a socially responsible business. The company has established collaboration with youth through education, with a focus on research and development and innovation (R&D+I), collaborating with people with different capacities through training and providing employment opportunities through culture, gastronomy and sport.

Environment matters

In its activities related to protecting the environment, Cosentino works in the areas of processes, products and people:

- Production processes: in a single operation, preventing environmental damages and using resources efficiently.
- Support processes: by employee example, training and practice, responsible use internally of material and energy resources.
- Products: through research and minimizing and/or preventing potential damage to the environment and people.
- People in general: by promoting new attitudes and behaviours, making rational use of its own resources.

All initiatives carried out in relation to sustainability demonstrate the company's ongoing commitment to achieving economic, social and environmental well-being in the areas where the company operates and is present:

- To treat 98 per cent of the emissions generated in its central facilities.
- To recover nearly 97 per cent of the water used in production processes.
- To use specific gadgets to optimize and minimize operating costs, such as systems based on infrared thermography or electric vehicles for transportation inside the industrial park.
- To apply the well-known three Rs strategy: reducing the amount of waste generated at work stations; reusing the waste it can by lengthening the useful life of products and packaging or buying products in returnable packages; and recycling in the various stages of the production process:
  - Raw materials are extracted from the quarries efficiently, enabling the company to use up to 95 per cent of the material extracted.

  – Waste from stone leftover from the production process that cannot be reused to make other products is processed to make aggregate, such that nearly 100 per cent of this waste is recycled for other uses.

● Quarry and tip restoration projects are being carried out in order to recover the landscape and environment.

The path to building the triple bottom line

Cosentino's purpose – to improve the quality of life for people in its value chain and nearby – has created a platform upon which to build a business that people can easily support.

Economically, Cosentino shows us that results can be obtained while maintaining values, respecting rights and being energy efficient. Similarly, it shows us that respect for the environment is the result of properly managing natural resources, seeking sustainability in order to improve people's lives and acting both at the local and global level.

With regard to its social profile, it seeks to improve people's standard of living through education, creating opportunities and responding to the specific needs of their community.

Last and not least, Cosentino has established an international verification process for its mining operations in order to ensure there is no child/slave labour, which continues to be a common practice in the industry in certain developing countries. For Cosentino this demonstrates on a daily basis, with facts, that the company's work is governed by humility.

Online conversations that flow like pebbles

At Cosentino the work is co-produced and co-created together with various external stakeholders. As a result the organization responds to a volatile world through observation, anticipation and execution. This is the new paradigm that enables a flow compared to the static image of the traditional business cycle based on control, planning and management.

Virtual stones

At the end of 2007 Cosentino's marketing department began to take interest in and place importance on new technologies. Fundamentally, the department knew that it was a new situation and that they should learn how to interact through practice: 'It seems to me that we are approaching a point in history where there will be no difference between the offline and online world and, if it is done properly, it should enrich the dialogues we have with our various stakeholders. We should learn to take advantage of it; I think an infinite number of possibilities open up for us,' said Santiago Alfonso, Cosentino's marketing director.

So, in early 2008 the marketing department already had its own corporate social network. It was called Recyecology and it was aimed at establishing a more fluid relationship with environmentally conscious people. Sustainable architecture, ecological gastronomy, sustainable innovation and so on were discussed. Offline events were organized that were streamed on the network – and it even had sections such as a Wiki.

However, people were aware that Cosentino was behind the social network. From the start, the network was not commercial but was rather to share ideas about people's hopes and aspirations for their future – albeit linked to the company's business and social activity.

In 2011 it had reached 30,000 visits from nearly 2,000 cities in more than 100 countries around the world, with high levels of participation. The time spent on the network was twice as long as the average time spent on comparable sites. It is also worth pointing out that more than 60 per cent of new visits originated due to references from other websites, without any type of advertising effort being made.

Almost simultaneously with the corporate social network, Cosentino began a new initiative, this time maintaining a clear balance between the offline and online world, which in some way complemented Recyecology. This project was known as 'Shape' and its goal was to encourage debate and reflection on architecture, food and healthy habits – issues that are ongoing concerns of the company with the general public.

Today, Cosentino continues its conversations through various websites and generalist social networks such as Facebook and Twitter, and it also has an online television channel on YouTube. Although these sites, because of their particular features, also lead to the communication of commercial matters, their continued social nature and interest remain evident, showing and demonstrating its flexibility, sensitivity and accessibility – values that the company puts into practice in its day-to-day operations. It translates into a constant invitation to participate and converse, where Cosentino speaks, but above all, actively listens.

Co-creation without stumbling on stones along the way

In 2011, after serious reflection and verifying what was going on, Cosentino decided that it should reposition its corporate brand.

The efforts it had made up until that point had produced great business results through the Silestone commercial brand; however, the company's other activities continued to go unnoticed. New product launches had to explain that the new products were made by Cosentino – the manufacturers of Silestone – and it diminished the capillary effect of the presence of the Cosentino centres in the world, which at the time exceeded 50.

Cosentino needed to redirect its actions, strengthen its dialogues with various stakeholders beyond its customers and the geographic areas where it traditionally had a presence, and back international growth and new product launches as a corporation.

This project was handled (of course) in a co-creative manner with the support of all of its key stakeholders, from the owners to senior management, to the employees in general, to channels, the customers, to opinion leaders and the consumers of its products. Over five months, more than 2,800 people from 25 different countries voluntarily participated, dedicating thousands of hours to searching for and creating an idea that could represent Cosentino.

In addition to the type of analysis carried out in a repositioning project for a corporate brand, it also carried out more than 20 workshops in Spain and the United States, with distributors from Europe and Latin America, more than 40 in-depth interviews, teleconferences with employees of various levels and from five continents; plus an online social platform that proposed and discussed various concepts.

In several areas the results were more than encouraging:

- First, all stakeholders recognized the social work that Cosentino has been carrying out coherently and consistently for more than 35 years. This is also the reason that the participation of external stakeholders was so enthusiastic and generous.

- Its early entry into the online world allowed it to swiftly open a channel of conversation about subjects of mutual interest with various stakeholders, who accepted it with pleasure and ease.

- In the end, they came to the conclusion that simplicity, familiarity and significance represents the implementation of Cosentino's shared vision.

- In 2013, Cosentino launched a new product, Dekton, without the traditional reference to the Silestone brand.

After the brand was repositioned, and considering it a strategic platform for the business, the owners decided to internally adapt the company's mission and vision, which now reflect and transmit the concepts behind 'imagine and anticipate'. And that is exactly the way in which Cosentino's marches into future adventures – by imaging and anticipating, together with all its stakeholders.

Reflective questions

- Are family-run brands more conscientious?
- Should companies become more transparent? Or is being authentic enough?
- Is your company prepared to empower others as a result of new technologies?

Building a caring organization

09

SUDHIR JOHN HORO IN COLLABORATION WITH
SHYAM VASUDEVAN ON TATA STEEL

○ *Corporate governance is only crucial when the system fails.*

○ *It is not about brands or business.*

○ *First give and then take back; that's the order for a caring organization.*

I was born in a small village (now a bustling town) almost 170 kilometres from Jamshedpur, the home to Tata Steel. Our village lacked a modern school, and so my aunt, who was employed as a teacher in one of the many schools run by Tata Steel for the children of its employees and citizens of Jamshedpur, took me in at the tender age of four. Soon, I was in Jamshedpur, a city very different from the rest of the cities in the erstwhile state of Bihar (now Jharkhand). The city was clean and very well maintained, with well-managed amenities – housing facilities with 24/7 electricity and water supply, well-paved roads, green boulevards with parks and ample greenery against the backdrop of an iconic steel factory.

I grew up studying in Loyola School, an institution run by the Jesuits. Thanks to my aunt, at home I was often exposed to the activities in schools run by Tata Steel. I fondly remember the days when my aunt used to bring home packets of hard-boiled sweets on every third day of March. Each of those sweet packets bore a print of Jamshedji Tata, the founder of Tata Steel, and as a young child the benign face left an indelible mark in my mind.

During my 12 years of growing up in Jamshedpur (1981–92), everything that the city offered to me seemed to be normal. It was only after I stepped out of Jamshedpur and moved to other parts of India that I realized that all the small things that Tata Steel took care of to run a town like Jamshedpur – water, electricity, roads, parks, cleanliness, health care and education (all these services usually in the domain of a government body), things that we took for granted in Jamshedpur – seemed to be less accessible to citizens across the country. Looking back now, Jamshedpur easily is one of the best-managed cities in India and the entire credit goes to Tata Steel.

After stepping out of Jamshedpur, and having lived in various parts of the country, I still fondly remember Jamshedpur in shaping who I am today. I had the good fortune of growing up in a city that recognized excellence – in academics as well as extra-curricular activities and sports – and fostered a great sense of secularity, community living and togetherness.

So, when Sandra Horlings suggested that I write on an Indian brand with a conscience, I immediately jumped at the prospect of writing on Tata Steel (though it is only a division of the Tata Group, a much larger corporate conglomerate), as I believe I am a beneficiary of the philosophy of sharing and caring at Tata Steel in Jamshedpur. This also gives me an opportunity to pay tribute to Tata Steel for having shaped my life.

Writing this story enabled me to look deeper into this remarkable institution and its contribution to society in an objective manner. Being a more visual person and with very little writing experience, I must also thank Shyam Vasudevan, my colleague at Ideaworks Design and Strategy Pvt Ltd for having ably assisted me in putting together this story.

An overview

'In a free enterprise, the community is not just another stakeholder in business, but in fact the very purpose of its existence.'

JAMSHETJI NUSSERWANJI, FOUNDER, TATA GROUP

'Winning' is not just a word in Tata's dictionary. It is a habit, one that has been rubbed into the veins of the enterprise. Its 36,200 employees in India form a massive profit machine. The whole idea of having a sustained engagement programme with the community is to shape future societies and rub the sense of achievement into each citizen around its plant and facilities. The past employees of Tata Steel created these societies. The present employees of Tata Steel live in these environs. The future employees of the enterprise are likely to come from there. Therefore it makes massive sense to deploy your resources in developing this whole ecosystem.

And that is what makes Tata unique in the world. A transformative purpose, consistent delivery and a set of guiding principles to support everyone actively involved in Tata.

The most important guiding principles

Clause 1: national interest

The Tata Group is committed to benefit the economic development of the countries in which it operates. No Tata company shall undertake any project or activity to the detriment of the wider interests of the communities in which it operates.

A Tata company's management practices and business conduct shall benefit the country, localities and communities in which it operates, to the extent possible and affordable, and shall be in accordance with the laws of the land.

A Tata company, in the course of its business activities, shall respect the culture, customs and traditions of each country and region in which it operates. It shall conform to trade procedures, including licensing, documentation and other necessary formalities, as applicable.

Clause 3: competition

A Tata company shall fully support the development and operation of competitive open markets and shall promote the liberalization of trade and investment in each country and market in which it operates. Specifically, no Tata company or employee shall engage in restrictive trade practices, abuse of market dominance or similar unfair trade activities.

A Tata company or employee shall market the company's products and services on their own merits and shall not make unfair and misleading statements about competitors' products and services. Any collection of competitive information shall be made only in the normal course of business and shall be obtained only through legally permitted sources and means.

Clause 4: equal opportunities employer

A Tata company shall provide equal opportunities to all its employees and all qualified applicants for employment without regard to their race, caste, religion, colour, ancestry, marital status, gender, sexual orientation, age, nationality, ethnic origin or disability.

Human resource policies shall promote diversity and equality in the workplace, as well as compliance with all local labour laws, while encouraging the adoption of international best practices.

Employees of a Tata company shall be treated with dignity and in accordance with the Tata policy of maintaining a work environment free of all forms of harassment, whether physical, verbal or psychological. Employee policies and practices shall be administered in a manner consistent with applicable laws and other provisions of this code, respect for the right to privacy and the right to be heard, and that in all matters equal opportunity is provided to those eligible and decisions are based on merit.

Clause 8: health, safety and environment

A Tata company shall strive to provide a safe, healthy, clean and ergonomic working environment for its people. It shall prevent the wasteful use of natural resources and be committed to improving the environment, particularly with regard to the emission of greenhouse gases, and shall endeavour to offset the effect of climate change in all spheres of its activities.

A Tata company, in the process of production and sale of its products and services, shall strive for economic, social and environmental sustainability.

Clause 9: quality of products and services

A Tata company shall be committed to supply goods and services of world-class quality standards, backed by after-sales services consistent with the requirements of its customers, while striving for their total satisfaction. The quality standards of the company's goods and services shall meet applicable national and international standards.

A Tata company shall display adequate health and safety labels, caveats and other necessary information on its product packaging.

Clause 14: use of the Tata brand

The use of the Tata name and trademark shall be governed by manuals, codes and agreements to be issued by Tata Sons. The use of the Tata brand is defined in and regulated by the Tata Brand Equity and Business Promotion agreement. No third party or joint venture shall use the Tata brand to further its interests without specific authorization.

Setting a winning mood

In August 2013, Purnima Mahato,[1] a 39-year-old accomplished archer and coach, went to meet the president of India to collect the coveted Dronacharya award.[2] She stepped on to the dais and greeted the head of state with great pride and a sense of achievement. At the function, she rubbed shoulders with some of the most accomplished sportspersons, members of parliament, ministers and other distinguished guests. She felt elated. Her life had hit the bull's eye.

That evening in New Delhi, as she accepted the memento from the president, she was the proudest woman in the world. Back in her home state of Jharkhand, she was ever more important. She was the first woman from the state to claim the prize – for excellence in mentoring sportspersons. It had also made her institution proud.

She had been practising and teaching her sport to students at the Tata Steel Sports Academy in Jamshedpur since 1994. At the institute, she trained herself and other archers such as Deepika Kumari, who won laurels for the country. But Purnima is not an accidental genius. The archer is the fifth coach from the Tata Steel stable to bag the coveted Dronacharya award. Earlier, Illyas Babar and K O Bosen (both athletes), Pullela Gopichand (badminton) and Sanjeeva Singh (archery) had received the honour.[3] These coaches trained aspiring Indian athletes to make a mark on the world stage. It also served as a great inspiration for the locals. Some young people, many of them of tribal origin and from villages across the state, thronged the gates of the JRD Sports Complex and toiled until late in the evening under the watchful eye of coaches like Purnima in order to win a medal in their sport of choice.

Her success had originated 110 years earlier. At the beginning of the 20th century, Jamsetji Tata, the founder of Tata Sons, travelled to Pittsburgh. He had heard the great Thomas Carlyle declare to the world 'the nation which gains control of iron soon acquires the control of gold'.[4] Inspired, he held meetings with some of the greatest steelmakers of the time and wanted to transplant the graft of the Industrial Revolution into India. Tata found promise in the geologist Charles Page Perin. He brought him home to India. In 1904 the search for a place rich in the raw materials for steel – iron ore, coal, limestone and water – began in great earnest in the forests of Madhya Pradesh, thick jungles of the British Raj where generals from its army and the erstwhile kings and princes of India went on hunting sprees shooting tigers, lions, cheetahs and deer. Visualize orgies of blood and violence that lasted several weeks. Their bungalows and palaces were filled with the trophies of their violence. Stuffed carcasses, horns, heads, claws and bones filled the walls and hallways. Men competed with each other to show off their pagan roots, taking great pride in opulent displays of their capability to kill and destroy.

In such a day and era Perin's party, a motley crowd of two dozen men, travelled through these thick and dangerous jungles testing soil, water, air and everything that looked promising to them. In Perin's age, chemistry was crude and geology was an adventure sport, let alone a science. Nature revealed its secrets to only the most curious eyes and keenest minds. There was no computer-aided analysis. The only bird's-eye view of the topography had to be glimpsed from atop the tallest tree. Perin and his team followed the forest floor like ants. After three years of intense scouting, in 1907 Perin settled on a site near the village of Sakchi on the Chota Nagpur Plateau, at the confluence of the rivers Subarnarekha and Kharkari. The village's only claim to fame was a temple dedicated to the Mother Goddess (and now the birthplace of a leading multinational company).

Jamsetji's son Dorabji Tata had added two more prospectors to his company by then – C M Weld and Shapurji Saklatvala, both businessmen and investors. The work on India's largest integrated steel plant began in 1908. The first ingot rolled out on 16 February, 1912.[5] India had produced steel on its own; Tata's hunt for gold had begun. Thomas Carlyle's vision of 'iron begetting gold' was realized time and again. The 2013 winner of the Dronacharya award, Purnima Mahato was only one such in the long line of gold medal winners. Thomas Carlyle, Jamsetji, Dorabji and Perin shared a smile yet again in their graves.

An alternative legal structure

Today, the Tata Charitable Trust holds majority shares of the group – a whopping 66 per cent of group equity of Tata Sons, the holding company. It is thus probably the world's only operating enterprise run by a dynamic charitable trust! The group owns and manages some of the world's most interesting brands such as Tetley Tea in the UK, and the Jaguar and Land Rover brands of automobiles. Make no mistake, although it is a trust it is an agile and nimble business operation led by trained and well-respected professionals. And, the same professionalism is reflected in the company's approach and attitude to corporate social responsibility (CSR).

Tata's US$100 billion-plus revenues, more than half coming in from 80 countries overseas, has over 450,000 employees in 100 operating companies with interests ranging from tea to telecom, software to hotels, wristwatches to missiles, and coffee to power and steel. It is the largest private-sector employer in India and the UK. The group aspires to rake in US$500 billion in revenues by 2025.

Building brand Tata

In 1912, Tata's engineers worked from the forest. A shantytown with a state-of–the-art steel plant had virtually no amenities for its people who chugged in the tonnes of iron ore, limestone and coal. So Dorabji set out to build a city around his steel plant. His father Jamsetji did not want a city that looked like workers' hutments as in the West. He had grand ambitions. Jamsetji wrote to his son 'be sure to lay wide streets planted with shady trees, every other of a quick-growing variety. Be sure that there is plenty of space for lawns and gardens; reserve large areas for football, hockey and parks; earmark areas for Hindu temples, Mohammedan mosques and Christian churches.'[6]

So Julin Kennedy Sahlin from Pittsburgh was hired to prepare the first layout of the city of Jamsehedpur.[7] The firm created a grand plan and the Tatas implemented it with great panache. The result – it is India's only city with a million-plus population that still has no municipal corporation. In 1980, the state wanted to take over the reins of the city, but was voted out by a public outcry. In 2005, a similar attempt met with the same fate. The people did not want to switch. They were happy with Tata managing the place. Jamshedpur Utilities and Services Company (JUSCO) was carved out of Tata Steel from its Town Services Division in 2004. JUSCO is today India's only comprehensive urban infrastructure service provider.

Jamshedpur was declared the seventh cleanest city of India for the year 2010, according to survey by the government of India.[8] It has been predicted as the 84th fastest-growing city in the world for the time frame 2006–20. A major part of the city is run by Tata Steel itself. Jamshedpur has been selected as one of the cities for the Global Compact Cities Pilot Programme by the United Nations, the only one to be selected in India as well as South Asia. For a little over a century now, the city has reflected the ethos of the Tatas.

Its tryst with sports continues. Jamshedpur is said to be the sports capital of Jharkhand, where Tata Steel's interest in promoting sports brings athletes and players from far and wide. The city's private clubs provide opportunities for sports and games such as golf, tennis, squash, billiards, horse riding and water scootering.

'We also make steel', said a campaign for Tata Steel in the 1990s.[9] This enterprise is at the heart of the group. Most of Tata's value systems originated here. The founders also got to build a city and the enterprise from the ground up.

Brands serve three essentials – or the three Cs: cash, clutter and consistency. The brand ensures that your cash register keeps ringing in the future too. A good brand ensures that the enterprise stands out from the clutter of competition and, at the same time ensures consistency of excellent experience to the stakeholders. Tata understood this very early. He ensured that the institution he built will excel in all three of these facets through 'service'. He made it the core of his enterprise.

Tata's vision

Jamshetji Tata founded the group in 1868. And it was his vision that is still the foundation of this world-leading giant. Jamshetji, often referred to as the father of Indian industry, had a global vision for Tata. By 1892, he had earned enough profit to fund young Indians to visit and study in foreign universities. He even supported Gandhi's anti-apartheid movement in South Africa. The Tatas are known for having introduced many pioneering labour welfare schemes such as maternity leave, accident compensation, etc. The British Parliament enacted them many decades later.

Tata Steel: proven mettle in philanthropy

Through the whole 20th century Tata Steel carried on in the established way of the founder. Tata Steel pioneered several labour welfare benefits long before they were enacted or ratified by law. These include an eight-hour working day, free medical aid, establishment of a welfare department, leave with pay, workers' provident fund scheme, workmen's accident compensation scheme, maternity benefits, profit-sharing bonus and retiring gratuity. Most of these introductions were enforced by law decades later, and incorporated as part of various Acts, such as the Factories Act and State Insurance Act.

And Tata is still leading the way. In July 2004, the current Tata Steel chairman made another bold declaration. His company would not work with suppliers and businesses that did not match their standards of 'giving'. Tata Steel was exhorting a whole ecosystem in the steel industry to stand up and take notice. Tata ran a corporate social responsibility (CSR) check on each supplier and the small ones can work with Tata on community initiatives. Suppliers now realize that it is important to have a good CSR programme running in order to do business with Tata.

Against the 2 per cent mandated by the government of India, Tata Steel spent 3.31 per cent of its profit after tax on the community, having substantially enhanced the corpus for several schemes. As the revenues from the company's India operations saw a 14 per cent increase from US$7.39 billion in 2012–13 to US$8.1 billion in 2013–14, Tata Steel's CSR spend soared from US$28.5 million in 2012–13 to US$35.5 million in 2013–14.

Tata Steel delivers to the community

Tata Steel lives on a legacy of giving. Over the last century, it has perfected an ecosystem of delivering good to the public – almost parallel to, and far more efficient than, the government in the delivery of public good. In just one year, the company achieved the following milestones:

- Covered 5,032 acres through agriculture development initiatives.

- Created 92 ponds and 400 tubewells, 123 borewells, 152 irrigation structures and four rainwater harvesting structures.

- Under the National Wasteland Development Mission converted 13,000 acres into productive land.

- In 2013–14 about 200 metric tonnes of cashew grown by farmers earned them US$200,000.

- 2,357 additional lights illuminated 600 villages in 2013–14.

- Centres set up for IT, hospitality, textile, cosmetology etc, with partner organizations.

- Jyoti scholarships for meritorious students from economically and socially challenged families continued to be scaled up in 2013–14, accounting for 3,169 scholarships awarded in the reporting year against 2,477 in 2012–13.

- Pre-matric coaching classes were also expanded to cover 10,372 students in 2013–14, up from 5,006 students in 2012–13.

- To enhance the quality of education in government schools Tata Steel has sought to adopt 1,000 government primary schools in Odisha, touching the lives of 150,000 children.

Tata Steel and legacy giving

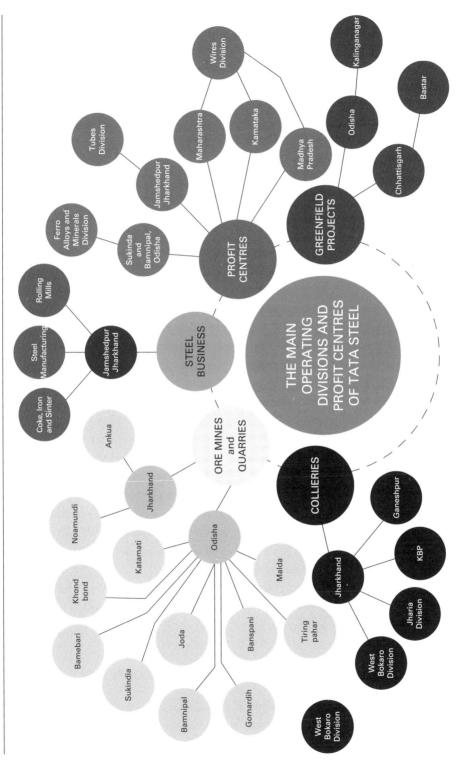

THE MAIN OPERATING DIVISIONS AND PROFIT CENTRES OF TATA STEEL

STEEL BUSINESS

PROFIT CENTRES
- Jamshedpur Jharkhand
  - Tubes Division
  - Wires Division
- Maharashtra
- Karnataka
- Sukinda and Bamnipal, Odisha
  - Ferro Alloys and Minerals Division
- Madhya Pradesh

GREENFIELD PROJECTS
- Odisha
  - Kalinganagar
- Chhattisgarh
  - Bastar

Jamshedpur Jharkhand
- Steel Manufacturing
- Rolling Mills
- Coke, Iron and Sinter

ORE MINES and QUARRIES
- Jharkhand
  - Ankua
  - Noamundi
- Odisha
  - Katamati
  - Khond bond
  - Bamebari
  - Sukindia
  - Joda
  - Bamnipal
  - Gomardih
  - Banspani
  - Malda
  - Tiring pahar

COLLIERIES
- Jharkhand
  - Ganeshpur
  - KBP
  - Jharia Division
  - West Bokaro Division
- West Bokaro Division

SOURCE: Tata Steel

Tata Steel and legacy giving

Tata Steel's CSR initiatives do not fall into any relevant models of CSR. The company's activities are spread beyond conventional CSR activities. It has transformed itself into a 'caring' organization. A caring organization is an organization that does much more than mere CSR. It has already created a legacy for itself through years of investing in social well-being.

The litmus test for legacy giving is a process that the authors call '*the future minus me*' test. The process is to answer one single question: what happens when your enterprise does not exist in the future? Firms are by nature very fragile. Take the top stock-market indices of the world. Every twenty years, index companies change across the world's leading stock exchanges. Companies either opt out, or the technology change in the market drives them out of business, they go bust or change their business altogether. As the speed of growth of knowledge increases, the technology and product life cycles get proportionately shorter. Enterprises vanish into thin air. So what happens to all your CSR initiatives when you are gone?

The process of answering this simple question is extremely complicated and varies from firm to firm. Most enterprises with 'legacy giving' (or the notion that the social good that they have created will outlast them with minimal external intervention) will admit that it was created by a series of unplanned events over time. This is where Tata's archery academy is important. Senior archers get together to train and inspire junior archers. The trainers arrived there as junior sports people, loved the cause and stayed on. They took it to ever-greater heights. Over the years, Tata has managed to attract the right talent to propel its cause. Every year, it produces a crop of people who are keen to pursue excellence. That is what success is – a psychological chase of small, incremental changes for the better; albeit slow, but steady. It needs an attitude shift. It is not just about giving away goodies, but inspiring the creation of good life for the masses.

The difference between conventional CSR and legacy giving is huge. It is almost the difference between a chicken farm and a rainforest. They have two different key result areas (KRAs) as far society is concerned.

Legacy giving is not just about social conscience

Sustaining good work takes a lot of effort, especially when you are a steel manufacturer. The most important words in the expansion of the acronym CSR are the terms 'corporate' and 'responsibility'. It is here that you have to make the adjustments to transform yourself into this goodness-giving behemoth. To create legacy, you need three things – an overarching vision, a strategy that calls for continuously reinventing your enterprise, and teams capable of designing and implementing tactical operations.

Tata Steel starts with spelling out an indemonstrable, yet inspiring vision:

> Our vision is to be the global steel industry benchmark for value creation and corporate citizenship.

What they created for our archers is value, which was derived from deep-seated values embedded in an organization's vision – values of self-esteem and honour in achieving the impossible through sustained effort and hard work. Thousands of tribal youth who get to go to Tata-run schools in Jharkhand experience that vision every day. Tata Steel does not expect any of these students to join their enterprise. They want them to do good for themselves and the society. Many children who studied in schools owned or run by Tata don't join the company. They grow up to be doctors, engineers, professors, artistes, filmmakers, bureaucrats, entrepreneurs, artists and others. They are each creating value for themselves and the society through their lives. Imparting excellence is part of inspiring society to reach for greater goals. That is a strategy to create a legacy – continuous, selfless, inspiration.

Tactical operations to support this vision are the most important thing. Not everyone who sees a garden full of beautiful flowers gets to see the bees working hard to make it work or the constant buzz in the beehive. Yet it is in this beehive of activity that the layout of the garden is planned and executed. For Tata Steel, 'caring' does not stop at its doors. Sustainability has been woven into this firm's fabric.

To create a sustainable organization means to secure sustainability in inputs, processes, external and internal environment and output of the firm. Sustainability is a dynamic equilibrium. It requires the organization to be nimble footed, to change every minute and adjust to both internal and external environments. Tata Steel's tactical model captures the busy beehive that it is.

Each of the smaller circles in Figure 9.2 denotes a tactical imperative. Each area needs attention because these parts add up to make what the organization itself is – a caring organization that focuses on legacy CSR cannot ignore any of these verticals. Tata Steel has also got the advantage of designing its own township around the factory. The city of Jamshedpur was essentially built and is still run by Tata for the most part. Many enterprises do not get the opportunity to intervene at such great lengths. What role does each tactical vertical play in the case of Tata Steel?

The Tata Steel tactical model

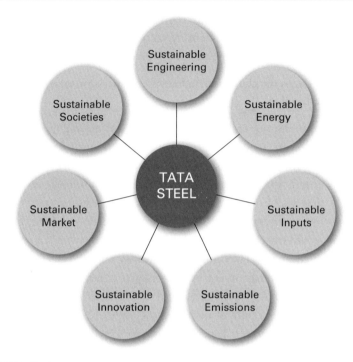

SOURCE: Tata Steel

Sustainable inputs

Tata Steel's operations stretch end-to-end, from the mining of coal and iron ore to serving the end consumer of steel. The company works on all opportunities at its mines along the value chain to ensure the sustainability of its inputs. Its efforts are driven by its objective of minimizing the environmental footprint of its operations. Accordingly, the coal and iron ore beneficiation projects continuously push the frontiers of technology in effectively using every tonne of natural resource mined. Tata Steel is today amongst the world's lowest-cost producers of steel. The company is also striving to be among the greenest metal producers in the world.

Sustainable emissions

Tata Steel is one of the lowest-cost producers of hot metal in the world and the national benchmark in the iron and steel industry for specific energy consumption CO_2 intensity through the BF-BOF (blast furnace–basic oxygen furnace) route. This achievement notwithstanding, the company had set targets for matching emission levels to global benchmarks. It also adopted the audacious target of confining overall dust levels to those achieved before the commencement of the expansion projects in the past six years. This has yielded a gradual but clear sustainable trend in Tata Steel's environment performance.

Sustainable innovation

Tata Steel's research and development efforts to reduce the coke rate led to the development of dual flux pellets, a first in the world, and continuous improvements in the quality of pellets. It also achieved an improvement in lime quality and the reduction of lime fines in its new kilns thereby improving material efficiency. The company has been continuously working to achieve breakthroughs in the areas of process and product technology and innovation. India needs Tata Steel in order to use the best minds to catapult itself to a path of high growth and sustainable development.

Sustainable societies

Tata Steel has contributed significantly to the cause of human development; not only in India, but also in several countries across the world where it has operations. With its majority shares controlled by the Tata Trust, it has built some of the finest institutions in India such as the Indian Institute of Science, Tata Institute of Fundamental Research, Tata Institute of Social Sciences, etc. It has also established schools and hospitals, which serve millions of people across India every year.

Sustainable markets

Tata Steel focuses on creating value for its future customers today; value creation for automotive customers through enhanced offerings. The unique Driving Steel seminar exposes steelmakers and engineers to challenges and opportunities in the original equipment manufacturers that use Tata's steel to manufacture automobiles.

Significant investments are also made in order to enhance capacity and quality augmentation of service. Centres of EPAs along with source authentication needs for Tata Astrum customers have been established separately. The sales team conducts a retail value management (RVM) programme to increase its reach in Tier 3/4 cities and rural areas. It is taking special care to enhance branded, automotive and value-added industrial product segments in order to stay ahead of the commodity curve.

Everything that Tatas does is now connected to the three Cs explained earlier; cash, clutter and consistency. Sustainability helps the enterprise to bring in cash through better profitability. Its stress on the environment helps it to build strong consumer connect and thus stand out of the clutter. The emphasis on creating value for the planet as a whole creates a culture of excellence and respect for the environment amongst all its team members. Thus 'sustainability', like 'service', gets ingrained in the core of Tata's brand values.

Transforming into a caring company

It is difficult and challenging to stick one's neck out as a caring company. Being in the CSR basket is relatively easy. One gets to strategically align one's business to its own CSR initiatives and derive benefits from it (as stated at the beginning of this chapter). Most enterprises would see shareholder wealth maximization (or stakeholder wealth maximization) as their only goal. To such enterprises, beginning to care for society seems to be a parallel stream of business. Yes, it is so. Caring for society, or creating a legacy CSR, is not everyone's cup of tea, however. It needs a new strategy.

Tata Steel has realigned its processes, goals and ambitions with the larger life goals of its people. The community around Tata Steel perceives it to be a caring organization. This makes it easier for Tata to undertake mining and acquire large plots of land for its projects. People trust the brand. They know that Tata will not short-change them. This lowers the company's cost of doing business. Tata Steel commissions social workers to live and work in the hinterlands. Thus governments want their social welfare programmes to be aligned with Tata Steel's because it ensures both coverage and better efficiency of money spent.

The employees of Tata Steel know that an enterprise that takes care of the world around them will take care of them too. They are motivated and dedicated. In fact, a large number of Tata Steel employees are second- and third-generation workers at the plant. Clients of Tata Steel are often invited to be part of Tata's social interventions. This ensures that clients remain committed to the activities of the company and are motivated to do more for their enterprise. Tata's commitment to social welfare and goodness has won them many friends abroad. When Tata made a bid for Corus Steel (UK), their employee unions supported the Tata bid as they liked the company's practice of aligning social goals with each one of the company's goals and their stress on achieving both of them.

The community-first model has served them well

Every enterprise has to reinvent itself every day. Even enterprises that have monopoly markets have to do so. Even if the name of the firm does not change, everything inside has to change since the market swings with the times. Companies cannot always insist on emphasizing the society-first rule. However, enterprises like Tata Steel are moving along a different trajectory. This community-first model has served them well. There are others in India and abroad who have tried to emulate Tata and failed.

> The community-first model is not, of course, solely found in Tata's organization. The Indian Space Research Organization (ISRO) is India's space agency. They are renowned for their frugal engineering capability. Their mars mission '*Mangalyaan*' was the world's most ergonomic space programme. They also hold the world record for the largest number of satellites launched with one single rocket. Despite all these technological breakthroughs, when their director was asked to list his enterprise's achievements, the first thing he remembered to tell the journalists was 'we have helped over 100,000 drought-hit villages to spot underground water supplies'. That is social orientation. These villages will continue to get water from their wells irrespective of ISRO's future performance or existence. The benefits of their efforts will continue to flow and nourish another generation of villagers. That is the 'future minus me' test. That is how caring organizations are built. Each time our archers hit their target, there is a steely resolve at work behind it.

Building an organization of the future: how is Tata Steel shaping itself?

It takes a steely will to produce a generation of iron-strong winners. Sport and games make a great way to produce outstanding, competitive people. Tata Steel does not count its return on investment by the number of medals it wins alone. In fact, medals are just one way of assessing your social impact. The real assessment is the decline in the number of registered criminal cases and an increase in the school and college tenures of its enrolled students. It keeps the community engaged in a positive manner. At the end of the day,

Tata Steel is not just a steelmaker. It is an aggregator of good for the community. It is here that the company's claim 'We also make steel' is set in the right context. No other company has had the good fortune to create a city for its factory and turn that into one of the world's finest places to live. Tata Steel built Jamshedpur brick by brick. And it didn't keep that city for itself. It is a thriving centre of commerce for the state of Jharkhand and its economy.

Over the years, Tata Steel has branched out into more places. The company is counted among the world's largest producers of steel. Asia's first integrated private-sector steel company is among the top 10 global steel companies today, with an annual crude steel capacity of over 29 million tonnes per annum. It is now the world's second-most geographically diversified steel producer, with operations in 26 countries and a commercial presence in over 50 countries. The Tata Steel Group, with a turnover of US$25 billion in 2014, has over 80,000 employees across five continents and is a Fortune 500 company.[10]

Tata Steel's larger production facilities comprise those in India, the UK, the Netherlands, Thailand, Singapore, China and Australia. Operating companies within the group include Tata Steel Limited (India), Tata Steel Europe Limited (formerly Corus), Tata Steel Singapore and Tata Steel Thailand. Underpinning its vision is a performance culture committed to aspiration targets, safety and social responsibility, continuous improvement, openness and transparency.

In 2008, Tata Steel India became the first integrated steel plant in the world, outside Japan, to be awarded the Deming Application Prize for excellence in Total Quality Management. In 2012, Tata Steel became the first integrated steel company in the world, outside Japan, to win the Deming Grand Prize instituted by the Japanese Union of Scientists and Engineers. It is this pursuit of excellence that has created a niche for the enterprise and its people.

The group company is aiming for a turnover of US$500 billion by 2025. The new group chairman has laid down several strategic initiatives to achieve this figure. What does it mean for Tata's social giving? As an enterprise owned and run by a charitable trust, Tata Steel has itself become a role model for other companies to follow. When the company's revenue goes up, much of it will surely be diverted back into social goodness.

The Tata Code of Conduct is a set of principles that guide and govern the conduct of Tata companies and their employees in all matters relating to business. First elucidated in 1998, the code lays down the ethical standards that Tata employees have to observe in their professional lives, and it defines the value system at the heart of the Tata Group and its many business entities. The code is a dynamic document that reinforces the Tata canon of honourable behaviour in business. While it has remained unaltered at its core, the code has been modified down the years to keep it in step with changing regulatory norms in the different parts of the world where Tata companies now do business. These modifications have reinforced the code, and enable it to reflect the diverse business, cultural and other factors that have a bearing on the health of the Tata brand.

So with the pursuit of excellence as part of the company's DNA, and a guiding Code of Conduct, everything else just fell into place.

Conclusion

Today, India is a very exciting place, poised to achieve many years of growth and prosperity. Its incumbent government is laying great stress on flagship programmes such as Make in India (to catalyse growth of the manufacturing industry so that it can generate revenues as well as employment), Clean India (or *Swacch Bharat*), Skill India, Women's Empowerment, and more, so that the country and its citizens may benefit from the outcomes of each of these national drives. It is interesting to note here that one such company in this very country had already envisioned these missions and has been actively contributing towards Make in India, Clean India, Skill India and Empowering Women. It has been for 100 years!

Over the years, what Tata Steel has perhaps managed to achieve is what brands actually dream of – creating an absolute buy-in and loyalty from its stakeholders. And it has clearly managed to do that and earn their trust, by primarily focusing on and investing in its people and then in its business, as can be best summarized in one of its popular publicity jingles – '*We also make steel*'.

(Many of Tata's new businesses are at a nascent stage in India and may enter the rapid growth phase over the next decade to 2025. However, its conventional businesses are facing an uphill future. Steel is facing cost pressure induced by the Chinese meltdown. Its car business is floundering. One half of Tata's revenue comes from outside India and is thus affected by the global slowdown. However, the group has exited all loss-making businesses. It is well positioned to tough its US$500 billion revenue by 2025 provided the global economy gets back to and sustains a growth momentum of 3.5 to 4.5 per cent per annum).

Reflective questions

- What leading multinationals do you know that grew thanks to their commitment to society?
- Will there be an end to the growth of Tata Steel?
- How do the values of Tata Steel reflect India's culture?

Notes

1 Z News [accessed 2 December 2015] Purnima Mahato, Narendra Saini recommended for Dronacharya [Online] http://zeenews.india.com/sports/others/purnima-mahato-narendra-saini-recommended-for-dronacharya_766705.html

2 The highest honour conferred to coaches and mentors of sportspersons by the government of India. Given by the president of India at a glitzy ceremony held at his residence in New Delhi, the award is named after the famous Guru Dhronacharya who trained the princes of Delhi in the great epic Mahabharat

3 The Telegraph [accessed 3 December 2015] Tata Fetes Drona Awardee Purnima [Online] http://www.telegraphindia.com/1130903/jsp/jharkhand/story_17303070.jsp#.VafyjUXLCf4

4 *Ultimate Handbook Guide to Jamshedpur: (India)*, travel guide by Ma Bunkley

5 Tata Steel [accessed 3 December 2015] History [Online] http://www.tatasteel100.com/heritage/history/history07.asp

6 Lala, R M (2004) *For the Love of India: The life and times of Jamsetji Tata*, Viking, India

7 Dutta, M (1977) *Asiatic Society Jamshedpur: The growth of the city and its regions*, Asiatic Society, Calcutta

8 Rank of Cities on Sanitation 2009–2010: National Urban Sanitation Policy [Online] http://pib.nic.in/archieve/others/2010/may/d2010051103.pdf

9 Fernando, A C (2009) *Business Ethics: An Indian perspective*, Pearson Education, India

10 [Online] www.tatasteel.com

No targets, no budgets and little marketing – and yet, multiplying branches in Britain

SIMON PATERSON AND ERIKA UFFINDELL

An example of a conscious, sustainable, bank brand

Handelsbanken is one of the oldest and most successful banks in the world and one of the few banks that proves you can be conscious and successful, over the long term. Founded in 1871 in Sweden, Handelsbanken sets out its purpose and sustainable principles on its website:

> A long-term perspective and stability... the latest global financial crisis has clearly shown that, for a bank, the most fundamental criterion for sustainability is survival. Handelsbanken is – and will continue to be – a bank with stable finances, which manages without support from the government or central banks, a bank that, regardless of the situation in the world around us, is there for our customers. Handelsbanken is convinced that sustainable long-term growth and shareholder value can only be achieved if the bank creates long-term value for its customers at the same time – and also society as a whole.

Handelsbanken's performance in the UK demonstrates these principles well. The bank has been in the UK since 1982, but its growth only really took off in the past decade. In 2001 it had six branches in Britain. By the end of 2006 that had risen to 26, then to 104 by the start of 2012 and 200 in 2015. The UK is now the bank's second largest market, overtaking Norway.

How has the bank done this?

No targets, no budgets and little marketing

First, there are no concrete targets, no budgets and there is no centralized marketing department. As the UK CEO, Anders Bouvin, says:

> We don't do fixed planning at all. I have no plan. But the way things look now we will continue along this path for the foreseeable future. I cannot see at this stage why we would want to change anything.
>
> Our overall corporate goal is to have a higher return on equity than the average of our peers, which we happen to have had now for 43 consecutive years, and of course the way of achieving that is to have a top-level customer satisfaction, as well as being thrifty and cautious with costs – only spending money on the things that give value to customers.

Decentralization and freedom of authority

Handelsbanken is highly decentralized and gives freedom of authority to its managers. Typically a new branch is set up when an existing branch in a town reaches around 12 staff, at which point it is deemed to be at the limit of its size if it is to retain the feel of a local branch, and it splits off a new bank in the same area. On average that new branch becomes profitable in 18 months. It operates on what it calls the 'church-spire principle', a model it has followed since the 1970s under which each branch is given total freedom to decide how to deal with its customers.

'The larger we get, the more decentralized we get, the closer to the customer we get,' said Mr Bouvin. 'As responsibility always lies with the local branch and only for the geographical area that surrounds the branch, the more we have, the more decentralized we become... The more branches we open, the more our reputation among customers grows and we find it increasingly easy when we open new branches to get them going.'

Prudence and long-term thinking

One ultimate limit to the bank's growth is that the bank is keen to focus on 'prudent' lending, keeping down losses on bad loans rather than branching out into shorter-term relationships with customers. That means getting to know its customers well and sticking with them over the long term.

The bank also takes the long-term view about the sweep of history and the human tendency to quickly forget the lessons of the past. Referring to the 140 years of board minutes that lie in the basement of its Stockholm headquarters, the main lesson that Anders Bouvin draws from them is that about every 17 years there is a financial crisis: 'Depending on the fact that the business cycle is so long, and memory is not always so long, we know we have to prepare ourselves for bad times...'

The value of direct human contact

Handelsbanken does not have call centres. Instead, customers have their bank manager's mobile phone number and can call at any time. That manager remains their main point of contact in all their dealings with the bank and they are not forced to deal with centralized departments for loans, for example.

Innovative and open-minded

Despite all the branches, Handelsbanken has not neglected the digital side of banking. The combination of smartphone apps and branches allow it to lower costs and boost efficiency. The bank also looks beyond banking for ideas. Inspired by the example of fashion retailer H&M, Handelsbanken started a video channel on its website that became very popular as a way for customers to receive news.

No bonuses, no temptation

Crucially for a bank, Handelsbanken does not pay bonuses to its staff. Instead they benefit from the collective performance of the bank over the long term. Every year that the bank's return on equity beats rivals, staff are awarded an equal share of profits. These flow into a foundation that owns 10 per cent of the bank's shares. No one can withdraw any money until they turn 60.

'The reason we don't do bonuses is that it is not compatible with our long-term customer-centric way of running our organization. If you are to take customer satisfaction seriously, if you really believe that customer satisfaction is the main reason for achieving superior results, you really have to eliminate any kind of steering mechanisms that could push one of your employees to do something that is not in the interest of customers,' Bouvin says.

Having a wide and socially useful purpose

Underlying all this is a belief that a bank should not be a drain on society but a helper, providing credit to people and businesses. It underscores why Handelsbanken is keen to avoid taking help from governments.

'In order for our branches to succeed in their communities and gain the trust of people, it is very important we behave in a responsible way. The ethos of the bank is: a bank should be an asset to the community, not a liability,' Bouvin says.

Handelsbanken's purpose suggests that it is a highly conscious organization that can sense and respond to where the organization is going. It is simple but responsible practices that replace the machinery of plans, budgets, targets and incentives.

Slow but stable growth

The lack of state aid and little marketing mean that growth is slower than it could be, but it is also more stable. It is precisely this outcome that shows Handelsbanken understands the true value and benefit of being a conscious and sustainable brand – being satisfied with enough, not more; benefiting from the sense of continuity that taking the long-term view provides; trusting its people to do the right thing, but not putting temptation in their way; and, consequently, balancing different measures of success: economic, human, social and environmental.

Sources

Milne, R, Handelsbanken is intent on getting back to the future, *Financial Times*, 20 March 2015

Wallace T, No marketing? No plan? How Handelsbanken hit 200 branches in the UK, *Daily Telegraph*, 9 September 2015

Branding the place and growing the good life

10

NIKOLAJ STAGIS ON PLACE BRANDING

○ *Place branding is not only about attracting new people, it's also about improving the quality of life for current residents and businesses.*

○ *Place branding needs particpation and resolute, tenacious leaders who can overcome difficulties and win in the long run.*

○ *Deeply rooted, authentic identities are the key to successful implementation.*

Around the world cities, regions and even small towns are embarking on place branding journeys. They all want to become attractive places that function as a source of the good life, as a cradle for innovative entrepreneurs and profitable businesses. Local authorities, businesses and institutions all want development, growth and prosperity for their area. This might explain why cities and regions are campaigning in the media and through events and festivals to show their advantages to the world. But some of the most attractive place brands do not advertise or campaign at all. Instead they try to create the best possible conditions for a good life by utilizing their identity and offering a unique approach. They continually try to define and refine value creation rather than publicize their benefits.

Urbanization is changing places around the globe

The mobility and growth of populations have created new conditions for the development of places and also created new challenges. As more people move from the countryside to the edge of towns and into cities, traffic congestion and air pollution have become evident – while the focus on public health, life quality and life expectancy is increasing, people are getting sick with stress and many have a hard time living up to the expectations of modern life. On a global scale there is growing attention on sustainability – environmental as well as social – which influences politics, city planning and the narratives of place brands.

These new concerns set certain agendas for leaders of cities and regions. Many local governments have to balance a wide range of competing needs and demands:

- planning that combines homes and business;
- regulating traffic so that people can commute quickly and efficiently without polluting;
- attracting business that is not noisy or polluting;
- creating more jobs and financial development in the local area;
- taking care of senior citizens while enhancing health and living standards;
- setting the bar for using organic food and CO_2-neutral energy in the city.

... All the while keeping costs and taxes low. Clearly, then, what 'living a good life' actually means is rather complex.

These challenges are especially notable in rural areas that do not have the financial resources to develop comprehensive policies and deliver in every field of responsibility. When resources are scarce, how do you define and develop a conscious and sustainable place brand that can create the setting for 'the good life'?

Yet, some cities and towns are achieving just that in spite of their financial restraints, small size or limited resources. Especially in Europe, a considerable number of cities are becoming more sustainable, more green, socially responsible and conscious. And by creating the best possible living conditions they also become successful place brands.

Copenhagen – green smart thinking

Copenhagen is Denmark's capital and home to 600,000 people in the city and some 1.2 million in the urban area. It is not a big or well-known city in comparison to the likes of London or New York, but it has become a city brand with an interesting image and reputation. Hailed three times in the past seven years by the international magazine *Monocle* for its quality of life, Copenhagen has, by many measures, become a more conscious and sustainable city brand that can compete with cities throughout the world. 'In the 1980s the city's economy and the liveability was terrible. Residents were moving out of the city and the population was in decline. The mayor and government in those years were exploring ways to get out of that crisis. If it had been a corporation, they would have called it a turnaround,' says Frank Jensen, Lord Mayor of Copenhagen, who has been the city mayor since 2010. Back in the 1990s, the mayor decided to embark on a new journey, creating a new story for Copenhagen that has since been praised in media such as *Monocle* magazine and *The Oprah Winfrey Show*. Today, Copenhagen is a social, green and innovative city with a vibrant cultural and architectural scene. Flying into the city you will notice a long curve of wind turbines in the ocean outside of the city – a well-chosen functional symbol for the image that the city wants to promote. The local tradition and awareness on sustainability, social responsibility and smart city planning have given new attention to Copenhagen as one of the best places to live and as a cultural and creative hub of importance. But how could a capital change so drastically in reputation and attractiveness over a period of 20 years?

'This city has always been known for tolerance, openness and collective social responsibility. You have to remember, this city hall was the first in the world to marry a gay couple in 1989. I'm very proud of that, and I think it's a good example of the identity that we've continued to build on,' explains Frank Jensen. The issue that became important for the local politicians in the 1990s was the narrative of Copenhagen: 'Who are we?' and 'Who do we want to become?' Copenhageners like to take social responsibility and show that they are able to act together – and those cultural values became a primary driver in the development of the sustainable city. The city council decided that they wanted Copenhagen to be a climate frontrunner delivering 'liveability'. From 1995 to 2005 the CO_2 emissions were reduced by 45 per cent and in 2009 the city council set the ambitious goal of becoming the world's first CO_2-neutral city by 2025. One of the initiatives that makes the reduction possible is the central-heating distribution system built on excess heat from burning waste. 'When there is something we really want to do, we go ahead and do it. More than 99 per cent of the homes in Copenhagen are heated by central heating because we have decided that everyone is obliged to use the system. In many places that would be considered an infringement of personal freedom,' says Frank Jensen. Politicians have tapped into the collective interest in social and environmental responsibility.

The Copenhagen narrative means that the city has become a 'smart city', which means that the city planners believe in the principle that solutions should always solve two or three problems rather than one. The new street layouts have cycle lanes that are wider than the lanes for cars and buses, which enhances the opportunity to cycle. The benefits are less traffic, less air pollution, better public health and higher life expectancy. And because people exercise more they are less sick and that saves money on the public health-care budget. The massive investment in becoming a great cycling city means that Copenhagen has more than 370 kilometres of cycle lanes and recently was given the title as the world's best cycling city in competition with Amsterdam. 'We continually have to invest in making our city more efficient by using data and developing more innovative solutions. One of the ways we can do that is by thinking more holistically,' says Frank Jensen. The Copenhagen narrative is about balancing several factors to create a great place to live and the liveability becomes the primary experience and message of the Copenhagen place brand.

Lejre – the organic municipality

Lejre is a Danish region and home to 27,000 inhabitants – the town Lejre itself only has 2,300 citizens. Just like other rural areas in many parts of the world, the region of Lejre is threatened as inhabitants of the small towns migrate to the big cities. The countryside of many Northern European countries has been changing rapidly over the past few decades, and even though Lejre is less than an hour's drive from the Danish capital Copenhagen, Lejre's politicians are concerned about the future of the place. Statistically, a rural area like Lejre could end up with fewer people, less business and a situation where the local government would have to shut down schools and cut welfare expenses as a consequence of migration. Many areas around Europe and other parts of the world suffer the same difficulties and ask themselves: what would attract new businesses and people to move to our part of the country? How can the area keep developing in spite of the global trend towards large cities and the abandonment of the countryside? How do we create the basis for a good life?

Elected as mayor of Lejre in 2009, Mette Touborg has a mission to build a conscious community with ecology, organics, social welfare and health high on the agenda. 'When I ran for the elections my personal mission was better ground water, creating a national park and a vision about starting a community that makes it possible to create a good life in the countryside. You see, when you live in the countryside you have to come together to create the content of a meaningful life,' says Mayor Mette Touborg. With a community of residents who were already shaping their lives towards an organic and ecological lifestyle, Lejre seemed like the right place to succeed.

When the Danish Environmental Protection Association approached Lejre to do a live full-scale experiment to see what would happen if an organic lifestyle became the mission of the region, Mette Touborg quickly got involved and made it her mission to create the organic region of Denmark. Yet getting others to join in was a political and organizational challenge: 'Many think that an organic lifestyle is an ideological or political choice, but I made it very clear that every employee in the municipal organization had to follow suit. This wasn't a choice of liking or disliking the idea, this brand was the definition of the organizational identity and the way to do the job,' Mette Touborg explains. 'Most politicians are good at speaking up in front of a large crowd, even when a case is difficult, but when you want to roll out a new strategy it is extremely important that you communicate clearly to the municipal organization what you want them to do. At our initial kick-off meeting I spoke directly to each of the directors in front of all our 50 leaders. I asked every director explicitly to return to me with their ideas on how they would implement our new vision in each of their areas of responsibility.'

One of Lejre's strategies in creating a powerful place brand was to partner up with appropriate organizations to create the necessary grounding and backup for the new place brand. The idea came from the Danish Environmental Protection Association and soon Lejre also teamed up with the Organic National Association and the Danish Agriculture and Food Council – a large, prominent organization but also thought of by most as a conventional institution. The collaboration showed public approval of the idea.

In the last five years Lejre has undergone a tremendous change. Projects and experiments run by passionate locals seem to pop up everywhere and today the widespread activity throughout the region seems to be its most important strength. Today, if you live in Lejre, you can borrow chickens so that you can see what it is like to keep your own chickens, laying eggs at home. Local entrepreneur Johanne Schimming got the idea because she wanted more people to have their own chickens. Mette Touborg recalls a meeting for local entrepreneurs: 'We sat at a large round table. Johanne was telling how she wanted to let people lease chickens. And I thought to myself, what is she saying about those chickens? I didn't quite get it and I wondered what the other entrepreneurs were thinking. Her dream was to have a lot of chickens and let people try to have chickens at home before they bought them. And everyone was quite fascinated by the idea.' Now customers at the chicken leasing company can lease a chicken to bring home or follow their personal chicken or lamb by daily newsletter. Recently Johanne Schimming began to deliver chickens and eggs to the world's most sustainable restaurant, Relæ in Copenhagen, founded by former Noma chef Christian Puglisi. She is just one of the entrepreneurs in Lejre who are living their dream based on the organic mindset of the place brand.

The political commitment is carried out with integrity. For instance, Lejre supports organic farmers over conventional farmers – even if it costs the municipality money. 'We set a minimum price for the leasehold of farming land. And any bid above that level is evaluated and selected depending on how organic the farming will be if they get the land. We prefer organic farming and our lowest priority is conventional farming that uses pesticides,' explains Mette Touborg. This political choice means that Lejre may get less money for the lease of the land as they prioritize organic farming over the extra money they may get from a conventional farmer.

In the process, some may have thought that Lejre was becoming a bit of a hippie place with these alternative ideas. Recently, however, four local organic farmers from Lejre got a deal with the nationwide supermarket chain Føtex and are now selling the milk brand 'Milk from Lejre' across Denmark. 'Now, when I meet with other mayors at different venues, I certainly enjoy a different kind of respect. I think they've realized that this is also a matter of business,' says Mette Touborg with a grin. The initiatives and development mean that Lejre has a unique brand but more importantly it has changed the lifestyles and habits of the people in the area. 'We are creating consciousness among the broader audience. The core and the potential was already here, but our percentage of farmers producing organically is 12 per cent, whereas the national average is only 6 per cent. We also know that today the consumers in Lejre buy 18 per cent organic foods which is 7 per cent above the national average,' says Mette Touborg. Last year 10 families were looking for a place to create a living community focusing on ecological sustainability and they chose Lejre as the right place to settle down and build their houses.

The Citta 'Slow' movement focuses on quality of life

Another example of a different way of thinking about place is the Citta 'Slow' movement, founded in Orvieto in Italy in 1999 and with more than 200 certified cities around the world. The primary focus of the movement is to 'enlarge the philosophy of Slow Food to local communities' but the charter of the organization reaches far beyond food. Citta Slow cities work actively on policies regarding energy, infrastructure, quality of urban life, agricultural, touristic and artisan policies, hospitality and social cohesion. But first and foremost, the Citta Slow movement is about authenticity – both in the sense of going back to the roots of quality and the good life and in the sense of finding the inner meaning of a place. The first sentence of the charter says: 'The development of local communities is based on the ability to share and recognize their intrinsic specific traits, of regaining their own identity, visible from outside and deeply lived within.'

One of the early cities to join the movement was Sokndal in southern Norway. They say that the idea is to 'stop the chase, turn down the pace and prioritize life quality and the good life. In Sokndal it is the law to be a bit different and a bit crazy. We have our own "love week" and focus on the things close to us. We have no tourists – only guests!'

In Svendborg, a medium-sized city in southern Denmark, in 2008 it was decided to certify as a Citta Slow municipality. The city is concerned with the amount of people getting sick due to stress. The local administration has been working on numerous Citta Slow projects but finds the wording difficult to communicate. 'This is a general trend that many young people and families find attractive,' says Søs Grützmeier, a communication officer from Svendborg municipality, 'but we find it a bit difficult to communicate. Some of the locals say that they really don't think we are slow – they cannot see themselves in this idea. If we had just said, Svendborg is a blue city by the sea it might have been easier. But I'm not sure that would have moved us either,' Søs says while pondering the right move for the city. The kindergartens and nursing homes in Svendborg have been implementing the idea. They take the children on day trips by bicycle; and the nursing home is a real home, rather than an institution that looks like a hospital. The schoolchildren in eighth to tenth grade learn to cook a slow, healthy lunch called LOMA. It stands for local food and sounds a bit like Noma – the world's best restaurant.

Creating conscious uniqueness

Place brands are ecologies that are large in scale, complex, have long histories and traditions and therefore take tremendous efforts and time to change and develop. Merely understanding them and creating an overview can be a difficult task. The cultural identities of places are rather stable – for good and bad. Unlike companies and most organizations, the leadership, power and control of a city or region is dispersed among many different stakeholders and parties, which makes it difficult to form a common idea about what the identity is and what purpose it serves. Consequently, it is quite difficult to form a strategy, goal or vision for a place that everyone can support and benefit from.

The official objectives of cities and municipalities are defined in part by national legislation, and the range and delivery of services are delivered in much the same way, as the legislative directives are quite specific. It causes the claims and messages of one place to be the same as another, which is contrary to the primary aim of place branding: creating unique differentiation. When it comes to creating unique brand identity, the administrative organizations are in a sense designed to efficiently deliver homogenization. The unintended side effect is a commodified service and a homogenized place identity. In spite of this general homogenization some towns, cities and regions are able to create a unique mindset and deliver the mandatory services in their own way. These places deliver services and carry out their mission differently because of their sense of identity.

Democracy as a differentiation paradox

In the most developed, democratic parts of the world, cities and regions are managed by a diverse, democratically elected city council or regional council that represents the citizens of the area and has a wide range of positions and approaches to what is needed in order to develop their area. The ability to listen to many viewpoints and find common ground for conscious decisions are seen as fundamental and positive values in democracies. But sometimes contrary viewpoints lead to political and strategic compromises, which cause weak stances and a middle course that makes it difficult to stand out in the competition with other places. In a recent study of Danish city slogans, more than half of the 70 slogans or bylines in the study failed to create any external differentiation and did not give any internal sense of identity or direction: 'In the middle of possibilities' (Ringsted municipality); 'Willing to grow' (Assens municipality); 'We do it – together' (Syddjurs municipality); 'We create solutions together' (Furesø municipality); and 'Look forward' (Viborg municipality).[1] They point to the need for growth, that there are many possibilities and to the community or collective effort of the place. However, it is very difficult to draw any differentiation or direction out of them – most places in the world consider themselves as holders of possibility, will and togetherness. Some of the most efficient place brands make unique claims, offers and ideas that draw on the characteristics of the local authentic culture and identity. Think of such original expressions as 'Keep Austin Weird', from Austin, Texas; 'I ❤ NY' by Milton Glaser from New York City (this has since been copied by hundreds of destinations, expressing the lack of differentiation in the place marketing industry); or the slogan and vision of Kolding, Denmark: 'We design life'.

Obviously, slogans, names or other brand expressions are not the only terms in which place brands can be evaluated. To the contrary, many other characteristics may be more important in creating an image and expressing a narrative of a place brand. However, slogans are condensed stories that specifically aim to show the uniqueness of a place, and that is why they illustrate how difficult it is for leaders of place brands to find, define and express that uniqueness of the brand identity.

Conscious means involvement and interaction

One of the most essential problems with place branding is that any city or region holds such a diverse group of people and interests that it is very difficult to define any one thing that defines a place, helps it to stand out and gets support from everyone in the area. If you want to create a place brand that resonates with the people that live and work in the area, and delivers unique meaning externally, you have to build the brand position on strengths that are somehow represented inherently in the culture of the place. In order to find and underpin those culturally and locally defined strengths you have to understand, challenge and further develop the assets of the culture and the place.

Where brands have been a managerial and marketing responsibility earlier on, there is now a growing tendency towards involving local leaders as well as residents and local businesses in defining and developing the brand. This way of involving and interacting with stakeholders in the early phases of defining the essential characteristics and the narrative of the brand can lead to a more conscious and more efficient implementation. This type of development thinking entails a governance rather than administrative mindset, as public institutions have to manage networks across conventional boundaries involving public employees, citizens, volunteers and private businesses.

Discovery and involvement as brand design tools in Kolding

In the case of the municipality of Kolding, the fundamental platform for a new vision and brand was a two-month ethnographic research study with citizens, business leaders, politicians and people working in the public institutions. The team from Stagis, a brand consultancy working out of Copenhagen, wanted to find the authentic strengths of the place. What does the history and heritage of the place mean in the present time? Are there activities, beliefs and cultural traits that could become something more unique if only they were further developed? And where are the fireballs and passionate people who communicate what Kolding stands for?

Six authentic strengths that represented the essential characteristics of Kolding emerged from the research. The primary authentic strength that really stood out in comparison to other places was 'design'. In many different ways, Kolding uses design methods and design thinking but this force was underutilized and hardly exposed to the outside world, even though it seemed an obvious opportunity. 'The analysis of the authentic strengths was something that really resonated – it really felt true for Kolding,' said Jørn Pedersen, Lord Mayor of Kolding municipality.

Involving leaders as well as citizens in defining the essential narrative or the vision of the place can lead to a more conscious, sustainable and efficient implementation of the brand. In Kolding 100 opinion leaders worked on the region's future strategy and explored the consequences of three possible visions, all variants of using design thinking to empower the potential of the area. Later in the process, 600 citizens participated in the development process by discussing possibilities, effects and concrete ideas for the future. Finally, the essence of the brand was decided by the local government. In its shortest form the vision that served as a basis for the future development of Kolding read: 'We design a better life through entrepreneurship, social development and education.' The vision was also expressed in the slogan 'Kolding – we design life'. Kolding has become a design city that is now aiming to create better lives for the area's 92,000 residents by using design thinking and design methods in the municipality's everyday planning and problem solving. The sense of engagement and inspiration that was generated through the process contains both bottom-up and top-down initiatives. The discovery of the culture and the involvement of multiple stakeholders ensures the delivery of inspiration and makes implementation possible. The process and final decision among directors and politicians is a classic top-down process, which makes it possible to take a stance. Without a clear standpoint and the courage to choose, the brand will never stand out.

Several initiatives prove that the place is moving in a unique and common direction. The University of Southern Denmark campus in Kolding has incorporated the idea of design thinking into their courses, so that management and economy courses now include design methods. The municipality has hired several designers and established a design vision secretariat to implement design thinking in the organization and into the policy-making processes. This includes teaching leaders how design thinking can be used to solve problems in their public institutions.

Design methods are now being implemented as useful tools and ways of thinking about solutions for public services across the 9,000 employees in the municipal organization. The conscious city brand is not only something you talk and write about but something you do as you go about your everyday tasks as a manager or employee. 'We used to think in a more old-fashioned way as a public authority where residents come in to ask for permission and we say "yes" or "no", to now a more proactive attitude where we say, "come and join, play with us",' says Thomas Boe, director of city planning and development in Kolding municipality. In the year after deciding on the 'we design life' vision, the city planning department scheduled the opening of a new area of housing plots for potential inhabitants. But instead of deciding on the layout and dividing the land into lots, they gathered people who took an interest in the area and asked them, 'how should the place be developed and what should the layout be'? Rather than selling plots, they invited people to develop the place through an open design process. Since then many developments and decisions take their starting point in this new understanding of 'who we are' in Kolding. 'The fact that we can identify with the vision – and that our vision is forming our identity and the way we think and present ourselves to others – makes it strong,' says Thomas Boe. Kolding now 'owns' the design city position in the country, competing with the capital, Copenhagen. The primary use of the design-thinking positioning is a political and managerial approach in developing new solutions.

Morality as a primary force in the conscious city brand

The conscious place brand considers the identity and the actions of the place as being equally important as creating a good external image and attracting businesses and tourists. Goals are balanced between different factors: quality of life, economy, long-term sustainability, attracting tourists and creating business. When these factors include quality of life for a wide range of the population, and the redistribution of wealth, there is also a moral element of judgement and taking action on beliefs that everyone may not agree with.

Consequently, a part of the conscious city brand is teaching the population about a different lifestyle in order to achieve better conditions for the residents and a better reputation outside of the city. In a sense, the political leader becomes a teacher and radical peace activist rather than an administrator, because the ideological place brand that is not able to implement its beliefs and create the necessary changes is not really going to prove its value. Some of the most noticeable brands have demonstrated their political commitment and willingness to change through experiments and initiatives that have changed the people and the place for good.

Bogotá – a city of change

Bogotá has gone through dramatic changes over the past decade, one of the primary forces being the famous politician Antanas Mockus who was an important part of the transformation of the city after being elected as city mayor in the mid-1990s and again from 2001 to 2003. During his campaign, Mockus swore to use his powers to diminish crime and benefit humanity – just like Superman. And when he was elected mayor of Colombia's capital, he appeared in a spandex Superman suit and cloak with a giant 'S' for Supercitizen on his chest. Mockus's intention was to inspire the residents of Bogotá to join the fight to improve their lives and the environment.

If an authentic brand is one that practices its beliefs in real life, then Bogotá has certainly become more authentic under the leadership of Antanas Mockus, who changed the city's perception of itself through an impressive string of social experiments and initiatives, many of them driven by a desire to implement a more conscious and responsible behaviour among the city's 6.5 million inhabitants.

One of Mockus's famous initiatives included firing a large number of traffic police officers and hiring 420 mimes to teach good behaviour in the busy city traffic by making fun of traffic violators, as he believed Colombians were more afraid of being ridiculed than fined. Another active way of nudging the residents to behave and act more nicely was to hand out 350,000 cards to the residents to let them vote 'good behaviour' and 'bad behaviour' to one another. Consequently, traffic fatalities dropped by over 50 per cent in Bogotá.

When Antanas Mockus asked residents to pay a voluntary extra 10 per cent in taxes to make local improvements, 63,000 people did so. Under Mockus's leadership, Bogotá saw tremendous improvements. Water usage dropped 40 per cent, the homicide rate fell 70 per cent and clean drinking water was provided to all homes (up from 79 per cent in 1993). Antanas Mockus takes these rather unorthodox methods to teach the general public a different set of values and a different lifestyle. He acts more as a teacher and trainer than what is usually expected from a politician. Mockus takes on the role of a radical peace activist, promoting morality as a primary force in transforming the identity, community feeling and expression of the city and hence the city brand.

Developing the conscious place brand

Every city and every region can become more aware and conscious about their authentic identity and the strengths that a place holds. By discovering the local and cultural potential and the characteristics of the place, it becomes possible to define and further develop the brand identity of any place. Some of the most successful place brands have actually found something truly unique about themselves and tried to emphasize those particular traits.

In Lejre, organic had been popular for many years, but it only became an integral part of the place brand when a group of passionate individuals used their human and political willpower to make it come alive. I asked Mette Touborg if she could create the same movement and brand identity for any other place. She said, 'There is a method, but I can't say that the idea about being organic would work everywhere. Because it depends on the culture of the area. Of course I have been running things in a particular direction but there is an authentic identity base focusing on organic lifestyle here, which was present before I started this process. There are other regions where the idea about the organic region would be more difficult to realize.' Embedded in each and every place in the world there is already the potential for an identity that can be developed. Someone just has to see it.

Key learnings

- Placebranding is about attracting new people and improving the quality of life for all
- Success comes from participation and resolute, tenacious leaders
- Deeply rooted, authentic identities are the key to successful implementation

Reflective questions

- Can you define the most relevant reasons and goals for place branding?
- What are the most important stakeholders where you live, and how can they get involved in the place brand?
- Which cultural characteristics are unique and hold the potential to develop your place brand?

Note

1   Research by Stagis brand consultancy, Copenhagen, October 2015

Cork – big on life

MALCOLM ALLAN

In May 2013 key stakeholders from the city region of Cork in south-west Ireland started down the road on a continuing journey to raise awareness of the region, what it has to offer and the experience of living, working or studying there.

The year before, in 2012, Cork City Council had commissioned consultants to prepare proposals for the regeneration of its outdated former docklands area, running from the city centre along the River Lee towards the Atlantic. A key component of this work was to create a destination brand strategy for the area.

But this was no easy task. The strategy that emerged recognized that while a brand could be developed for the docklands area the real challenge lay in changing market perceptions of the city as a whole and, indeed, the region around the city.

As Tim Lucey, the city manager of Cork, Pat Ledwidge, head of economic development, and Martin Reardon, the manager of Cork County, recognized, 'there was no point in launching a brand for the docklands if the surrounding city did not reflect its values and propositions'. They also recognized that a city-wide and regional brand and marketing strategy would be a much more powerful vehicle for the economic development of the whole region than one just for the docklands area.

Conor Healy of the Cork Chamber of Commerce, a member of the steering committee, also thought, correctly as it turned out, that a major challenge for the people and organizations being consulted would be 'understanding where the process would lead and that it was serious'.

Tower of Babel

The first phase of research brought to light that the region had a comprehensive offer for businesses seeking an Irish location, a strong and supportive business community, a strong tourism and education offer (at further and higher education levels) and a valued quality of life as a place to live and visit. However, there were so many messages being communicated about these offers and experiences to so many people in too many places that it was difficult to 'hear' them. Unintentionally the region had created a 'Tower of Babel' effect. As I say, 'you cannot tell all of the people, everywhere, everything about your offer all of the time'.

And there was no consistency in the marketing collateral and in the channels to market being used. As a result there was confusion in the market locally, nationally and internationally about Cork and its distinctiveness as compared with Dublin, and major and second-tier cities in Europe. Nor was it clear what Cork was good at.

So there was an urgent need to bring clarity to the offer, raise awareness of it through more effective marketing and messaging, and change international perceptions of the place.

Involve the community

Everyone involved in the steering group was very committed to mobilizing the support of the regional business community, to get it actively involved in the development of the brand strategy and to give them the opportunity to be actively engaged in its implementation. It became clear that if the strategy was to be truly owned by a wider community then that community had to be encouraged to play a role in funding its implementation.

With hindsight, this looks like the natural thing to do: 'It is for the benefit of the community that we are strategizing – or it should be. They can make or break a brand strategy, by wholeheartedly supporting it and investing in it – with their money and time – or they can ignore it, decide to move or simply bad-mouth it when they feel ignored, frustrated or forgotten.'[1] This is why place branding is such a delicate process of multi-stakeholder management, rather than traditional brand management. But it is easier said than done.

In order for the whole region to get on board with this project, the core team recognized that they had to create a common 'hymn sheet' in order to sing a compelling song about the qualities and attractions of the place – 'The Song of Cork' – a melody of key messages for use in promoting Cork to industry and inward investors, international talent and students. The words of the song are set out in a brand book, publicly available for all those involved and interested.[2]

A compelling and uplifting melody

The proof of the pudding is in the eating, so you have to motivate people to visit Cork and see it. The brand proposition for Cork is that it is a place that combines agile, energetic and entrepreneurial local and global business success and a tradition of independent learning, great ideas, contemporary innovation and collaboration.

However, the brand-testing process identified that people ranked the region's quality of life as the most important aspect of the brand – followed by economy, education and visitors.

Based on a considerable number of responses to the question 'What makes Cork different', posed during the testing of the brand proposition, the recurring sentiment was that Cork is *'big on life'* – it is a place to live life to the full, a place to make it big. It is a very compelling song to sing.

The brand book describes in detail the other key messages to be used for a variety of target groups. It helps to bring together, for the first time, in a coherent and coordinated way, the economic development strengths of the Cork region. It sets out what makes Cork unique and attractive and how the Cork region should communicate, promote and share this story in Ireland and with the world. By working together and using this book to communicate a common set of messages about Cork and its strengths, Cork's stakeholders can now consistently position it in the same way and enable it to compete more effectively to deliver business growth, jobs and wealth – for Cork and for Ireland.

However, this is just work in progress.

Roger Hobkinson, director of destination development at Colliers International in Dublin, summed it up: 'We are being ambitious but not over-promising. We want the brand to be authentic and understood by Cork people and for them to really take ownership of it. Cork and the eventual vehicle/structure for delivering the brand and promoting Cork will need to ensure it remains flexible and is used appropriately – the volume is turned up or down for various brand values for different audiences.'[3]

The 'Song of Cork' could be heard quite clearly at the Financial Times Foreign Direct Investment Forum in September 2015. This was the second FT event of this nature – a global gathering of practitioners in the field of attracting inward investment and the places who want to capture it. If you are an aspirant place, this is a key forum to get your message over to those who advise international companies on new locations.

And it was here, at a stroke, that many perceptions of the offer of Cork changed for the better.

And how about you? Are you interested to come and see for yourself?

The Cork region brand pyramid

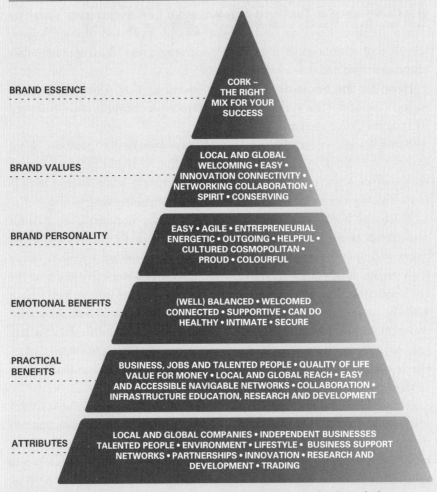

SOURCE: Colliers International Destination Consulting, Place Matters, Fuzion PR Marketing

Notes

1 Quote from interview with Malcolm Allan in the placebrandobserver.com, 2015
2 www.corkbrand.ie
3 Roger Hobkinson

Exploiting leadership to better the world

11

ENRIC BERNAL

This is not a book on how to build a brand. It is a book on how to change the world through business. And all the stories related are somehow interconnected on another theme: that of leadership, exhibited by founders and managers, and captured in their conscientious approach to business. Possibly, it is a book about conscious leadership.

Similarly to leadership itself, conscious leadership has to be understood in four different yet complementary domains: intrapersonal, interpersonal, organizational and societal. And each domain has two levels on their own – the level of consciousness, or in other words awareness, concern or attention; and the level of leadership, which is the intention, decisions and actions to do something about it.

Corporate social responsibility

In this book, the most obvious domain is the **societal** component. It is about having the awareness our actions and those of our brands have on society and the environment. This involves some big-picture and some systemic understanding: why do things happen the way they do? What are the basic laws of humankind? Corporate social responsibility (CSR) is great if it is not only an external facade. It has to be rooted in deep beliefs and values that you are willing to act upon. Similarly, to the other components of conscious leadership, the **societal** one cannot stop at the awareness level and needs to get into action. It is not enough to complain about child slavery in the chocolate supply chain. You have to work privately and publicly to help it be eradicated (as in Tony's Chocolonely story).

Examples of societal conscious leadership:

- You deeply care about planet Earth and you behave responsibly – using, reusing and recycling materials (as do Dr Hauschka and Lovechock).

- You take a voluntary assignment to help those who need it most without worrying about your personal benefits (eg Cosentino).

- You care about AIDS in the world and start an initiative to prevent it (Star for Life).

- You believe that inequality is unnecessary when you are able to share value where it is created (as did Dilmah Tea).

- You understand that the world has some systemic problems that can only be solved at a systems level over a long term (Tata Steel).

Three more levels

Let's consider the other three complementary components of conscious leadership (CL):

- the intrapersonal domain;
- the interpersonal domain;
- the organizational component.

The **intrapersonal** domain is the most basic level and the only one that looks inwardly. It involves you being aware of your thoughts, your emotions and your behaviours. Being aware of your inner debates, hot buttons, motives and values help you to understand your actions and reactions. And of course it is about leading yourself in a way that respects and reflects such consciousness. Think about the effect of food on our well-being – physical and emotional: cultivating and growing food equals the shared joy of consuming it (as in Slow Food's chapter).

Think of intrapersonal conscious leadership when:

- You are not willing to do something just because everyone else does it (Merci).
- You leave a company because your values are not in line with those of the corporation (Vegetalia).
- You exercise regularly as you know it positively affects your mood.
- You eat healthily to increase your sharpness and resilience (Slow Food).
- You understand the natural polarities of darkness and light, warmth and cold, movement and rest, as a way to balance yourself (Dr. Hauschka).

The **interpersonal** domain is about being aware of the impact that your behaviours have on others. Your actions may make people feel inspired or anxious, committed or resistant, enthusiastic or bored. It is about showing humility and empathy and about being able to build trustful and successful personal and business relationships. Again, it is not only being aware of this but also doing something about it.

Examples of interpersonal conscious leadership:

- You listen attentively when you know you tend to interrupt.
- You quickly understand and empathize with others.
- You recognize that wealth is about saying thank you (Merci).
- You contain your emotional reaction in the face of a problem or a crisis.
- You acknowledge your employees as shareholders, besides being stakeholders (John Lewis Partnership).

The last component of conscious leadership – **organizational** – is primarily about understanding your brand and your organization as a complex interrelated system and doing something about it. It is also about having the consciousness for what it is like to work at your company: what is the employee value proposition? Are employees engaged in all parts of the organization? Why or why not?

Examples of organizational conscious leadership:

- You have the desire to make your company the best place to work (John Lewis Partnership).

- You make sure your company cannot be sold or bequeathed, because its capital does not belong to an individual (as in Dr. Hauschka's story).

- You realize the impact that your production process has on the pollution of the planet and you take responsibility in cleaning it up (H&M and adidas).

- You see that the world runs on a neurotic masculine energy and decide to empower feminine energy as a gentle sense of nurturance (Alqvimia).

Bold steps that have impact

All of our 'brand with a conscience' stories relate great success stories about leaders that took a visible bold step forwards, from a societal or organizational consciousness perspective. But when you read such stories and pay close attention to the leader (or leaders) behind these brands you will discover it is about people acting on an intrapersonal and interpersonal level of consciousness.

Whether you are aware of it or not, something bigger drives you. It is as if you are only an actor in a larger plan. And when that happens you cannot ignore this calling; you are neither happy nor satisfied by accumulating material possessions or by pursuing your own well-being and you want to help the world to be a better place. If you are compelled by a mission grander than your own existence then you are a conscious leader.

Rethink: all of us are capable of making a difference in this world. At the end it is simple: leave the world better than you found it. It is your choice! It is your legacy!

How to be a brand with a conscience

12

ORIOL IGLESIAS AND NICHOLAS IND

Before we discuss *how* to be a 'brand with a conscience', we need to answer the question 'why'? Beyond a warm feeling of contributing to the world is there a strong rationale for why organizations should bother to emulate the spirited and committed approach of the companies and movements to be found in this book?

We believe there are two strong business reasons why companies should do so. First, is to realize that business does not exist solely to meet the needs of shareholders. This might be anathema to some, but the idea of the dominance of the shareholder is a recent invention. It was in the 1960s when there seemed to be unlimited resources that the needs of shareholders began to dominate as a principle. This shift of perspective was affirmed in Jensen and Meckling's influential 'Theory of the firm' (1976), in which they argued quite explicitly for the pre-eminence of the shareholder over other stakeholders.[1] While the shareholder perspective has held sway during the last 40 years, it is questionable what it has really delivered for shareholders. There are question marks over the shareholder perspective both in its failure to recognize the interconnectedness of different stakeholders (is it possible to ignore the links between consumers, employees and shareholders?) and in the tendency towards short-termism.

The counterpoint to the shareholder focus is to explicitly recognize that it is not possible to sacrifice the needs of employees, customers and citizens on the altar of shareholder returns: 'companies have to recognize their accountability not only to shareholders, but to all audiences and to society as a whole'.[2] We would argue that the business organization and its various stakeholder groups are not independent of each other. The impact of employee perceptions affects the delivery of service standards to external audiences, while external reputation impacts back on the sense of self of employees. Companies such as Tata Steel, Dilmah Teas and Unilever all recognize that their businesses are intimately intertwined with the societies within which they operate and they work to forge close links that both help them to sustain their success and to benefit communities. As Freeman, Harrison and Wick advocate, the business organization should be a vehicle for 'a joint and cooperative enterprise of creating value for each other'.[3] Once the connectivity of stakeholders is recognized it becomes essential that organizations do not promote one stakeholder group over another, but rather aim to meet the mutual interests of all stakeholders. That in turn has implications for the way that organizations are structured and the way success is measured.

Second, business has become participative. The old way of viewing consumers and other stakeholders as passive recipients of products and services seems more than passé. Forward-thinking organizations recognize that there is no longer a sharply defined boundary between the inside and the outside of their operations, but rather an increasingly porous membrane. Consumers have started to actively participate in the development of the brands they use through online communities, ambassador schemes and crowdsourcing. Employees write blogs; discuss ideas online with suppliers, buyers and consumers; and take part in live events where the future of a brand is co-created. The implication is that 'managers need to recognize that although they have responsibility for shaping a brand's identity, the process will evolve with the participation of many other stakeholders'.[4]

When different stakeholders participate it enhances their feeling of proximity to a brand and their sense of ownership. This involvement, when well managed, can contribute significantly to a brand's strength because it provides deeper insight into the needs of stakeholders, contributes to the intellectual capital of the firm and reduces innovation risk. Yet participation only works when companies are open, trusting and honest. They have to demonstrate an ability to listen and to show humility – not traits that are normally encouraged in most business education, but can be seen in brands with a conscience. As soon as businesses start to instrumentalize their stakeholders, the motivation to participate starts to crumble. It is when businesses treat their stakeholders as partners in a voyage of discovery that they reap the benefits of being an integral part of society.

Now... how?

While the writers of this book started out with some core ideas about what might constitute a brand with a conscience, we did not set out to test any specific hypotheses. Rather, through the cases our goal was to let the theory emerge. Thus the task falls to us to synthesize the ideas contained within the chapters and to create a model that both reflects the emergent themes and provides a usable idea that can help guide managers in their quests to become more sustainable in the way they think and act. There is of course great diversity in the cases – from a cause such as the Slow Food Movement to a campaigning brand like Tony's Chocolonely to a global business-to-business brand like DNV GL – but there is a common pattern that can be traced to a greater and lesser degree through the cases.

Brands with a conscience not only have clarity of purpose but are driven by deeply rooted principles that guide the ideas and behaviour of leaders

Brands with a conscience must be driven by principles

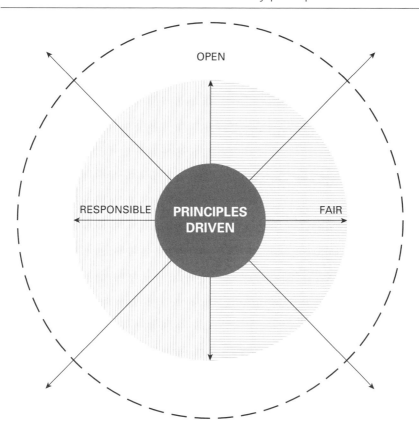

and employees. This is the centrepiece of the brands with a conscience model. That the principles resonate so strongly is because they are appealingly human and humane. Brands with a conscience are both fair to the needs of their different stakeholders and responsible. These brands recognize the impact they can have on the world and act to achieve positive benefits for all. Finally, brands with a conscience are open. This is important because it makes them highly influential – able to sway other organizations and individuals to follow their lead. It encourages them to be accountable for their actions and to be transparent.

Principles driven

Brands with a conscience have a desire to transcend their licit business objectives and make a positive transformative impact on the world. In this sense, brands with a conscience are built inside-out – led by a founder or leader's commitment to a cause or principle that is independent from consumer trends or competitor actions. Even though brands with a conscience are externally aware, they are fundamentally internally driven. Not surprisingly, the commitment to a set of principles makes such brands very persistent and leaders often show a willingness to fight for what they believe against the odds. For instance, Fernando from Dilmah Tea fought for his and the company's principles despite the pressure from Western companies and the resistance from people in his own country, who could not understand his vision. Similarly, Tony's Chocolonely has been fighting for its principles against big multinationals and publicly denouncing, over and over again, the use of child slavery in the chocolate industry.

Chocolonely and Dilmah have a clear stakeholder perspective, as does Cosentino. All these businesses are very explicit in their commitment to fostering economic and social development. Similarly, Tata is committed to benefit the development in the countries in which it operates. As Jamshetji Nusserwanji Tata, founder of the Tata Group, argues: 'In a free enterprise, the community is not just another stakeholder in business, but in fact the very purpose of its existence.' Tata see themselves as a caring organization and this is the reason why, in 1912, the founder created the city of Jamshedpur next to the steel plant. Jamshedpur is nowadays India's only city with a million-plus population and no municipal corporation. Tata runs the city services for their employees and has turned it into one of the world's finest places to live. As an indication of their stakeholder orientation, Tata measures its success by their legacy giving. They even have the 'future minus me' test that tries to ensure that the transformational projects that they promote could continue even if Tata disappeared.

Being principles driven means focusing and aligning brand, corporate and innovation strategies behind them. At Dilmah Tea, both the corporate and innovation strategies concentrate on developing the competences that sustain and empower the Dilmah brand. In the same way, the Slow Food brand drives all the different activities that have been undertaken under its umbrella: the Ark of Taste, the Slow Food Foundation for Biodiversity and the Terra Madre Network. When a brand has strong, shared principles that are culturally embedded they not only guide the choices that leaders make but also steer employees in their behaviour and interactions with different stakeholders. Thus, principle-driven brands, such as John Lewis Partnership, empower their employees to act in the best interests of the organization and what it stands for.

Fair

Brands with a conscience are human and humane. In the words of Beltman, from Tony's Chocolonely, being human means being serious about people. At Chocolonely they think about everyone who is involved with the brand (directly and indirectly) throughout the value chain and work for their well-being – for example by opposing slave labour (still a common practice in the cocoa-production industry of some countries). Beltman's argument is that the problem can be solved simply, by paying fair wages at the beginning of the production chain. In another sector, which still sometimes uses child and slave labour in some developing countries, the Cosentino Group has launched an international verification process for mining operations to ensure that none of their partners use this type of labour.

Therefore, one of the guiding principles of brands with a conscience is that all the participants involved in the development of the product and the local environment should benefit from it. For example, Dilmah grows premium tea ethically. This means picking tea leaves manually – in the traditional manner – and paying fair wages to the pickers so that they can live a decent life and prosper (rather than enriching the company at the expense of the pickers, as still often happens). The ultimate goal is to fairly distribute the profits of the tea business among the various stakeholders and contribute to the development of the territory – in this case Sri Lanka.

Being fair means taking into account the perspectives of other stakeholders and finding a balance between various interests. For instance, Slow Foods envisions a world in which everyone can access and enjoy food that is good for them, good for those who grow it, and good for the planet. This implies the need for accessible prices for consumers and fair conditions for producers, so that producing communities can flourish. Sometimes organizations also try to balance the needs of different interests by adopting new and fairer models for sharing ownership and profits. Tata Group, most of whose shares are owned by the Tata Charitable Trust (an impressive 66 per cent) aims to ensure that the activity of the company is in line with its principles and that contributions are made to help develop communities. Similarly the John Lewis Partnership has an employee ownership model that aims to be fairer for all while overcoming some of the challenges of a shared and consensual decision-making approach. The partnership combines employee ownership with business agility by encouraging senior company executives to make decisions with the necessary speed while making them accountable to the members of the partnership – the employees. Finally, Dr Hauschka is a firm that has a human approach to business with a long-term perspective that considers all its employees as partners and consequently provides significant benefits (including a share in company profits) for them. This has led to employee turnover rates being half those of the industry and extremely low after five years' employment.

Responsible

Brands with a conscience understand that they cannot pursue unlimited growth at any cost. We live in a consumer society in which most consumers seem to need more products and services in order to be happy, and where companies are pressurized by shareholders into pursuing and achieving steady and rapid growth. The logical question we should ask ourselves is how can we balance the desire for infinite business growth with the suffocating pressure applied by finite resources? Is such a reconciliation possible?

A company whose strategic approach challenges the quest for unlimited growth is Handelsbanken. From its foundation the bank decided to operate with its own resources and refuse public aid. This lack of state aid and limited marketing investment has meant a reduced growth rate, but also greater stability and fidelity to its principles. Moreover, the bank balances various measures of success, not only economic, but also human, social and environmental.

Such brands with a conscience have a long-term vision that goes beyond short-term economic goals and aim to develop responsible and sustainable relationships. At Tata there is a responsible long-term commitment to stakeholders, which delivers a strategy based on sustainability in their value chain. Similarly Cosentino treats 98 per cent of the emissions generated in its facilities – recovering nearly 97 per cent of the water used in production processes. Nearly all of the waste from leftover stone is recycled for other uses. At Dr Hauschka, all production activities are based on environmental principles that ensure responsible handling of natural resources and recycling – and only substances or raw materials from sustainable sources are used. Some companies have even adopted sustainability as the centrepiece of their corporate vision. DNV GL aims at making a 'global impact for a safe and sustainable future' by bringing sustainability to the core of its offering and aligning all employees around this commitment.

Open

Brands with a conscience are transparent and accountable for their actions. They act on their principles and they demonstrate the importance of their beliefs and actions to internal and external audiences. However, this is only the starting point. While brands with a conscience are principled they are also receptive to the ideas of others.

Dr Hauschka is a brand that is very open to the influence of its employees and considers them as key partners in generating an open culture that fosters continuous improvement. Employees are encouraged to share their ideas and suggestions for improving the company and have a high degree of freedom. Cosentino are open to the influence of potential customers. The company has its own corporate social network called 'Recyecology', which aims to create a continuous discussion with people and customers sensitive to environmental issues who wish to share their thoughts on subjects such as ecology, innovation, sustainable architecture and gastronomy. Other brands are not only open to the influence of their customers and employees, but also attempt to include and understand the views of the community in which they operate and aim to generate a positive transformative impact. An interesting case is Kolding in Denmark, a place that co-created its identity together with its key constituents.

In addition to being open to the influence of various stakeholders, brands with a conscience also try to influence stakeholders by promoting a particular way of understanding the world and contributing to its transformation. DNV GL lives and acts according to its principles and so adopts an evangelizing role, both in its own right by challenging its customers to embrace sustainability and adopt responsible practices, and through its work with organizations such as the United Nations. In the same vein, adidas aims to raise awareness about environmental issues. One of the latest initiatives is a shoe made from plastic waste recovered from the ocean.

A new role for brand leaders

To encourage the development of more brands with a conscience, we need to educate and cultivate conscious leaders: executives who can drive this transformation are those who have developed a conscious leadership approach that includes four key dimensions: 1) intrapersonal – enabling a leader to act according to his or her conscience and convictions; 2) interpersonal – enabling a leader to be aware of the impact of their actions on others; 3) organizational – reflecting the ability to understand the systemic and complex nature of organizations; and 4) societal – enabling a leader to be aware of the impact of an organization's activities on the environment and society.

This is undoubtedly a task in which business schools should be playing a key role – not least because many of the company directors who fed the financial bubble were shaped by these schools. Business schools must rethink their educational objectives and role in society. Some institutions have already started to move in this direction. At ESADE business school in Barcelona, Spain, the claim is 'We do not train the best managers *in* the world, but the best managers *for* the world.' Students at ESADE have to understand the context of business, the needs of society and the potential positive impact that businesses can have.

Changing the way that managers approach their role is vital to deal with the many challenges we face: a growing shortage of natural resources; excessive pollution of our natural environment; an intolerable economic inequality between regions; a growing distrust in the ability of capitalism to build a fairer world; a progressive loss of confidence in many public and private institutions; as well as an exponential technological revolution that is transforming the way we communicate, interact and organize. We have to recognize the scale of these challenges, but also work to change the way that people think and behave, both through what they do and the influence they exert through others. It is up to us as individuals to emulate the work of brands with a conscience and to think how we can contribute to improving the world we live in.

Notes

1 Jensen, M and Meckling, W H (1976) Theory of the firm: managerial behavior, agency costs and ownership structure, *Journal of Financial Economics*, 3 (4), pp 305–60

2 Ind, N (ed) (2003) *Beyond Branding: How the new values of transparency and integrity are changing the world of brands*, Kogan Page, London

3 Freeman, R E, Harrison, J S and Wick, A C (2007) *Managing for Stakeholders: Survival, reputation and success*, Yale University Press, New Haven, p 6

4 Iglesias, O, Ind, N and Alfaro, M (2013) The organic view of the brand: a brand value co-creation model, *Journal of Brand Management*, 20 (8), p 685

AUTHOR BIOGRAPHIES

Nicholas Ind: 'a lobby for change'
Editor of the book
Author of DNV GL and Influence at adidas
Co-author of How-to be a brand with a conscience
Nicholas's mission is to change the way people work, which he discovered after reading Thomas Gad and Annette Rosencreutz's book *Managing Brand Me*. He was also inspired by meeting (and writing about) the employees of outdoor clothing brand Patagonia.

Nicholas attended the first Medinge meeting in 2000, where the aim was to respond to the critical assessment of branding in Naomi Klein's book *No Logo*. 'I felt we could have a say in what branding is, to make it different and to be a lobby for change.

DNV GL was an interesting case because their "Greener, smarter, safer" slogan felt more genuine than most companies' statements.'

Nicholas is a partner at the consulting firm Equilibrium Consulting and an associate professor at Oslo School of Management. He has written 11 books including *Living the Brand* and *Beyond Branding*.

Sandra Horlings: 'driven by expansion'
Editor of the book
Author of Tony Chocolonely and Lovechock happiness inside
Sandra says, 'I'm driven to make the way we work better because I really like it when things evolve, when we apply what we learn every day. And use our intelligence and talent in as many ways as possible to do this.'

She joined Medinge in 2011. For her, Medinge continually provides food for thought and the ingredients to provoke new ways of thinking. Medinge truly is a learning platform. And a dear group of business friends.

Sandra says that the Tony Chocolonely brand appealed to her because it is a Dutch brand with potentially worldwide influence. 'It is a bold brand that challenges the status quo to make the supply chain better and improve the way we make chocolate. And it is done in an optimistic and fun way.'

Sandra is a values-based, insight-driven brand strategist. She developed the sustainable marketing model as founder of 'World Marketers' within the Dutch Association of Marketing and has written *Bridging the Gap Between Brands: Consumer demand and sustainablility*, on sustainable marketing.

Contributors

Malcolm Allan: 'passionate about cities'

Author of Cork – big on life

Malcolm's mission is to help places to understand what place brand strategy can do to help them gain the knowledge and skills to develop, implement and manage brand strategies for the benefit of the people who live there. Malcolm has a passion for cities. He thinks they are endlessly interesting and constantly surprising.

Malcolm joined the Medinge Group in 2002 in Amsterdam. 'All at once I was in the company of people who were ethical in their approach to branding, people who were giving substantial and creative thought to the creation of brands with a conscience, people who shared my passion for honest and truthful messaging on place.' With three others participants in that Amsterdam workshop Malcolm formed Placebrands, possibly the world's first dedicated place brand agency.

Malcolm chose to write about Cork City Region in south-west Ireland as he has been on a journey with the city for three years helping its officers, councillors, businesses and institutions to think about their offer and what they want to do together to improve and expand it.

Malcolm studied town planning and urban design in Scotland where he benefitted from a liberal arts education that also introduced him to interior design, textile design and graphic art. He regularly blogs on city branding for the Place brand Observer and City Nation Place.

Enric Bernal: 'developing leaders, transforming cultures'

Author of Exploiting leadership to better the world

Enric is driven by personal development and growth, his own and those with whom he interacts. His personal mission is to help increase the level of consciousness in the world (notice the word 'help') and he is set to accomplish that by influencing organizations by designing and facilitating powerful engagements and workshops. And by publishing his thoughts and innovative yet simple models. He believes that organizations have the power in today's economy to change the world to be more humane, sustainable and fair to all.

Enric joined Medinge in 2010, its 10th anniversary, to expose himself to brilliant minds and a great team atmosphere of like-minded individuals.

An accomplished international senior leader, he is currently a senior faculty member at Center for Creative Leadership (CCL) where he leads the design and delivery of custom leadership programmes for global clients.

Enric was Director of Corporate Education at EADA Business School and an executive at HP for 13 years.

Peter Brown: 'multiple talent to make a positive change'
Author of Slow Food

'A desire to make a positive change, by supporting and advocating those whose passion and purpose in life is positive social change' – that is what drives Peter Brown, who joined Medinge for the shared value in conscious, sustainable brands.

For the last few years Peter has worked closely with organizations active in areas such as education, old age and homelessness, as well being on a board of a food-based social enterprise, Eat Club. All are organizations whose brands have conscience, authenticity and purpose.

We asked Peter to write about Slow Food. And he gladly accepted. As a board member and head of strategy and development for Eat Club – designed with the principles of Slow Food in mind – Peter was very familiar with the philosophy of Slow Food, particularly the importance of food as culture and the benefits of eating together in a social setting.

Peter is an international strategist, strategic marketing and communication professional. He works around the globe, with a special focus on Europe and the Near and Middle East. And you can find him acting on stage, with Questors Theatre and the Tower Theatre Company in London and Theatre Proteus in Surrey.

Guiseppe Cavallo: 'creating happiness'
Author of Vegetalia and Alqvimia

Happiness. That is what drives Giuseppe. And what he thinks brands should deliver. With this in mind, Giuseppe has developed new branding tools to help leaders and organizations stay faithful to their original vision and benefit their stakeholders. He has written a book about happiness marketing – *El Marketing de la Felicidad* – a manifesto for businesses built on values.

In joining the Medinge Group, he sought and found a group of like-minded professionals who strive to contribute to a better world, one where the well-being of people and the expression of their talents are at the centre of business life.

Giuseppe spent most of his career, over 25 years, in marketing and public relations positions at multinational brands such as Colgate, Palmolive and Nissan. He served as Marketing Director Europe of the Light Commercial Vehicles division of the Japanese manufacturer and then created and managed its Global Communications department. His passion for marketing is as profound as his interest in wisdom traditions, the vedic and buddhist among them. Giuseppe is also interested in photography, an art that he considers a way to connect with nature through an appreciative contemplation.

Thomas Gad: 'ahead of the game'
Co-author of Sustainable fashion at H&M
Nowadays Thomas can be found in Silicon Valley almost more often then back home in Sweden. Inspiring exponential organizations with the conceptual idea of branding... how to build a consistent company and define shared principles to generate growth. This is what really makes Thomas happy: being at the forefront of transition. Always driven to find 'what's next'.

This was also his motivation to found Medinge in 2000; stunned by Naomi Klein's book *No Logo*, Thomas invited some friends in the field of branding to discuss it at Medinge Sæteri in rural Sweden. The group's debate turned into a heartening call that brands can be a force for good. Ever since, Medinge Sæteri has been the home for good debates for a group that developed into Medinge, a think thank on branding.

Thomas interviewed Catharine Midby of H&M, together with Brigitte Stepputis, to learn how much progress H&M has made since Thomas nominated H&M for the Brands with a Conscience award in 2008.

Ava Hakim: 'curiouser and curiouser'
Author of Changing the relevancy of business and the role of brand leaders forever
One key thing drives Ava – curiosity about technology and the future. It is why she works at IBM – 'The nice thing about my work is it's always changing and I get to work with really smart people. It's never boring. It's groovy.'

Why Medinge? Ava says that it's the same as IBM only a lot smaller. She finds joy in being challenged by people who think about brands in a different way. And she says that 'the core values of Medinge are my own values as well. It means I can be true to myself.'

Ava thinks that writing the opening chapter was a little scary: 'It not only sets the tone, but also determines whether people will read the rest of the book.' But she thinks that it has also been a lot fun to do and an opportunity to learn – 'a real eye opener'.

At IBM, Ava's role is to bring a business perspective to complex technical ideas; to be creative in an analytical culture and to have the opportunity to demonstrate the incredible power that business has to change the world.

Sudhir John Horo: 'designing communities and societies'

Author of Tata Steel

Sudhir John Horo has worked on brands at a very high level, including the nation brand promotions of India during the World Economic Forum since 2006, UN General Assembly and other international platforms. He has also worked on public diplomacy initiatives of the British High Commission and the Embassy of France in India and conceptualized INDIAFRICA: A Shared Future, India's largest engagement programme with Africa for the government of India.

An alumnus of the National Institute of Design in Ahmedabad, he began his career as a graphic designer. Like so many creative people, he says each new assignment gives him 'the opportunity to experience a sense of joy and fulfilment and at the same time be in a position to effect change for communities and societies'.

Although new to the network of Medinge, Horo enjoys meeting like-minded branding colleagues from different parts of the world and working to leverage each member's expertise, for the benefit of society.

In this book, Horo looks at Tata Steel, a company he knows well, having grown up in Jamshedpur, Jharkhand, the 'Steel City' founded by industrialist Jamshedji Tata. He grew up with the brand and knows many people who work with Tata Steel.

Oriol Iglesias: 'back and forth inspiration'

Co-author of How to be a brand with a conscience

Oriol says 'I'm a professor because it allows me to inspire others and be inspired by them.' He is driven by the charm and intellectual challenge of a good discussion.

Oriol enjoys the eclecticism of the Medinge group, as well as the professional, ideological and geographical diversity of its members. He especially appreciates the deep and provocative conversations that take place which always also balance respect and positive criticism.

Oriol loved the challenge of writing the 'How to' chapter where he has to synthesize the overall key learnings from the cases presented in the book. He also enjoyed developing a theoretical model that can be used by companies and brands who want to transcend their traditional profit orientation and make a positive impact in the world.

Philippe Mihailovich: 'endless discoveries'

Author of Merci 'destination store', Paris

Philippe has always been anti-greed but admits to having a greed for living life and tries to live many lives at the same time. As such, he tries to live in London, Paris, New York, Riga, Johannesburg, Belgrade, Hamburg and Geneva, all at once. He thinks he should have been an investigative journalist or social anthropologist because of his curiosity.

Growing up in South Africa made Philippe very sensitive to inequalities and he has always tried to create projects that will give something back to society. He was delighted to have the chance to meet Medinge member Sicco Van Gelder, whose brand models Philippe uses to provide a foundation for his luxury brand content strategy models. Philippe appreciates the intellectual challenges of Medinge.

The Merci 'destination' store in Paris inspired him through its 'wonderful creativity and philosophy'. He felt it was close to the Trade for Aid concept he had created with Donna Karen in the late 1990s but much better and stronger. Inspired by Merci, he challenged Medinge members to create their own *brands with a conscience*. With his partner, Caroline Taylor, they proceeded to show the way by creating a chocolate brand in order to provide a sustainable income to the Home of Hope in Johannesburg.

Simon Paterson: 'useful and desirable'

Co-author of Handelsbanken and co-author of John Lewis Partnership

Simon strongly believes that a business should have a clear purpose that provides the opportunity for fulfilment for employees and customers. As a consultant he gets the chance to help organizations to do this: to uncover and then express the real purpose and meaning of what they do.

Simon has been a member of the Medinge Group since 2006. He likes the natural and meditative environment of the place in rural Sweden where we meet every year. And he identifies with the humanistic ambition of the group – 'It always gives me food for thought and the opportunity to learn.'

Simon says that the John Lewis Partnership is interesting because it is an organization with a distinctive business model, a long-established purpose and a focus on people. 'It's a successful business that has kept true to its roots, but has also adapted to a changing world.'

Simon has taught at the Royal College of Art (RCA), been a member of the advisory panel for Glasgow City of Architecture and Design and has worked as a brand consultant for a broad variety of international businesses.

Annette Rosencreutz: 'helping individuals to grow'
Author of Star for Life

Annette likes working with people to help them to develop and grow. She thinks that too often organizations limit opportunities, but the key is to liberate and then focus individual energy so that it benefits the business and the individual – 'to encourage the entrepreneurial spirit in all of us'.

Annette feels that there are some special things about the Medinge Group: the opportunity to acquire new insights and to learn; a time for reflection; ego-less discussion; and an environment that inspires and builds confidence.

Annette says that Star for Life shows how you can solve a big issue when you engage people. For Annette, the important thing is not presenting solutions, but inspiring people to change themselves. 'When you help children to fulfil their dreams you generate joy and happiness for everyone.'

Annette enjoys the freedom or her work as an advisor to individuals and organizations. It creates the opportunity to travel, to transform the practices of managers and to deliver visible change in people's lives.

Cristián Saracco: 'action-inspiring curiosity'
Author of Cosentino

Cristián is always looking for new intellectual challenges that allow him to learn and grow. However, he highlights that his curiosity is inextricably linked to action. He is curious because he wants to learn and use this knowledge to make things change.

He joined Medinge because he was interested in how companies could transcend their focus on profits and develop a consciousness grounded in the respect for people and the environment.

Cristián is passionate about the Cosentino case. He has know the company and its founders since 2003, when he established his own consultancy firm and started working with them. He was surprised since the first day by their intelligence, energy and humility. Moreover, he is inspired by their commitment and consistency to make a positive impact on the environment and to help people to live a better life.

Nikolaj Stagis: 'creating better lives'
Author of Place branding

Exploring cultural identity and converting deep understanding into a purpose for a company, organization or city – that's what makes Nikolaj tick. 'I love when the integration of a purpose, the culture of the company and its design and services all come together and express the core of the organization.'

Nikolaj attended his first Medinge meeting in 2011 on a cold winter day in Paris. 'I had difficulties finding out what the Medinge Group was, but we're just a very diverse group with many backgrounds and interests – that gives many viewpoints on brands and which makes our discussions interesting.' For Nikolaj, Medinge is a place separate from everyday life – a space for inspiration and sharing ideas.

'Place branding and city branding have been part of my practice for about six years. You can make a real difference. And you help people in creating better lives.'

Nikolaj is the founder of the Danish brand consultancy Stagis. He has written numerous articles and the successful book *The Authentic Company* (2012) (in Danish). He talks and gives lectures on strategy, identity, authenticity and brand.

Brigitte Stepputtis: 'pursuing outside interests and activities makes me better at my job and a more rounded person'

Author of Dr Hauschka and co-author of H&M

Brigitte says, 'I am curious by nature, because that's the way for me to stay inspired and to get a better understanding of the world we live in.'

This is the reason she joined Medinge, after having met lifetime member Stanley Moss, who made her understand that branding is at the heart of her work: making the vision and values of Vivienne Westwood noticeable and identifiable in her work with the brand.

Brigitte chose to write about Dr Hauschka for personal reasons; the brand reminds her of her youth, growing up in South Germany, where Dr Hauschka is based. H&M was a particularly interesting case for her because it is a distinctive fashion brand with a commitment to sustainability.

Brigitte's passion for art, beauty and politics comes to life as Head of Couture at Vivienne Westwood and she is also a director at the Ethical Fashion Forum. Her German roots and London life meet in her role at the board of the German – British Forum.

Erika Uffindell: 'a belief in compassion'

Co-author of John Lewis Partnership and co-author of Handelsbanken

Erika's quest is to help organizations fulfil their potential, embrace conscious business principles and be a force for good. She works with leaders to transcend their egos and 'see the world through the lens of compassion'. She thinks leaders would make different decisions if they did this – if they were truly awake to the implications of their beliefs and actions.

Erika is a long-term member of Medinge and believes that brands can play a powerful role in transforming the world by living out 'right thought, right action' and sharing knowledge, ideas and wisdom. She chose to write about the John Lewis Partnership because she believes that the organization lives out conscious business principles and brings a great sense of integrity and humanity to the way it works – something that has enabled it to deliver value to its employees and customers.

Erika adopts a systemic approach to business and branding and through her work as a director of the Global Centre for Conscious Leadership she works to inspire others to change the way they work. She blends contemporary leadership thinking with her passion for wisdom, principles, energy systems and equine-facilitated learning to bring about positive transformation.

Jack Yan: 'leader and pioneer'

Author of Dilmah Tea

Jack's quest for excellence gives him an edge in his field of work and he has many firsts to his name – the first digital typeface designer in New Zealand, publisher of the first online fashion magazine in New Zealand and even the first designer (perhaps) to run for mayor!

Jack is a publisher, designer and an entrepreneur. Apart from writing for his publications, he has written on various genres in some of the leading journals in the world and spoken at many important platforms.

Jack fondly remembers April 2002 when he drove to Sweden from Paris to attend his first Medinge meeting and was highly impressed with the collection of experts specializing in humanistic branding and social responsibility. And he has since then been a very active member of Medinge.

Serendipity led to his meeting Merrill Fernando, the founder of Dilmah Tea, a Sri Lankan international brand. The meeting generated conversations on how Dilmah has practised the culture of sharing and giving, as the brand has grown.

INDEX

Italics indicate a figure